AA

explor

EGYPT

Anthony Sattin and Sylvie Franquet

AA Publishing

Written by Anthony Sattin and Sylvie Franquet
Original photography by Rick Strange and Steve Day
Edited, designed and produced by AA Publishing
Maps © The Automobile Association 1996

Distributed in the United Kingdom by AA Publishing, Norfolk House, Priestley Road, Basingstoke, Hampshire RG24 9NY.

The contents of this publication are believed correct at the time of printing. Nevertheless, the publishers cannot be held responsible for any errors or omissions or for changes in the details given in this guide or for the consequences of any reliance on the information provided by the same. Assessments of attractions, hotels, restaurants and so forth are based upon the author's own personal experience and, therefore, descriptions given in this guide necessarily contain an element of subjective opinion which may not reflect the publishers' opinion or dictate a reader's own experiences on another occasion. We have tried to ensure accuracy in this guide, but things do change and we would be grateful if readers would advise us of any inaccuracies they may encounter.

A CIP catalogue record for this book is available from the British Library.

ISBN 0 7495 1029 3

Published by AA Publishing (a trading name of Automobile Association Developments Limited, whose registered office is Norfolk House, Priestley Road, Basingstoke, Hampshire RG24 9NY. Registered number 1878835).

Colour separation by LC Repro
Printed in Italy by Printers SRL, Trento

Cover picture: Temple of Hathor, Abu Simbel (Tony Stone Images)
Page 2: detail from a Koran cloth
Page 4: a *felucca* on the River Nile
Page 5 (top): sunset at Giza
Page 5 (bottom, left): relief from the tomb of Seti I, Valley of the Kings, showing Seti with the goddess Isis
Page 5 (bottom, right): street scene, Isna, Upper Egypt
Pages 6 and 7: in an Egyptian market
Page 9: a guardian of the temples of Abu Simbel
Page 27: relief carving, Saqqara
Page 169: statue of Ramses II at Abu Simbel
Page 241: the Path of our Lord Moses, Mount of Moses

Sylvie Franquet, who studied Arabic at the universities of Ghent, Tunis and Cairo, has lived in Cairo for six years, working as a model, translator and tour manager. She writes a column for the Belgian newspaper *De Morgen*. **Anthony Sattin** is the author of *Shooting the Breeze* (a novel) and *Lifting the Veil*, a history of travellers and tourists in Egypt from 1768 to 1956, the editor of Florence Nightingale's previously unpublished *Letters from Egypt, 1849–50* and a regular contributor to the *Daily Telegraph* and *Sunday Times*.

They met in Cairo and now divide their time between London and the Middle East, travelling and writing.

The entrance to the Temple of Hathor, Abu Simbel, Upper Egypt

How to use this book

This book is divided into five main sections:

❏ Section 1: *Egypt Is*
discusses aspects of life and living today, from politics and religion to Egyptians and the River Nile.

❏ Section 2: *Egypt Was*
places the region in its historical context and explores those past events whose influences are felt to this day

❏ Section 3: *A to Z Section*
is broken down into eight regional chapters, and covers places to visit, including walks and drives. Within this section fall the Focus-on articles, which consider a variety of topics in greater detail

❏ Section 4: *Travel Facts*
contains the strictly practical information that is vital for a successful trip

❏ Section 5:
Hotels and Restaurants
lists recommended establishments in Egypt, giving a brief résumé of what they offer

How to use the star rating
Most places described in this book have been given a separate rating:

▶▶▶   **Do not miss**

▶▶   **Highly recommended**

▶   **Worth seeing**

  Not essential viewing

Map references
To make the location of a particular place easier to find, every main entry in this book is given a map reference, such as 176B3. The first number (176) indicates the page on which the map can be found, the letter (B) and the second number (3) pinpoint the square in which the main entry is located. The maps on the inside front cover and inside back cover are referred to as IFC and IBC respectively.

Contents

5

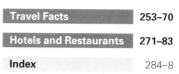

Quick reference

This quick-reference guide highlights the features of the book
you will use most often: the
maps; the introductory features;
the Focus-on articles; the walks
and the drives.

Ahdaf Soueif
Ahdaf Soueif was born in Cairo and educated in Egypt and the UK. She writes articles, reviews and stories for various English and Arabic magazines and newspapers. She is the author of *In the Eye of the Sun* (Bloomsbury 1992 and Vintage 1993), a novel set in Egypt and England, and *Sandpiper and other stories* (Bloomsbury 1995). She now divides her time between homes in Cairo and London.

My Egypt

by Ahdaf Soueif
Western friends who visit Egypt usually start out with six or seven items on their agenda: the Nile, of course, and the Pyramids, the Valley of the Kings at Luxor, maybe Groppi's and the site of the old Shepheard's Hotel in Cairo. All there, and all well worth seeing. But there is so much more.

Often I've been asked by a guest I'm driving in from the airport 'What's happening? Is there a festival?' No, it's just the normal street life of Cairo; coloured lights decorate buildings to draw attention to the pastry shops on the sidewalk. Giant gas-lamps illuminate stalls where fruit is balanced in delicate symmetry. And people – everywhere people, going about their business but always ready for a chat, to give directions, or ask about your country or how you like theirs.

For me, Egypt is the most varied place on earth – and the most friendly. Stop and watch a wedding in the lobby of a grand hotel, or watch another in the narrow streets surrounding the Citadel of Saladdin and you will be swept away into the world of the Arabian Nights. Sit and drink green tea in el-Fishawi by the mosque of el-Hussayn, get your shoes polished and listen to a wandering musician. Eat Mediterranean prawns in Alexandria and feel that graciously ruined city tugging at your heart-strings. Explore the coral reef of the Red Sea or spend a breathlessly quiet day in a desert oasis. Ther is so much to be beguiled by; all you need is a little *money* and an impressionable heart.

My Egypt

by Mohamed Salmawy
The land of Egypt has been my home for the past 7,000 years. During that time I have known many visitors whom the history books would call conquerors but who, in fact, all ended up being converts. I remember a young man called Alexander who came more than 2,000 years ago as an ambitious soldier eager to enlarge his empire, but ended up declaring himself the son of Amon, the god of the land.

In more recent times a Frenchman, equally ambitious, called Napoléon, stated that 'Egypt is the most important country in the world'. He started an expedition to take control of the land but ended up falling in love with the history and its many secrets.

In between those two I have known thousands. Some came and went, others stayed. Among that latter group were the Arabs who, though equally enriched by my heritage, have added a new aspect to our multi-faceted identity. Throughout its history Egypt has maintained its ability to absorb all other cultures and yet sustain its own.

When you visit Egypt, therefore, I advise you not to skim through the surface for a day or two and then say in all confidence, 'I have done Egypt', but to spend time looking into layer after layer of its infinite history. To 'do' Egypt you will need to give it a few thousand years of your life.

Mohamed Salmawy
Born in Egypt and educated at home and abroad, Mohamed Salmawy is the Executive Editor in Chief of *Al-Ahram Hebdo* newspaper. He is a prominent Egyptian writer and journalist, and titles from his pen span topics as diverse as political affairs, journalism and literature. His novel *Coloured Beads* was turned into a serial on Radio Cairo, and his most recent play, *The Flower and the Chain*, is the first literary work on religious terrorism.

9

Gift of the Nile

■ **Egypt is defined by its geography. Bordered by the Red Sea to the east, the Mediterranean in the north, and the Libyan and Nubian deserts in the west and south, most of the country is desert. But running through the middle of all this is the world's longest river, the magical Nile.....■**

The Nile Valley Egypt occupies 3.3 per cent of Africa's land mass, but 95 per cent of Egyptians inhabit only about 5 per cent of their country, most of it near the Nile. The Nile runs through rainless Egypt from south to north and irrigates it like the blessed river that Muslims believe runs through the gardens of paradise. It is worthy of praise: flowing out of the lakes of Ethiopia and Uganda, it is over 6,400km long and for the last 2,700km of its course through Sudan and Egypt, it has no tributaries and receives very little rainfall. So vital is it to the country that Egypt is defined according to its direction of flow. The south of the country is known as Upper Egypt, while the north is called Lower Egypt, and when asked for directions, Egyptians will often refer to the river: *gibli*, towards the mountains in the south and *bahri*, to the sea in the north.

The river's course One of the icons used by the ancient Egyptians to depict their watery lifeline was the lotus plant, with its thin stem and a fan-shaped bud. The river still looks very much like that when seen from the air. In southern Egypt, its valley is extremely narrow in places as the river passes between harder rock formations which it has been unable to erode, but further north, where the rock formations are softer, the river averages more than 800m in width, while its valley stretches some 10km from east to west. After passing Cairo, the Nile splits into the branches that have created the Delta.

The Delta In antiquity the Nile had seven branches, but now there are only two which flow into the Mediterranean near Rashid (Rosetta) and Dumyat (Damietta). Between

them is some of the most fertile land in the country: low-lying, irrigated by a network of canals and intensively farmed. The Delta has been an inspiration to Egyptians to reclaim land from the desert, but even a river as powerful as the Nile has its limits and beyond its reach lie the rock and sand of the deserts.

The Western Desert To ancient Egyptians, the west was the place of

the dead, so it must have seemed appropriate that threats to Egypt's security often came out of the Western Desert, from the Libyans in antiquity to the Germans in World War II. The desert here is relatively flat, with depressions which have created oases. Ironically, it is to the west that some Egyptian strategists look for the country's development, having found oil fields under the desert in the north and underground water reserves in the south near the Sudanese border.

The Eastern Desert Unlike the Western Desert, the narrower stretch of land between the Nile Valley and the Red Sea coast is mountainous. The Red Sea mountains rise to a height of 750m and, as the ancient Egyptians knew, are rich in gold and other minerals.

Although close to the Nile Valley, the Red Sea mountains were almost considered another country, where hermits went to retreat from the world. Only recently were the last of its semi-nomadic tribes settled.

Holy desert The Sinai desert offers an even more dramatic landscape than the Eastern Desert. The peninsula is flat along its coastal plains, rough and rugged in the south and the centre. The sacred Gebel Musa (Mt Sinai), where Moses is said to have received the Ten Commandments, rises to 2,285m while the neighbouring Gebel Katerina is Egypt's highest mountain at 2,642m.

With most of their country covered by desert, Egyptians farm intensively along the Nile

11

Politics

■ **Egypt has been a republic since the overthrow of the monarchy in July 1952. Although it practises a limited form of democracy, the country is still effectively ruled by a handful of very powerful people who take their orders from the president.....■**

The state Egypt is an Arab republic, headed by a president who has the power to appoint a government and its ministers. The government is aided by the People's Assembly, a legislative body elected every five years. The state proclaims the right of freedom of thought and religious practice. Islam is the state religion and *Sharia* (Islamic law) provides the precedent for state laws.

The government Hosni Mubarak won the last presidential election in 1993 with around 95 per cent of the votes cast. As with each election since he became leader on President Sadat's assassination in 1981, he was unopposed. Mubarak has been called the most democratic leader Egypt has ever had, but he has been criticised abroad for not offering real democracy to his people. The president is head of state and of the armed forces and also has the right to appoint all government ministers. In all respects, he runs the country. As a recent presidential spokesman explained, the president holds 'sovereign power in his hands' with the cabinet 'serving as his administrative hand'.

When President Sadat's assassin called his victim 'pharaoh', he echoed popular opinion.

Political parties Until recently, the National Democratic Party was the only political organisation that had access to power and it still holds the upper hand. But in response to growing unrest, President Mubarak has allowed a wider range of political opinions and parties that have long been silent are again being heard. However, he stopped short of lifting the ban on the Muslim Brotherhood and other Islamist organisations. In response, they have built power bases elsewhere, as in such democratically elected bodies as the lawyers' syndicate.

The actuality of power Egypt has had only three rulers in the past 40 years. President Mubarak was the heir-apparent to his predecessor, but he has yet to give his sign of approval to a visible successor, nor, at present, is there a democratic system in place to elect one. His supporters explain that the president is in the process of transforming the entire political system. In the meantime, when events such as political scandals threaten stability and raise the prospect of the present regime falling, there are fears of extremist Islamic groups being swept to power or of the army stepping in to maintain order.

Top: Abdin Palace, the presidential residence. Left: the Egyptian flag, symbol of a modern Arab republic

Human rights In May 1993, Amnesty International reported 'grave human rights abuses amid political violence' in Egypt. Mass arrests, prolonged arbitrary detention, reported torture of political opponents and police killings were all mentioned, though many of these reports were unsubstantiated. Since President Sadat was assassinated the Egyptian government has ruled with emergency powers, effectively suspending ordinary Egyptian law along with much of their accountability, and it is clear that these powers have been used by the authorities in their struggle against opposition groups.

Foreign policy The ministry of foreign affairs recently moved into an impressive and very visible headquarters on the Nile in Cairo, a sign of its

President Hosni Mubarak has enjoyed the role of international statesman and has mediated between Arabs and Israelis

importance. Egypt runs a large diplomatic corps and has made the most of the ending of the isolation that followed the Camp David accord (see page 51), especially since the Arab League has moved its headquarters back to Cairo. The country is active in the United Nations, whose secretary-general, Dr Boutros Boutros-Gali, is Egyptian, and in the Organisation of African Unity, of which President Mubarak was recently chairman. Egypt's importance as a stabilising presence and a moderate link between the region and world powers was highlighted by its role in the Gulf War and in peace talks between Arabs and Israelis.

■ **Egypt is not an Islamic republic like Iran or Saudi Arabia, but Islam is the state religion and both laws and attitudes are shaped by it. The majority of Egyptian people are guided by Islam in all aspects of their lives.....■**

❑ Muhammad had many wives – he married another ten in the last decade of his life. But after he had married the last one, he received a revelation that a man should not have more than four wives, and that he can have the additional wives only if he can afford to support them and their children, and if he treats all of them equally. ❑

In the beginning The Prophet Muhammad was born around AD570 in Mecca and was raised by his uncle, a merchant. According to Islam, during his 40th year Muhammad had a vision in which he received the word of God through the archangel Gabriel. He began to read, although he was illiterate. The divine message soon

Cairene mosques prove to be too small when the faithful gather for the Friday prayers

attracted followers, but some members of his tribe grew nervous of his power and he was forced to flee to Medina in 622. This journey, known as *el-Hijrah*, is the starting point for the Islamic calendar. Muhammad's message was popular, but from the very beginning his followers had to fight for the right to worship and to fulfil Muhammad's vision that Islam was meant for all people, not just the Arabs. While preparing for a campaign in the north of the peninsula, Muhammad fell ill and died in 632.

The Quran (Koran) For 22 years Muhammad recited his revelations to his followers (*el-Quran* means the recitation), but it was only after his death that they were written down, their accuracy confirmed by those closest to the Prophet. Islam rests on the Quran, the word of God delivered directly and in the language of the people, and on the Sunna, the actions of the Prophet, which are unanimously agreed upon by Muslim scholars.

Sunni or Shi'a Muhammad died without naming a successor and soon after his death Muslims were divided. The Prophet's companion, Abu Bakr, was accepted as the Caliph Rasul-Allah, the Successor of the Prophet of God, but Ali, the Prophet's son-in-law, claimed that he was the natural inheritor of the throne. Ali and his son Husayn were both killed, but their followers, members of the Shi'a sect, believed that only Ali's descendants had rights to the throne. The Sunni refused to acknowledge any of the Prophet's descendants as caliph. The divide still exists today, and the majority of Egyptians are Sunni.

The final word The Quran sees Jews and Christians as 'people of the Book' who received the message of the one true God but, through weaknesses and corruption, have failed to be true to it. Muhammad is believed to be the successor of Moses and Jesus and the last of the prophets.

Islam Egyptian style Islam is in some ways practised differently in Egypt, particularly in the cult of the dead. The first Muslims, who arrived from Arabia, were buried simply in the desert, but before long the ancient traditions of tomb-building and grave-visiting were adopted by the Egyptian Muslims. Visible tombs encouraged the elevation of saints, although Islam had attempted to do away with the priesthood and saints, instead promoting a direct communication between the believer and God. Almost every Egyptian village now has its revered saint buried under a white dome or a tree – strikingly similar to the way that each village in ancient Egypt once revered its own god.

It doesn't matter where you are when it's time to pray

❏   The Five Pillars of Faith are these rituals, which every Muslim must perform: publicly declaring that 'there is no God but Allah and Muhammad is His Prophet', praying five times a day at specific times facing the direction of Mecca, fasting in the month of Ramadan, making the *hajj* (pilgrimage) to Mecca at least once in a lifetime and paying a religious levy for the ill or the poor, or for the defence of Islam. ❏

■ **About 10 per cent of Egyptians are Christians and a minute number are Jews. Although minorities are not persecuted by the state, as in some Islamic countries, their relationships with the Egyptians are just as turbulent today as they have been throughout their long histories.....■**

Coptic claims Egypt's estimated 6 million Copts are Christians belonging to the national Christian church (there are an estimated quarter of a million Christians of other denominations).The word Copt is a corruption of the Arabic word *Qibti*, which is in turn derived from the Greek *Aigyptos* (an Egyptian). Egyptians split from the rest of Christianity in AD451 after church rulers in Constantinople supported the edict of the Council of Chalcedon, which denounced monophysites – those who believed in the single nature of God rather than the Trinity – as heretics.

Real Egyptians Copts claim to be the direct descendants of the ancient Egyptians, and although the pharaonic world disappeared long before Jesus was born, they have preserved

With religious tension rising, soldiers are on guard outside most Coptic churches

in their language and customs some traces of that era which survived the Persian, Greek and Roman occupations. While the Coptic language is descended from ancient Egyptian, it is tempting to see parallels between the ancient religion and Christianity as the strongest link between past and present. It seems only a short step from pharaonic *ankh* to Coptic cross, from Isis suckling Horus to Mary comforting Jesus. Isolated from the rest of Christianity, the religion has evolved on its own, staying close to its original impetus and rituals, as a visit to monastery services makes clear. The Coptic spring festival of *sham el-nasseem* (sniffing the breeze) is a holiday throughout Egypt, as it was in pharaonic times.

Egypt's Jews Some of the earliest Bible stories concern the arrival of Jews in Egypt fleeing famine in Canaan, and their subsequent departure under Moses for the promised land. There had been a Jewish community in Babylon-in-Egypt (Cairo) for at least four centuries when the Holy Family is believed to have arrived to escape Herod. The synagogue of Ben Ezra that stands in Old Cairo is the oldest in the country.

Jews also played an important role in Alexandria. Encouraged to settle by the early Ptolemies, they became fully integrated, speaking Greek (the Old Testament was first translated into Greek for their benefit) and adding to the glory of the city; when it fell to the Arabs in AD641, the Arab general reported that there were 40,000 Jews in the city.

Modern Jews In the 1830s, Edward Lane estimated that there were 5,000 Jews in Egypt (and 150,000 Copts), of whom 3,000 to 4,000 lived

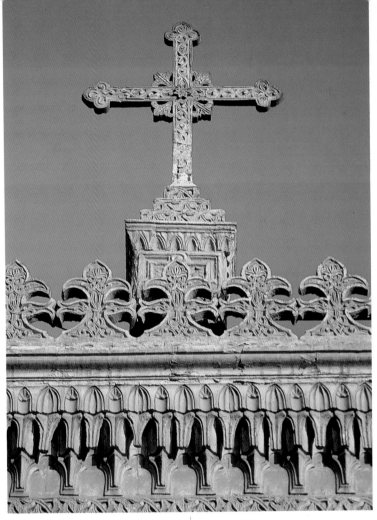

in Cairo. Although their numbers increased under the British, with many immigrants settling in revived Alexandria, the population was reduced to around 2,600 in 1967. In 1990, there were believed to be fewer than 60 Jews still living in the country, and too few of them in Alexandria for services to be held in the great synagogue.

Religious tension Current violence between fundamentalist Muslims and Copts is a new twist in an on-going struggle. Islam does not preach intolerance towards Jews and Christians, but politics, and groups using religion for their own ends, have led to increasing tension between fundamentalists and Egypt's minorities. The separate

The cross is the proud symbol of Egypt's Coptic minority

identity of the Copts has made them an easy target for extremists, though tension between the communities surfaces in other ways, not least in architectural rivalry. If you see a new church with a high bell-tower, there will probably be a higher minaret under construction nearby. Interestingly, the Coptic church has undergone an extraordinary revival just as Islamic fundamentalism has posed a greater threat. While dismay at Egypt's crushing defeat by the Israelis in 1967 and a sense of vengeance after the October 1973 war led to attacks on Jewish property, many Egyptians are tolerant towards the Jews living among them.

The economy

■ **Egypt's agriculture is guaranteed by a constant water supply and its manufacturers can draw on huge labour resources. The country also controls one of the arteries of world trade and contains some of the world's most interesting monuments. Yet only massive foreign aid keeps the country from economic collapse.....■**

Industries The Nile made it possible for civilisation to develop along the valley, and the Aswan High Dam made it possible to grow three crops a year. But the need to earn foreign currency to service massive international debts has led to the growth of crops that will appeal to an overseas market and made Egypt dependent on imports for up to 60 per cent of its food (figures vary and are a matter of dispute). Egypt's main crops include cotton, on which its 19th-century wealth was based, rice, sugar cane, grains and beans. In fact, agriculture now accounts for only 18 per cent of gross domestic product, industry for 30 per cent and services (including tourism and the Suez Canal) for 52 per cent.

Egypt's resources Egypt has offshore gas fields along the Red Sea coast, small oil reserves (Egypt is not a major oil producer), phosphates and precious metals, but its most valuable assets are its immense workforce, the monuments from its glorious past and the Suez Canal. The canal is the country's largest earner of foreign currency after remittances from Egyptian workers abroad and will continue to prop up the economy for as long as it is cheaper to transport goods through the canal than via the Cape. Even in antiquity, Egypt's monuments attracted visitors but then, as now, for many people it was a once-in-a-lifetime visit. New tourist developments along the Red Sea coast are attracting a different sort of

tourist, who comes to sun and swim and is more likely to return year after year. Perhaps Egypt's most important resource is its population, the largest in the Arab Middle East. If new regional economic policies come to fruition, many new jobs will be created, and with at least 20 per cent of its estimated 18 million workers unemployed, Egypt is well-placed to gain from this.

Workers abroad At the time of the Gulf War it was estimated that 1 million Egyptians were working in the region. Egypt's educational system had long been producing a surplus of qualified engineers, teachers and other professionals who were sought after, especially by other Arab countries. Under President Sadat, all university graduates were guaranteed a job, which led to job-sharing in Egypt, but some of them went to the Gulf, attracted by much better pay. For many years their remittances, sent home in foreign currency, bolstered Egypt's economy, supported their families and produced a housing boom as new buildings were commissioned for their homecoming. Their return to

Egypt because of the war meant a loss of their revenue and added another million to the large number already without work.

Aid Egypt is the second-largest recipient of US aid (only Israel receives more) and is reputed to be the second-largest recipient of all international aid. The country's need for aid is obvious and some of the more visible results – improved infrastructure, communications, health care and environmental awareness – suggest that some of it is having an effect. Some Egyptians have resented the involvement that aid donors have demanded in the country's policies. The World Bank in particular has regularly made suggestions as to how Egypt should be governed, and it has made loans conditional on the government pursuing reforms such as the reduction of food subsidies and the freeing of currency controls. But economic reforms take time and the growing population is expected to reach 65 million by the year 2000. With so many mouths to feed in a country that continues to be dependent on imported foodstuffs, the need for aid is not likely to diminish.

Some farmers still work the fertile soil of the Nile valley in much the same way as their ancient forefathers – a sharp contrast to the bustle of modern city life (below)

The Egyptians

■ Egyptians share a rich heritage, but they can't eat old stones (though some live off them in other ways). For many Egyptians life is a search for the basics, made tolerable because they are comforted by an extended family, consoled by religion and kept smiling by an irrepressible sense of humour.....■

Growing fast To Egyptians, children are a blessing and a security in their old age. There are now around 57 million Egyptians, but the population has been growing by up to a million every seven or eight months. Current hardships and longer life expectancy (from 41 years in 1960 to 61 years in 1990) are changing perceptions. In 1960 the average Egyptian family had seven children and it was thought lucky to have as many as

A boy selling green herbs grown in his parents' garden

ten; by 1990, the average was down to 3.8 children.

Families Egyptians identify strongly with their country, province and home town, but above all, at whatever age, the family is at the centre of their life. While the father is still very much the patriarch, a figure to be respected and sometimes also feared, it is usually the mother who rules as well as runs the house. It is also the women who keep up the traditions, preparing customary dishes for feasts and sometimes seeking help from saints or ancient shrines in times of trouble.

Young love On top of all the other obstacles to young love, people in Egypt, especially in cities, face the daunting task of finding themselves a home. At night they sit by the river, thinking about the difficulties. Many will have to wait for many years and take on night work to save enough for an apartment, which is why more Egyptian men are marrying later in life. Those who can't wait start married life living in the house of one of their parents.

Education Like other sectors dependent on government spending, education was underfunded while the Egyptian military rearmed after the wars of 1967 and 1973. The growing population, further stretching resources, has made the day short for most students, as schools run two or three shifts of classes to accommodate them. Although education is compulsory, a lack of enforcement means that many children, especially girls, will stay at home to help out. During the British occupation, several private schools were opened in Cairo and Alexandria, a trend that has continued to educated the children of the growing middle classes. But though illiteracy exists, some 10 per cent of Egyptians continue on to university or higher education colleges.

Electrifying President Sadat promised to bring electricity to every village in Egypt, and with it came television. Farmers whose days were regulated by the sun now stay up late watching American soap operas. TV has brought great changes, not least in taste, with more people aspiring to buy imported goods.

Great changes After receiving his Nobel prize, the Egyptian novelist, Naguib Mahfouz, announced that he

❏ A certain resistance to family planning is suggested by the fate of a recent US aid shipment of condoms: parents in Upper Egypt gave them to their children to use as balloons. ❏

could write no more: his subject, the Egyptian character, was changing too fast. One of the greatest shifts is in where people live. Fifty years ago most Egyptians lived and worked on the land, their lives ruled by the river. Since the revolution in 1952 and especially since the 1970s, a lack of employment for the growing rural population and the prospect of better-paid jobs has lured waves of immigrants to Egypt's cities.

Humour It isn't easy living in Egypt. Problems are many, opportunities are few. One thing that helps is a sense of humour. The Saeedis (Upper Egyptians) are the butt of many jokes. But in Egypt, everything except religion is a suitable subject, even President Mubarak.

Egyptians always have time for a good joke or a laugh

■ **Religious, courteous and patient, Egyptians have held on to their identity in spite of massive changes in their society, and neither mobile phones nor MTV have managed to shake their pragmatism.....■**

Trust in Allah One of Egypt's most commonly used words expresses a trust in God that foreigners find hard to understand. *Insha'allah* (literally, God willing) is used whenever some future event is referred to, as in 'We'll meet at eight, Insha'allah.'

Tomorrow and tomorrow Time is a commodity in which many Egyptians are rich. When *bokra* (tomorrow) is

referred to, usually with an accompanying *insha'allah*, it refers to a time in the future – not today, maybe tomorrow, maybe later. This applies to things they are promising to do, as well as the many blessings that life has so far failed to bestow upon them.

A little understanding *Insha'allah* and *bokra* reveal something about the Egyptian character, but another common word with even more uses is *ma'alesh*. It means 'Never mind.' Foreigners rarely use it, but when an Egyptian travels and the plane is late, the food cold or the only room left in the hotel faces a wall – in other words, when they can't get what they want – *ma'alesh* is their gracious and sympathetic response.

Separating the sexes Women can sit anywhere on the Cairo metro and Alexandrian tram system, but there are always coaches where men are not allowed. Sexual segregation is not a matter of legislation, but increasingly it is the norm.

Covering up Egyptian women tend to cover themselves up outside the house, so when Egyptian men see a girl's bare shoulder, or her figure in see-through clothes, they often consider it a sexual provocation and will stop to stare. Yet when a woman openly breastfeeds her baby in the street they will hardly even notice.

And finally Egyptians are pragmatic about death. It isn't hidden away, but is part of their lives, sometimes literally: many old houses contain tombs, and hundreds of thousands of people are now living in Cairo's cemeteries.

Many Egyptian women prefer to wear a headscarf rather than the traditional face veil

Etiquette

■ **The Egyptian people are renowned for their hospitality. They are also tolerant towards foreigners, but if you really want to fit in and get on, you'll need a few tips on etiquette.....■**

Greetings When Egyptians meet they don't just say hello. Greetings are elaborate and even if they are in a desperate hurry, very often one will force the other to stop for tea. In the café they will take time to swap stories with the owner before tea is served. The farewells will be as elaborate as the greetings. Foreigners who take time to ask after people's health are always appreciated.

Cleanliness Muslims are scrupulous about washing before prayer. Even if no running water is available, they will still attempt to wash themselves. They are just as scrupulous about eating and will only use their right hand, the left being reserved for cleaning themselves. Feet are also considered unclean (you don't know where they've been), so when a Muslim enters a mosque he takes off his shoes and when he sits down facing someone he makes sure the soles of his feet are not showing.

Photographs If you want to photograph Egyptians, especially women or religious people, you should always ask first (or make yourself understood). Children will sometimes ask for *baksheesh* (a tip), but otherwise you will be either waved away or given encouragement.

Gifts If you are invited to a house for a meal, it is polite to take your host or hostess a gift. Flowers will not do and wine is usually out of the question, but something that often goes down well is a selection of pastries.

Physical contact Egyptian men walk hand in hand down a street, but it is rare to see a mixed couple touch in public. Physical contact between foreign couples is also frowned upon. If you want to feel at ease, don't kiss or embrace in the street.

Muslims take off their shoes upon entering a mosque

23

■ Out of Egypt's early 20th-century struggles has come a profusion of artistic talent. The most populous country in the Middle East might not be 'Mother of the World' any longer, but it has certainly shown the way for the arts in the Arab world .....■

The spoken word Traditions of storytelling go back to long before the Arab invasion. Pre-Islamic stories were inevitably epics, long narrative cycles relating the adventures of heroes and the desperate acts of lovers. The *Hilaliya* (the story of Abu Zayd) and *Laila and Majnun* are but two examples of stories that are still in circulation today. The audience, assembled in cafés (or in houses for special occasions), would already know the story but would listen to enjoy the raconteur's embellishments. It was from this tradition that medieval European writers like Boccaccio and Chaucer drew their inspiration. Egyptian storytellers were popular until the advent of radio and television. Theatre director Hassan el-Geretly is currently engaged in recording as many of these epic narratives as possible in an attempt to preserve and reinvent the tradition.

Literature Introductions to novels and collections of short stories published in the 1960s and 1970s often cited the influence of European novelists and poets on Egyptian writers. Until the early 20th century, Egyptian literature was still an offspring of an oral tradition. But education, contact with foreign influences and political struggle led to experimentation by writers like Haykal and those of the so-called New School.

Tawfiq el-Hakim stands out as one of the leading figures of that period, but the writer who dominates the century is Naguib Mahfouz, who started writing in 1928. His winning of the Nobel Prize stirred up controversy in Egypt: it was claimed that other Egyptian writers had achieved more, and some Muslims felt that a man with a *fatwa* (religious edict) calling for his death because what he wrote was considered blasphemous should not be so rewarded. But Mahfouz has captured an Egypt that is only just out of sight.

Translated writers Many more Egyptian writers are now available in translation. Among the more notable are the older

Many of Mahfouz's characters come from the alleys of Islamic Cairo

24

generation of Mahfouz, Constantine Cavafy (*Collected Poems*) and el-Hakim. Waguih Ghali's only novel, *Beer in the Snooker Club*, is a bitter view of post-revolutionary Cairo that has never been available in Egypt. Nawaal el-Saadawi is often typecast as a feminist and her works are also controversial; like Gamal el-Gitani, el-Saadawi writes novels which are allegorical attacks on attitudes and government. Ahdaf Soueif is a younger novelist writing in English about contemporary Egypt.

Film and theatre Egyptians are proud of their cultural importance in the Arab world and nowhere is it more obvious than in film and television. Films created in Cairo's cinema city, and particularly the work of veteran film-maker Youssef Shaheen, have helped to shape Arab identity and attitudes. Some of the current stars have a huge following, which allows them to move easily between screen and stage. Entertainers such as Adel Imam or Fifi Abduh, like Umm Kalthoum before them (see page 26) can be seen on stage in Cairo at the same time as cinemas and television show their films.

Television has changed traditional family life

Television Egyptians are passionate television viewers. Streets were noticeably quieter for an hour each evening when American soap operas were first screened in the late 1980s. The main TV event of the year is the *Fawazeer* during the month of Ramadan. The programmes are full of stories, which are clues to a puzzle. At the end of the month, the person with the right answer wins an attractive prize. (The excitement is only mildly lessened by the knowledge that the answer can be bought on the street in Cairo some days before the end of the month.)

Visual arts Like all other art forms, painting and sculpture were transformed by Egypt's struggle for nationhood. Modernist artists like Mahmoud Mukhtar, Mahmoud Said and Muhammad Nagy were working in a period of mixed influences. While Nagy was in Paris with the Impressionist Claude Monet, Egyptologists were uncovering more of the pharaonic past. Egyptian art has developed out of these two influences, the innovation of the West and the burden of the past, and contemporary artists continue to explore these themes.

Classical Arabic music The reed pipe, drum, tambourine, oud and three-string fiddle – these instruments are at the heart of Egyptian music. The greatest names in classical Arabic music are Umm Kalthoum, who brought a previously unknown passion and bravura to the trilling, warbling vocals, and her one-time colleague Muhammad Abdel Wahab, who transformed the traditional thin *takht* music into something more like a big-band sound. While classical Arabic music is still performed today, it has been less popular since their deaths.

Umm Kalthoum sang about impossible love and passion

Umm Kalthoum Few performers have had such a devoted following as Umm Kalthoum, the magical *chanteuse* of Arab songs. Egyptians once sat beside their radio sets to hear the *Kawkab el-Sharq*, the Star of the Orient as she was known, sing her latest song about love and passion. Although she died in 1975, the legend lives on: mention her name and Arabs everywhere will smile, and maybe hum one of her tunes.

New sounds The latest changes have again been influenced by the west. *Shaabi* (people) music, as sung by Ahmad Adaweer, mixes protest lyrics with a strong back beat, while *el-Jeel* (the Generation) fuses disco beats to local rhythms as a backing for love songs. The newest movement, headed by Georges Kazazian, is a free-form 'New Age' fusion of Egyptian, Turkish and Hindi rhythms.

EGYPT WAS

■ Some 20,000 years ago the weather in Egypt became drier, which turned plains and forests into deserts. The people who had depended on the forests now depended on each other and worked together to cultivate the fertile land along the River Nile. In doing so, they created the world's first nation.....■

The Two Lands The spread of deserts in North Africa forced pre-dynastic hunters to settle around Egypt's oases and along the Nile. As communities developed, they learned that the annual rise and fall of the Nile would allow them to plant crops and therefore guarantee their survival. The need to make the best use of the Nile's flooding led to the creation of local administrators, who exercised power over the individual for the greater good of the community. These administrators became centralised over time and eventually developed into two opposing groups, one in the valley, the other in the delta, each with their own gods, capitals and leaders. They are known as the Two Lands of Egypt.

The Early Dynastic Period Facts about the people who lived along the Nile during this period (c 3100–2686BC) are hard to come by. Even material from the royal tombs, usually rich sources of information, is inconclusive: not only were the

tombs burned, but there appear to have been two of them for each king, one at Saqqara and another at Abydos. The Abydos tombs were probably symbolic, confirming the city's role as Egypt's spiritual centre. The tombs at Saqqara were surrounded by graves containing numbers of the pharaoh's subjects who appear to have been killed to accompany the king on his final journey.

The Old Kingdom The Old Kingdom – the reign of the pharaohs of the 3rd to 6th Dynasties (c 2686–2181BC) – was a period of growing power and wealth which saw the first great flourish of ancient Egypt. Funded by

Tributes are brought to the priest Ptah Hotep, Saqqara

❏ There is no proof that anyone by the name of Menes (or Narmer, as he is also known) ever lived, but whether man or symbol, what is important about him is that around 3100BC he achieved something rare in Egyptian history by reconciling the opposites and uniting the Two Lands. It was around that time that people from Upper Egypt conquered the north and founded a new capital, Memphis, at the border of the Two Lands, not far from present-day Cairo. They created a unified monarchy and the first Egyptian dynasty. ❏

A picture of contentment: the dwarf Seneb and his family

Imhotep, the architect of the 3rd-Dynasty pharaoh, Zoser, made the jump from the *mastaba* (oblong tomb chamber) to a series of *mastabas* built on top of each other – a step pyramid – which pharaohs of the 4th Dynasty perfected into the shining, limestone-clad pyramids of Giza. The pyramids prove the Old Kingdom's strong central authority, which maintained the large numbers of workers necessary for their construction.

The end of the old order Authority slipped away from the 5th-Dynasty pharaohs (*c* 2494–2345BC), as is obvious from the Pyramid of Unas, the last pharaoh of the dynasty. Constructed only three centuries after Imhotep built the Step Pyramid and a little over 200 years after the Great Pyramid was finished, Unas's complex was a work of inferior quality, built with a rubble core and limestone casing. It was restored by a son of Ramses II, but is once again in a state of dilapidation. By the 6th Dynasty, nobles were no longer buried near their pharaoh but in their own provinces, another step towards the end of central authority and therefore of the Old Kingdom.

the rewards of successful campaigns in Nubia, Libya and Sinai, and encouraged by a strong central authority whose main posts were occupied by relations of the pharaoh, Egyptians made significant developments, particularly in architecture with the development and perfection of the pyramid.

■ **For 150 years, the Egyptian ideal of statehood was torn apart by factional fighting between two main groups, centred around Thebes and Heracleopolis, near modern Beni Suef. Around 2050BC a strong ruler emerged to unite them. The Middle Kingdom is considered to end around 1786BC with the invasion of the Hyksos from the northeast.....■**

Unified lands The 11th Dynasty dates from *c* 2133BC, but the start of the Middle Kingdom is associated with the accession of Menthuhotpe II in 2010. He is also known as Sehertowy, or 'He who unites the Two Lands'. As during the Old Kingdom, political stability brought great rewards. Not only was the country quiet, but Egyptians were able to resume their military and commercial campaigns elsewhere. During this period they were active in Nubia and Qush up the Nile and around the Mediterranean as far as Syria and Greece.

Architectural wonders This new kingdom, its capital at Thebes (modern-day Luxor), saw great advances in Egypt's culture, as suggested by the paintings in 11th- and 12th-Dynasty tombs at Beni Hasan. There was also a revival of large architectural projects, one of the most famous being the Pyramid of Amenemhat III (1842–1797BC) in el-Faiyum. Little has survived, but the pyramid originally stood 58m high and was joined by a mortuary temple known as 'the Labyrinth', carved from a single rock. Herodotus, visiting Egypt around 450BC, found it a more impressive structure than the Great Pyramid at Giza.

Cult of the dead Another consequence of prosperity was that more people were able to pay for elaborate funerary rites, hoping to ensure a happy afterlife. The cult of Osiris grew in popularity during the Middle Kingdom, pilgrimages to the god's spiritual centre at Abydos became central in the annual cycle of festivities and, as with the Old Kingdom pharaohs, it became desirable to have a false tomb, or at least a *stele* (memorial stone) erected at Abydos so that the soul would be able to make the pilgrimage after death.

Top: the Rock Tombs of Beni Hasan. Left: Menthuhotpe II, founder of the Middle Kingdom

30

The New Kingdom

■ **The New Kingdom spanned three dynasties (18th–20th Dynasties, 1567–1085BC) and its ruins suggest that this was the golden age of Egyptian art and architecture. It brought widespread development, from the introduction of the chariot to the start of the Iron Age, and also produced some particularly famous rulers, among them Tutankhamun and Ramses II.....■**

❏ Tuthmosis I (1525–1495BC) made a radical break with tradition when he decided to hide his tomb. No Old Kingdom pyramid or Middle Kingdom labyrinth for him. He was the first New Kingdom monarch to be buried in a deep, rock-cut tomb which was intended never to be visited, neither by priests nor tomb robbers. The place where he was buried is now known as the Valley of the Kings. From Tuthmosis I's death until the end of the New Kingdom, this was where all but one of Egypt's rulers were buried. ❏

also among the finest architectural works to have survived from antiquity.

Revolutionary ideals Hatshepsut's nephew, Tuthmosis III, was one of the great generals of Egyptian history

Above: the death mask of Tutankhamun
Below: the impressive colossus of Ramses II at Abu Simbel

The Egyptian Empire Middle Kingdom pharaohs lost control of the north of the country to the foreign Hyksos people, who probably came from Syria, but the Theban ruler Ahmosis I overran their capital of Avaris in the Delta and, in 1567BC, chased them out of Egypt. The great Egyptian empire he founded had its capital at Thebes.

The importance of the temple
Rather than have the cult of the dead pharaoh centred on his tomb, secret burials in the Valley of the Kings focused attention on the mortuary temple. Queen Hatshepsut (1503–1482BC), who served as regent for her nephew, Tuthmosis III (1504–1450BC), and then ruled as pharaoh with him, began a revival of art and architecture with her magnificent funerary temple, built like no other into the side of the hill at Deir el-Bahri. The nearby mortuary temples of the later New Kingdom pharaohs Seti I, Ramses II and Ramses III are

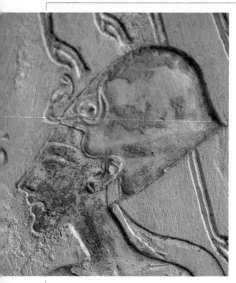

Queen Nefertiti enjoyed high status as Akhenaton's Great Wife

❏ When Akhenaton rejected the religion of Thebes, he also discouraged the old, formal artistic styles of his predecessors and favoured instead a naturalism previously unknown in Egypt. It is tempting to see the spirit of his reign expressed in the free and flowing representations of the royal family, full of affection, emotion and even bodily functions (the first depiction of vomiting), unlike anything else in ancient Egypt. They are among the most beautiful works to have survived from antiquity, the most famous of them being the head of Akhenaton's wife, Nefertiti (see page 124), now in Berlin's Egyptian Museum. ❏

and under his command the armies were victorious in Africa and Asia. Amenophis III (1398–1361BC) capitalised on his successes, and brought great wealth and power to Egypt and its capital, Thebes.

The priesthood used the massive donations of gold and land to extend its power and influence. It was perhaps as a result of this that Amenophis IV (1369–1353BC) moved his capital from Thebes to a new city he constructed at Akhetaton (modern Tell el-Amarna). Denouncing the state god Amun (and therefore also the priesthood), he promoted the sun god Aton, whom he worshipped as 'the one god' in an early instance of monotheism. He also changed his own name to Akhenaton.

The priests' revenge The priests of Amun had their revenge on Akhenaton when the crown passed to Akhenaton's son-in-law, the boy king Tutankhaton (1352– 1344BC). Akhenaton's general, Horemheb, and Tutankhaton's tutor, Ay, moved him and his capital back to Thebes, encouraging Tutankhaton to restore the god Amun and change his own name to Tutankhamun. As a reward, when the pharaoh died in the eighth

year of his reign the priests buried him in spectacular style. Tutankhamun's successors, Ay and Horemheb, consolidated the power of the priesthood of Amun but failed to preserve their own dynasty.

A classical revival As well as restoring the old capital and state religion, the 19th Dynasty revived classical art, but in an updated and refreshed form as monuments from the reign of Seti I suggest. Seti, a man of taste and ability, restored the empire by fighting the Libyans, Syrians and Hittites. His tomb in the Valley of the Kings and his temple at Abydos are particularly beautiful. The Abydos temple confirms the old order: the names of Akhenaton, Smenkhkere and even Tutankhamun were pointedly omitted from the list of kings.

The monumental builder One pharaoh stands out above all others as you move around the remains of ancient Egypt and that is Ramses II. His pre-eminence is partly due to the fact that he reigned for 66 years after Seti I's death. Although not as capable a general as his father, Ramses fought famous wars against the Hittites, particularly the Battle of Qadesh (c 1285BC), which is depicted on many of the buildings he erected. The fact that he married a Hittite

A shady 'garden' of fine stone columns in Karnak Temple

princess as part of a peace treaty suggests his victory was not so conclusive. Nor were his artistic achievements as notable as Seti's temple at Abydos, but his buildings at Karnak, Luxor, Thebes and Abu Simbel ensure the prominence of his name.

The last great pharaoh Some forty years and six pharaohs after Ramses II's death, Ramses III inherited a country threatened from the north by Libyans and the Mediterranean 'sea peoples'. Ramses III fought off external and internal threats throughout his 32-year reign. His mortuary temple at Thebes was built like a fortress and during the centuries of decline following his death, when the priests themselves finally took over the running of the state, it was often used for that purpose.

■ Egypt had lost its power long before the Assyrians sacked Luxor. After a succession of ineffective rulers weakened the country, Egypt was taken with little effort by Persian armies and then by Alexander the Great. But under the Ptolemies (323–30BC), who succeeded the young general, Egypt regained some of its glory.....■

Alexander the Great For the 700 years known as the Late Dynastic Period (1085–322BC), Egypt was fought over by a succession of rulers – some native, others from Libya, Nubia and Persia – who moved the capital from Thebes to Tanis to Sais to Memphis. In the end, Egypt became part of the Persian empire.

When Alexander the Great defeated the Persian king, Darius III, at Issus in 332BC, Egypt was his. Alexander was an idealist and a coloniser and he wanted to Hellenise the world. He founded Alexandria as a port that would link the old worlds of the pharaohs, of Babylon and of the Persians and Greeks.

The first Ptolemy When Alexander died in the East in 323BC, his Macedonian general, Ptolemy, met his funerary procession and, it is said, diverted it to Alexandria, where the dead hero was buried at the centre of his new city. Ptolemy, who had been governor of Egypt, became king, adding Palestine, Cyprus and parts of Asia Minor to his lands.

Ptolemy built temples, to familiar designs, at Edfu and Kom Ombo. These and subsequent works were meant to reassure Egyptians that their gods were being respected and to confirm the Ptolemies' status as rulers by divine right. But although he was energetic in administering and unifying the Nile Valley, Ptolemy I's real interest lay to the north. Alexandria, which he had helped Alexander to lay out and which he himself had built, was becoming geographically and intellectually the heart of a new world: ancient Egypt was dead.

The glory of Alexandria During the reign of the Ptolemies who followed, Alexandria became a world city. Their navy controlled the Mediterranean and trade flowed through the city from the east and north.

But while the rulers of ancient Egypt had channelled their resources into the pyramids and other visible monuments, the Ptolemies used theirs for the encouragement of science, religious thought and literature. Alexandria's reputation as a place of the intellect, centred around the fabled Mouseion (library), shone as brilliantly as her Pharos lighthouse.

Cleopatra The dynasty is named after its men, but apart from the first couple of Ptolemies, it is the women who come across as being the most exceptional, and none more so than Cleopatra (51–30BC). She was the last ruler until the modern era of an independent Egypt.

She was properly called Cleopatra VII Philopater, wife to her brother, Ptolemy XIII. Having seen her father, Ptolemy XII, humiliated by Rome, she used what she considered her most suitable weapon, her femininity, in an attempt to save Egypt for herself. When Julius Caesar defeated the Egyptian navy and her brother/husband was drowned, Cleopatra married her younger brother, Ptolemy XIV, and became Caesar's mistress, bearing him a son, Caesarion. After Caesar's death, she became the lover of his successor, Mark Antony. With Antony she blossomed, and with him she withered. The arrival of Octavius Caesar, known as Augustus, brought about the deaths of Antony, Cleopatra and Ptolemaic Egypt.

Top: the Temple of Isis, Philae
Right: relief in the Ptolemaic temple of Hathor, Dandara

■ **Unlike Alexander, the Romans had to fight to take Egypt and continued fighting to keep it. Alexandria consolidated her role as a centre of art and intellect, but much of the country suffered from the new rulers' indifference to anything but the size of the harvest.....**■

Augustan Egypt The Roman emperor Augustus captured a rich prize when he defeated Mark Antony and Cleopatra. Ptolemaic administrators had helped Egypt grow prosperous and the Romans left much of the system intact. But whatever happened elsewhere in Egypt, Alexandria and the Delta were too close to the Mediterranean, and therefore to Rome, to be left alone.

Augustus made changes. Greek continued as the official language, but he dismissed the Greek senate of Alexandria and, among other moves, granted Alexandrian Jews autonomy. There were riots in Alexandria after fighting between Greeks and Jews escalated; when Roman soldiers intervened, fires broke out in the harbour and the Mouseion's library burned down.

Rule from Rome Augustus ensured that Egypt was the emperor's private land, ruled by the emperor's deputy. Egyptians were subjected to a census and taxed, according to their numbers, in the form of grain. It was a valuable commodity for the emperor of a grain-poor country to control.

Augustus and the emperors who succeeded him maintained a sense of continuity in Egypt. Work was resumed on the great temples begun by the Ptolemies, older temples were restored and new buildings, like Trajan's beautiful 2nd-century kiosk at Philae, were started. Roman leaders were happy to follow the

Emperor Augustus, first Roman ruler of Egypt, in stern repose

example of Alexander in being identified with the Egyptian pantheon. Everything was done to encourage the idea that nothing had changed, except that now Egyptians were obliged to worship a divine Roman, rather than a divine Macedonian or Persian. There were even tangible benefits: around AD 115 the emperor Trajan had the Red Sea canal recut, linking the Nile to the Red Sea, and eastern trade flowed through Egypt, past the Roman garrisons at Babylon (Cairo) and Alexandria.

The habit of religion Egyptian civilisation was old before Rome was founded and the habit of religion ran deep. This, and the newer spirit of philosophical thought, produced extraordinary results when St Mark arrived in Alexandria to spread the word about a new religion: Christianity. Dates vary, but some time in the 1st century AD, Egyptians began converting; by late in the 2nd century, Christianity was firmly established alongside Judaism and paganism

In Egypt, Christianity attracted many converts, perhaps because religious texts had been translated into Coptic and therefore appealed to a much wider audience. Christianity spread just as Roman emperors like

36

Decius moved against it; Egyptian stoicism clashed with Roman intolerance and Egypt provided the Church with early martyrs, as well as its first hermits and monks.

The Coptic Church In AD391, less than 80 years after Emperor Constantine declared Christianity the state religion, Christians attacked the temple of Serapis in Alexandria, burning its library and smashing its gods. But there was a growing division among Christians concerning the nature of Jesus. Was he a man who became part of the Trinity, as the supporters of Arius suggested? Monophysites believed that he was God at all times and that the Arians, to whom Father and Son were two gods, were no better than pagans worshipping Osiris and Horus.

The debate continued into the 5th century, when an edict from the new imperial capital, Constantinople, declared that Christ was one person with two natures. Egyptians couldn't accept this and, ever since, the Coptic Orthodox Church has stood alone.

The simple beauty of an early Christian painting, now in the care of the Coptic Museum in Old Cairo

A fusion of Egyptian and Greek motifs on a Roman mummy case

■ **At the beginning of the 7th century a new force appeared, with dramatic suddenness, in the old imperial world. Arab Muslims came to spread the word and rule the world, and they ended up changing Egypt forever.....**■

38

❏ The Arabs were desert people and old habits died hard. Amr was terrified by the prospect of going on a boat, but the caliph, Omar, took his fear of water one step further. When Amr suggested maintaining the capital at Alexandria, Omar refused because there would be water between himself and his army. Amr retraced his steps and returned to his camp at Babylon-in-Egypt. ❏

Message from the East

Muhammad, born in AD570, was a member of the Quraysh tribe of Mecca, Arabia. In his 40th year he had visitations from the archangel Gabriel. Islam, the religion based on Muhammad's Quran (the recitation of these visitations), began to unite the various tribes of the Arabian peninsula until Muhammad's death in 632. The Prophet had appointed no successor, but Muslims were then led by the caliphs (from the Arabic *khalifah*, meaning follower), Abu Bakr (*d* 634), Omar (*d* 644) and Othman (*d* 656).

The new force

The people of this new religion were energetic in spreading their message and, happy to do God's work and gain power and wealth in the process, Arab armies moved north. The Byzantine and Persian empires, weakened by plagues and in-fighting, were in no state to resist the new force. Between AD636 and 649, the Arabs took all of the Persian and much of the Byzantine empires; by the end of this period of rapid expansion they had reached the Oxus River, the Caspian and Black Seas, crossed the whole of North Africa (only stopping

there, as the general said, riding his horse into the Atlantic, because there was no more land) and then turned north into Spain.

Amr Amr ibn el-As visited Egypt as a trader in his youth. In 639 he returned at the head of 4,000 horsemen, with whom he defeated a Byzantine army near the ruins of ancient Heliopolis. After a seven-month siege, troops at the fortress at Babylon-in-Egypt, key to the Nile and the eastern trade, surrendered in April 641. When Alexandria opened its gates a few months later, Egypt became a province of the Arab empire.

Arab rule Amr met little opposition to his rule once the Byzantine armies had been defeated. The native Egyptians, whether bitter over the Christian controversy that had left the Copts isolated or merely indifferent to another foreign ruler, made no protest. For some there were benefits. The Arabs had no desire to force converts to their religion and people were free to worship as they chose, on payment of a tax. No doubt Amr's popularity was helped by charging Jews and Christians lower taxes as 'people of the Book'.

E M Forster called him 'one of the ablest and most charming men that Islam ever produced' and Amr proved to be as able a governor as he was a general. He left Alexandria to the ravages of time and salt water, and made his capital at his old camp at Fustat, outside Babylon on the Nile, the seed from which Cairo has grown.

Tulun By 868, when Ahmed ibn Tulun was sent to administer Egypt, the caliphs were losing their grip on the empire. Ibn Tulun seized the

opportunity to exploit their weakness and founded the first independent dynasty in Egypt since Cleopatra: the Tulunids. In his new capital, el-Qitai, north of Fustat, Islamic architecture came of age. Ibn Tulun's son, Khomaruya, embellished the capital, making it the stuff of fantastic tales, but less than 40 years after ibn

The Ibn Tulun Mosque, Cairo, is impressive for both its grand scale and its extreme simplicity

Tulun's arrival, the caliph's troops were back in control. El-Qitai was destroyed and only ibn Tulun's mosque, one of the most perfect Islamic buildings, has survived.

Fatimid and Ayyubid

■ **Empires never stand still but are always either growing or shrinking, and while the caliphs in Baghdad were losing power, rival leaders in Tunisia were preparing to take it from them. Their rule was one of the most fantastic in Egypt's Islamic history.....■**

❏ On 5 August 969, the Fatimid general, Gohar, laid out the ground-plan for a new capital city. Ropes with bells were slung around the perimeter. At the most auspicious moment, to be determined by Gohar's astrologers, the bells would ring and the ground would be dug. But a raven landed on the ropes, the bells rang and the building of the city began. At that moment, the planet Mars was ascendant. In Arabic it is called el-Qahir, so the new city was called el-Qahira (the triumphant), which Europeans corrupted to Cairo. ❏

The Fatimids The Abbasid caliphs in Baghdad staked their right to power on their descent from the first caliphs. The Abbasids had been energetic about eliminating rivals but somehow, in what is now Tunisia, a powerful group had formed around the Fatimid rulers, people who claimed descent from Ali, the fourth caliph, and his wife Fatima, Muhammad's daughter. Their rivalry not only involved power; they represented a split in theology as well, for the Abbasids were Sunni and the Fatimids were Shi'a Muslims. When the Fatimid ruler, el-Muizz, invaded Egypt, his army met with little resistance. Weakened by the plague and disillusioned by their rulers, Egyptians welcomed change.

The Fatimid succession The Fatimid empire included North Africa, Sicily, parts of Syria and the

El-Azhar Mosque

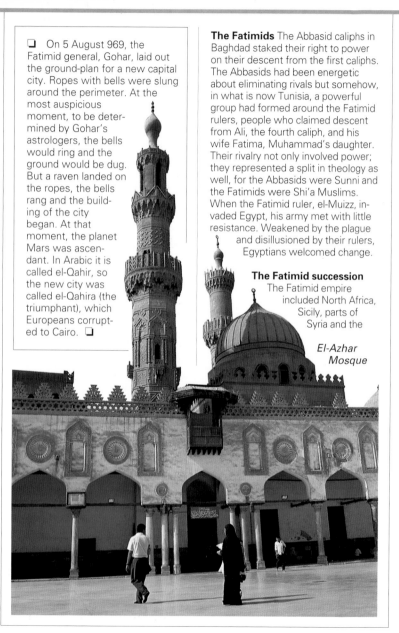

Crusaders make a treaty with Saladin

Hejaz. It contained great wealth, which the caliphs increased by good management. Fantastic palaces were built, as well as Islam's first university-mosque, el-Azhar. Its purpose was to educate Muslims in the way of the Shi'a, a task in which it failed; but, as the historian ibn Khaldun observed, by the time that was apparent, the dynasty had passed from innovation to exhaustion.

❑ Salah ad-Din is hard to separate from his legend, although his recorded achievements need no elaboration. He turned his back on the Fatimid palaces and built himself a defensible citadel above Cairo. He assumed the title of sultan, reinstated Sunni rites in Egyptian mosques and was happy to leave religious authority in the hands of caliphs in Baghdad.

By calling for and leading a *jihad* (holy war) to rid the Holy Land of Christians, he provided Muslims with a common cause. He recaptured Jerusalem and provoked the Third Crusade. In the peace treaty of 1192, the Crusaders saw their presence in the area reduced to a minor holding on the Mediterranean coast. Salah ad-Din had drawn a Muslim buffer across the great trade routes between Europe and the East. He died in 1193 and was buried in Damascus. ❑

Ayyubids On 10 September 1171, prayers were offered in Cairo's mosques for the Sunni caliph in Baghdad, not the Shi'a caliph dying in the fortress-city. Fatimid rule ended without a fight. Three years earlier they had been powerless to stop a Crusader army from attacking Egypt and only the intervention of forces from Damascus saved Cairo.

The Syrian troops were led by a young Kurd called Salah ad-Din, son of Ayyub. Having made the country safe, he founded a new dynasty in the name of his father and brought Egypt back into direct contact with the Muslim world from which it had been estranged.

Salah ad-Din, known as Saladin

■ **From the first Arab invasion to the downfall of the Fatimid caliphs, power in Egypt had always been legitimised by descent from the prophet Muhammad and his followers. With the coming of the Mamluks, succession in Egypt became a fierce and often bloody test of strength and ruthlessness.....■**

The Mamluks Mamluks were slaves, mostly Turks, who were brought to Egypt, converted to Islam, taught how to fight and given their freedom, at which point they usually joined the army of an emir. The most promising were given official posts as cup bearer, horse master, treasurer and so on. Without hereditary sultans, the country was ruled by the most powerful Mamluk emir, his right enforced by his Mamluk soldiers. The system encouraged loyalty and ruthlessness and succeeded admirably in its intention of providing Egypt with a supply of men to fight invaders in the north and east.

A Muslim queen Between the last Ayyubid and first Mamluk sultans, Egypt was briefly ruled by a queen (a rare thing in Islamic history). When Sultan el-Salih Ayyub died fighting the

The scale of Sultan Hasan's madrasa *was unprecedented. Begun in the 1350s, it epitomises the Mamluk period's bold and voluminous architectural style*

❏ The first 'dynasty' of Mamluk sultans (1250–1382), most of them Turks or Mongols, were called Bahri (or riverine) Mamluks because their barracks were on the river at Roda Island. They were succeeded by the Circassian Burgi (tower, or citadel) Mamluks (1382–1517) who were garrisoned in Salah ad-Din's citadel. ❏

Crusaders in the Delta in 1249, his son by an earlier marriage was in Syria. The death was concealed by his then wife, Shagar el-Durr (Tree of Pearls), until the prince returned, but once back in Cairo he was murdered and his step-mother was proclaimed queen.

When the Ayyubid caliph in Damascus heard the news he said, 'Woe to the nations ruled by women', and sent an army to remove her. To help her face the challenge, Shagar el-Durr married her Mamluk lover, Aybak

– insisting first that he divorce his wife – and on his victory he became sultan. Eventually, he too fell foul of this formidable woman and she had him killed in 1259. In retaliation, his Mamluks handed her to Aybak's first wife, who had her beaten to death with wooden bath clogs!

A matter of taste Although their lives were filled with violence, Mamluk monuments display a refined sense of taste. Inheritance of position was forbidden and inheritance of wealth was frowned upon, so the successful Mamluk had plenty of money to spend during his often short lifetime. Arab historians recorded the opulence of their houses, but Mamluks also expressed their power and hopes for remembrance after their death through public buildings. The inscription outside Qalawun's mosque in Cairo glorifies his name and lets us know how quickly it was built, speed being necessary so that the great project would be finished before the sultan met his end.

Much of the present-day appearance of Islamic Cairo was shaped during this period. Schools, hospitals, markets, caravanserai for visiting traders and public fountains were built and endowed, the Mamluks perhaps hoping to obtain good favour in heaven for their charitable works. The rest of the country also benefited from Mamluk taste and talent, and more citadels are now being uncovered across the Sinai desert.

The coming of the Ottomans The Ottoman Turks, another tribe that came out of central Asia, took Constantinople in 1453 and by the 16th century, they were threatening to move south to Egypt. The Mamluks, weakened by their own squabbling, were unequal to the fight and, only 19 years after the late flowering of Mamluk architecture under the Sultan Qaytbay, the Ottomans were in Cairo. The last Mamluk sultan was hanged from Bab Zuwayla and another long period of foreign domination began.

43

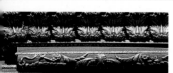

■ **The Ottomans showed little interest in Egypt. It was just one part of an immense empire, and their desire was that it should be quiet and pay taxes. Their gain was Egypt's loss.....■**

Egypt's many losses The independent Mamluk ruler of Egypt was hung in front of his people in 1517, and the last Abbasid caliph died in Cairo in 1538. By then, Europeans had sailed to the Americas and India and broken the Mamluk monopoly on eastern trade. Egypt, once a wealthy, independent state controlling a vital trade route, now found itself with reduced revenues and facing demands for tribute from an indifferent foreign ruler.

A land of legend Under the Ottomans, who periodically banned Christian ships from the Red Sea for fear of their involvement with the holy places, Egypt became isolated. In its seclusion, something strange happened: the monuments along the Nile were forgotten abroad, as well as the churches, mosques and palaces, and a country and people that Europeans had little difficulty in understanding some centuries earlier became a place of myth and legend. The 18th-century explorers, like James Bruce, who came looking for the source of the Nile, found themselves laughed at when they recounted their tales of travel – such things surely could not be!

Mamluks and janissaries Authority in Egypt was officially held by a governor appointed in Istanbul; it was enforced on the ground by janissaries – Ottoman troops recruited from the Balkans. But with no one to replace the tax-collecting, administrating Mamluks, the Ottomans had no choice but to perpetuate the system of purchasing and training slaves. A power game developed between janissaries and Mamluks, which weakened both of them and threatened to ruin the country.

It was then that the British and French, looking for faster access to their eastern colonies, considered the possibilities of passing overland through Egypt. The landing of Napoleon Bonaparte and a French army in 1798 brought an end to Egypt's isolation and, effectively, to Ottoman rule. Napoleon brought learned men as well as soldiers to Egypt. The *Description de L'Egypte*, the result of their researches, was the first attempt to systematically record Egyptian monuments.

A mashrabiya lattice window of the 16th- and 17th-century Bayt el-Suhaymi, one of Cairo's finest merchant houses

■ **Like the Ottomans, the French and British were drawn to Egypt because of its command of eastern trade routes. But while their sights were set elsewhere, a Macedonian-born commander in the Ottoman army had his eye on controlling the Nile.....■**

❑ Muhammad Ali's main rivals were the Mamluk beys (nobles). In March 1811, his position secure, he invited 470 Mamluk beys and their followers to a banquet in Cairo's Citadel. As they left, he ambushed them by the main gate. According to local legend, all were killed but one, who escaped over the walls on his horse. ❑

The European wars For nine years (1798–1807), Egypt saw a succession of foreign armies coming up the Nile shores in what the contemporary historian el-Jabarti called 'a period of great battles, of ghastly events, of disastrous facts, of frightful calamities, of constantly growing evils'. The French arrived as liberators under their idealistic general. The British followed them, also as liberators. Then the Ottoman sultan in Constantinople sent an army of mercenaries.

Visitors at the foot of the Giza Pyramids, c 1895

Muhammad Ali After the French army had been forced out of Egypt in 1801, the Ottoman troops attempted to change the balance of power by eliminating the Mamluks. But there was no money to pay troops in Cairo and a contingent of Albanian mercenaries mutinied. Their revolt became a rallying call for the many who were dissatisfied with Ottoman rule. In 1805 the people of Cairo insisted that Muhammad Ali, commander of the Albanian troops and the most powerful figure in Egypt, be made their ruler.

45

The making of modern Egypt
Muhammad Ali brought direct rule back to Egypt after three centuries and founded a dynasty that lasted until the revolution of 1952. During his reign as pasha from 1805 to 1848, Egypt was transformed, roads and railways laid, canals cleared, agriculture encouraged, industries started and the military reorganised. While his motives weren't entirely altruistic – he made himself owner of all land in Egypt – it was his inspiration that laid the foundations of modern Egypt.

■ **Egypt was too important for the 19th-century European powers to ignore. The Suez Canal, the cotton harvest, access to Africa and its potential as a market for European goods meant that foreign governments were unenthusiastic about Egyptian independence.....■**

❑ After Tawfiq's succession, a faction of the army objected to British and French advisers controlling Egypt's finances. To appease them one of their officers, Ahmad 'Urabi, was offered a cabinet post. But that didn't stop riots breaking out. On 11 July 1882, British ships bombarded Alexandria and a month later 20,000 British troops landed under the pretext of restoring peace. 'Urabi and his supporters were defeated at the battle of Tell el-Kabir. ❑

Railway or canal The vigour of Muhammad Ali's reign died with him. His successor, Abbas (1848–1854), sacked his foreign advisers and cancelled their projects, although the British-built railway was continued between Alexandria, Cairo and Suez. Abbas's successor, Said (1854–1863), was more sympathetic to French interests and granted De Lesseps the Suez Canal concession, but under terms that proved financially disastrous for Egypt. In order to meet the terms, Said had to borrow money from abroad, a move which subsequently made Egypt financially dependent on European backers.

Egypt developed In 1866, 3 years after coming to power, Muhammad Ali's grandson, Ismail, negotiated with the Ottoman sultan for a change in the succession to ensure that his own children would inherit his position. He also asked permission for Egypt to maintain its own army.

More important still were his plans to redevelop Cairo. Ismail had lived in Paris as a student, and when he returned there in 1867 he was so impressed by Haussmann's transformation of the old medieval city that he decided that his old Arab capital should be redesigned along similar lines. In the next couple of years, Ismail initiated a building boom which has left Cairo with broad boulevards, palaces, public gardens, Cairo central station, an opera house and scores of other buildings. Ismail explained his intentions at the opening of the Suez Canal in 1869 when he announced his belief that Egypt now belonged to Europe, not Africa. It did, but not as he imagined.

Queen Victoria's initials on the British Embassy gates, Cairo

The veiled protectorate Egypt earned enormous profits in the 1860s by meeting the shortfall in cotton caused by the American Civil War. But there wasn't enough to finance Ismail's plans, compensate for financial mismanagement and service Egypt's growing overseas debts. Egypt was broke and had already sold her shares in the Suez Canal to Britain by 1879, when the British and French governments persuaded the Ottoman sultan to depose Ismail. The throne passed to Tawfiq (1879–1892) and his son Abbas II Hilmi (1892–1914), but by 1882 a British consul-general and a corps of British civil servants were running the country in the name of the *khedive* (viceroy).

The independence movement There is no starting point for the independence movement. It grew among all classes of Egyptians, fuelled by increasing resentment at foreign presence and intervention in Egypt's affairs. When Turkey allied

The belvedere of the Edwardian-Moorish Old Cataract Hotel, on the Nile in Aswan

itself to Germany in World War I, Egypt, still officially Turkey's colony, was finally annexed by the British. In 1918, Egyptians approached London, not Istanbul, for their independence.

The Wafd Saad Zaghlul, a British-appointed minister for education, demanded the right for an Egyptian delegation to attend the international Paris peace conference of 1919. The British refusal led to an uprising. The force of that protest showed that discontent with British rule was widespread. Zaghlul and his Wafd (Delegation) party were at the forefront of the independence movement, and they won a landslide victory in the 1924 elections after Egypt declared itself independent. But the British remained, pulling their troops back to Suez Canal bases in 1936 and still hesitating over withdrawal 18 years later.

■ **As the dissatisfaction of Egyptians of all classes came to a head after World War II, the country became increasingly unstable. In 1952, the Egyptian army moved to restore stability and 150 years of rule by Muhammad Ali's dynasty ended.....■**

After World War II Egypt remained officially neutral throughout the war, although factions in the government showed support for the Nazis in the hope they would rid Egypt of the British. With the Germans defeated and the British still in place, Egypt was in turmoil.

King Farouk, who had come to the throne in 1936, alienated his subjects with his decadence and political mismanagement. The old establishment was corrupt and nepotistic, and the Wafd party had lost its credibility as champion of independence in 1942, when British tanks surrounded the royal palace to ensure the appointment of a Wafdist prime minister. Meanwhile, other parties were becoming increasingly active and the Muslim Brotherhood, originally a reformist Islamic group, adopted a political agenda encouraging violent struggle.

The Free Officers Several army officers were also opposed to the government and the British. The first aim of the Free Officers, Muhammad Naguib and the young Gamal Abdel Nasser among them, was to force the British out of Egypt. Meanwhile another disaster struck: in 1948–9, Egypt and its Arab neighbours went to war with the newly created state of Israel and returned home after a crushing defeat. Rumours of Egyptian soldiers fighting with defective arms increased sympathy for the dissidents. In 1948, the Muslim Brotherhood struck out and assassinated the prime minister, but a couple of months later the Brotherhood's founder, Hassan el-Banna, was killed, large numbers of his supporters were arrested and the group was officially outlawed in Egypt.

Black Saturday The British base at the Suez Canal was one of the world's largest military establishments and, as the situation within Egypt deteriorated, it became a target for patriotic groups. On 25 January 1952, retaliating against these attacks, British troops surrounded a police post at Isma'iliya and ordered the auxiliaries inside to surrender. They refused, and 41 Egyptians were

Anti-British rioters attacking the British Embassy in Cairo

killed in the fight. On the following day – known as Black Saturday – foreign interests were attacked throughout Egypt. Cairo's famous Shepheard's Hotel and the Turf Club were obvious colonial targets, and both were destroyed.

The revolution On the night of 22 July, the Free Officers and their supporters took over key posts and both the old government and the monarchy were toppled in a bloodless coup. It was a popular move, greeted with widespread celebrations. General Naguib was appointed president and prime minister of the new republic, with Nasser as his deputy.

The Nasser years Nasser was president by May 1954 and within six months had negotiated the withdrawal of British troops. The terms were something of a compromise, but agreement had been reached and he was seen as his country's saviour, the man who could guarantee Egyptian independence. Encouraged by this, he pushed through plans for building the Aswan High Dam and proposed to finance

President Nasser played the Russians against the Americans to get the Aswan Dam built

part of it by nationalising the Suez Canal, in which Egypt owned no shares. The move prompted a joint British, French and Israeli invasion. When Nasser stood up to them and they were forced to withdraw by international pressure, he became an Arab hero.

❏ On 26 July 1952, three days after the public announcement of the military coup, King Farouk was escorted aboard the royal yacht to sail into exile. His extravagances didn't end there, though. Living in exile in Switzerland, he maintained his reputation as a gambler and a cigar smoker. King Farouk died in exile, but was allowed back to Egypt for a quiet burial. He shares a tomb with others of his dynasty in Cairo's City of the Dead. His son, ex-King Fuad II, lives in exile in Europe. ❏

War and peace

■ After three damaging wars with Israel, Egypt risked the anger of its Arab partners by agreeing to talk to the enemy. The Egyptian-Israeli peace talks have made peace in the Near East a probability.....■

1967 In six days during the summer of 1967, Israeli forces defeated the combined armies and air forces of Egypt, Jordan, Syria and Lebanon. The Israelis took Sinai, crossed the Suez Canal and were ready to march on Cairo when cease-fire terms were agreed. Nasser, autocratic but ever popular, resigned after the defeat but mass demonstrations brought him back and he continued as president until his death in 1970. More than 3 million people attended his funeral.

Sadat's revolution

Vice-President Anwar Sadat assumed power on Nasser's death. A Free Officer, he was neither as charismatic nor as popular as his predecessor, and there were doubts about his ability as leader. But within two years of becoming president, Sadat was secure enough to push through sweeping changes and Soviet links were cut as Egypt turned towards the West.

Sadat's next move was more unexpected: in October 1973, Egypt attacked Israeli forces in Sinai. While the October War was not the great victory Egyptians sometimes claim, the Israeli defensive line in Sinai was breached and Egyptian forces were

still intact when the cease-fire was arranged. The myth of Israeli invincibility had been destroyed. As both the Israeli and Egyptian militaries managed to end the war with their pride intact, the way was left open for reconciliation.

Opening doors In November 1977, Sadat shocked Arab leaders and Egyptians, too, by speaking at the Israeli Knesset in Jerusalem. Many Egyptians saw it as an act of weakness and betrayal, but it led to the peace agreement with Israel, signed in 1979 at Camp David, and to Egypt receiving massive aid from the USA. Arab countries isolated Egypt, removing the Arab League headquarters to Tunis. This further

Egypt and Israel had been at war for over 30 years when the Camp David treaty was signed

❑ Egypt became embroiled in the Cold War when it turned to the Soviet Union for funds after the USA refused help with building the Aswan High Dam. Mementoes of the Soviet years litter Egypt – the Mugamma building in Cairo is one – but Arab socialism never strayed towards the Soviet model. ❑

encouraged Sadat's open door policies, attracting foreign investment and easing currency restrictions to revive Egypt's war-torn economy.

Sadat's downfall Sadat's economic policies created great wealth, but only for a minority; they widened the gap between rich and poor which the revolution was supposed to close. Inflation made the situation worse and conditions were so tense that when food subsidies were lifted in 1977, there were riots in the cities until the government changed its mind. The lack of foresight that led to the riots suggested that Sadat had lost touch with his country.

While economic policies led to social unrest, Sadat's easing of politi-

❑ By the terms of the March 1979 accord, signed at Camp David under US President Jimmy Carter's patronage, Israel and Egypt recognised each other's rights according to international law. The treaty has been widely criticised for not being explicit on important issues and both Israelis and Egyptians have complained of a 'cold peace' between them. But without Camp David as a precedent, other Arab-Israeli negotiations might have been more difficult to arrange. ❑

A worried President Mubarak

cal repression had more damaging effects for him. The Wafd regained some of its credibility as a viable opponent of the government, the Muslim Brotherhood came out of hiding and a host of other parties attracted supporters. On 6 October 1981, at a ceremony to celebrate Egypt's victory in the 1973 war, Sadat was assassinated. Egyptians cite his standing up to greet the soldiers who had come to kill him as proof of how little he understood the anger he had stirred.

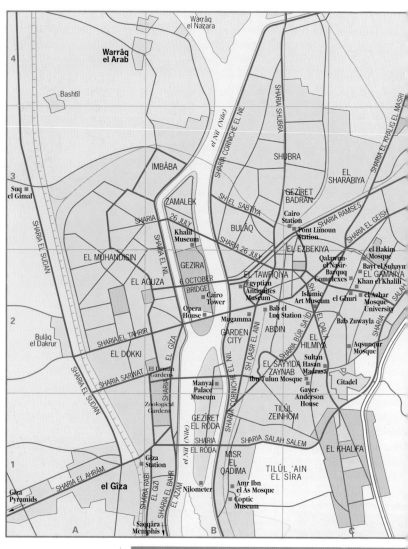

Warrâq
el Nazara

**Warrâq
el Arab**

Bashtîl

4

3

el Nil (Nile)

SHARIA CORNICHE EL NIL

SHARIA SHUBRA

SHARIA EL KHALIG EL MASRI

Suq
el Gimal

IMBÂBA

SHUBRA

EL
SHARABIYA

ZAMALEK

GEZİRET
BADRAN

SH. EL SABTIYA

26 JULY

SHARIA

Cairo
Station

SHARIA RAMSES

SHARIA EL GEISH

Khalil
Museum

SHARIA EL NIL

BULÂQ

SHARIA 26 JULY

Pont Limoun
Station

EL-EZBEKIYA

el Hakim
Mosque

EL MUHANDISIN

GEZIRA

EL TAWFIQIYA

Qalawun-
el Nasir-
Barquq
Complexes

Bayt el Suhaym
EL GAMAIYA

EL AGUZA

6 OCTOBER
BRIDGE

Egyptian
Antiquities
Museum

Khan el Khalili

Cairo
Tower

Islamic
Art Museum

el Ghuri

el Azhar
Mosque
University

Opera
House

Bab el
Luq Station

SH.

Bulâq
el Dakrur

Mugamma

SHARIA EL TAHRIR

GARDEN
CITY

ABDIN

SHARIA BÛR SAİD

Bab Zuwayla

2

SHARIA EL SUDAN

EL DOKKI

SHARIA SARWAT

SH QASR EL AINI

EL
HILMIYA

EL QAL

SHARIA

Aqsunqur
Mosque

El Urman
Gardens

SHARIA EL NIL

SHARIA EL GIZA

EL SAYYIDA
ZAYNAB

Sultan
Hasan
Madrasa

Manyal
Palace
Museum

SHARIA CORNICHE EL NIL

Ibn Tulun Mosque

Gayer-
Anderson
House

Citadel

Zoological
Gardens

GEZİRET
EL RODA

TILÛL
ZEINHÔM

SHARIA
EL RODA

el Nil (Nile)

SHARIA SALAH SALEM

EL KHALIFA

1

Giza
Station

MISR
EL
QADIMA

TILÛL 'AIN
EL SÎRA

SHARIA EL AHRÂM

SHARIA RABI

SHARIA EL GIZI

SHARIA EL BAHR

SHARIA EL AZAM

el Gîza

Nilometer

Amr Ibn
el Âs Mosque

Coptic
Museum

Gîza
Pyramids

A

Saqqâra
Memphis

B

C

*The Sphinx and the
Pyramid of Cheops,
Giza*

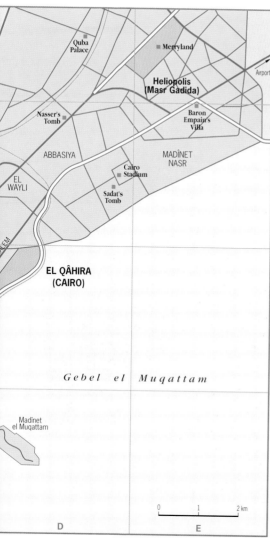

Quba
Palace

Merryland

Airport

Heliopolis
(Masr Gadida)

Nasser's
Tomb

Baron
Empain's
Villa

ABBASIYA

MADÎNET
NASR

Cairo
Stadium

EL
WAYLI

Sadat's
Tomb

SALEM

EL QÂHIRA
(CAIRO)

Gebel el Muqattam

Madînet
el Muqattam

0   1   2 km

D

E

CAIRO

First sight Many flights into Cairo (el-Qahira) arrive at night. From the air, Africa's largest city appears as a galaxy of movement and light, but by day, its size and complexity can be disorientating and that glittering night vision can seem illusory. However, in spite of the population explosion, industrial development, economic hardship and now terrorism, Cairo does still retain some of the qualities of 'the Mother of the World'.

Getting on top of the city One of the best ways to make sense of Cairo on arrival is to get on top of it. From the viewing platform on the Cairo Tower, or the terrace outside Muhammad Ali's mosque at the Citadel, it is possible to follow the city's lifeline, the Nile, identify its various landmarks and see how the desert hems it in. Another way to reach an understanding is via the city's origins.

Before Cairo There were settlements along the Nile long before what we know as Cairo came into existence, but you have to look hard to find them. Little remains at the early dynastic Egyptian capital of Memphis, 24km away, or at the Old Kingdom religious centre of Heliopolis. Persians and Romans left more of a mark, building fortified posts (the ruins at Babylon-in-Egypt) at what is known as Old Cairo, where the river was more easily crossed, and where a canal from the Red Sea joined the Nile. But it wasn't until the Arab conquest that the seeds of modern Cairo began to sprout.

At sunset thousands of muezzins call the believers for prayers

Cairo seems to go on for ever, a brown dusty sea cut through by the blue of the Nile

Old Cairo When the Arab general Amr took control of Egypt in AD641, the capital was at Alexandria. Amr would have been happy to keep it there, but the caliph, Omar, in Baghdad refused to allow the Nile to come between him and his general. So Amr went back and built his settlement where he first pitched his tent. The site, near the Roman emperor Trajan's fort at Babylon-in-Egypt, became known as Fustat (the camp).

Islamic Cairo The Abbassid ruler ibn Tulun constructed a new settlement, el-Qatai, at the end of the 9th century, but what we know as Islamic Cairo wasn't founded until 969, when the Fatimid caliphs from Tunisia usurped Baghdad's power and built their fabled palace enclosure, el-Qahira. When Salah ad-Din ended Fatimid rule in 1171, he recognised the difficulty of protecting the Fatimids' royal enclosure and built the Citadel on an outcrop of the Muqattam Hills. It has housed one of Cairo's most important garrisons ever since.

Modern Cairo The 19th-century ruler Muhammad Ali believed his family would remain in power as long as they continued to live in the Citadel, but his grandson ignored his advice. Ismail did much to develop Cairo along the lines of Europe's great cities and set an example by building himself the palace of Abdin down among the new developments in 1874. Five years later he was forced to abdicate. The 'Europeanisation' and more recently the 'Americanisation' of the capital has continued without much interruption for more than a century, which is why, at first sight, downtown Cairo looks so familiar to tourists.

Don't be fooled by appearances However familiar the city may seem, it is unique in its make-up. Built and rebuilt over a thousand years, it is home to people of the Nile Valley and the Delta, Bedouin from the deserts, businessmen, and Arabic and Islamic scholars from around the world and each community has its own gathering place. Downtown Cairo is the place where the city's sophisticates used to meet, which is why it looks familiar, but you don't have to go far from the centre to find yourself in an entirely different world. That is part of the city's attraction and one of the reasons why, if you can bear the pollution, it is so rewarding to climb down from the terrace or tower and walk around.

What's in a name?
The western name for the city – Cairo – comes from the Arabic *el-Qahira* (the victorious), supposedly given to the Fatimid city because Mars, the victorious planet, was ascendant when the city was founded. However, in Arabic both the city and the country of which it is the capital are known by an older name, Misr.

Mother of the World 55
'He who hath not seen Cairo hath not seen the world. Her soil is gold; her Nile is a marvel; her women are like the black-eyed virgins of Paradise; her houses are palaces; and her air is soft, as sweet-smelling as aloes wood, rejoicing the heart. And how can Cairo be otherwise, when she is the Mother of the World?'
Thousand and One Nights

Pharaonic Cairo

▶▶▶ The Pyramids of el-Haram (Giza) 52A1

18km southwest of central Cairo Site open 8–5 daily; Pyramid of Cheops closes at 4.30; Solar Boat Museum open daily 9-2. Admission fee.

Already in ancient times, the Pyramids of Giza were considered one of the Seven Wonders of the World. Today they are the only 'wonder' to have survived the ravages of time, almost intact. They are, without doubt, the most famous and probably the most photographed monuments in the world. But in spite of all the superlatives a first visit to the pyramids can be disappointing, perhaps because they have become so familiar that when you stand in front of them they can seem smaller or less impressive than expected. Pictures usually show the pyramids in the middle of the desert, but suburban Cairo has crept up to the foot of the Giza Plateau and takes away from the splendour of the view. It takes time, walking around them or watching them from the desert, before you realise how grand they are. The best time to visit is around sunset or sundown when it is cooler and the light is at its best, or at night when most of the camel drivers, touts and soft-drink sellers will have gone home.

The Great Pyramid of Khufu (Cheops)▶▶▶ (4th Dynasty) is the first pyramid to appear as you approach them along Pyramids Road. As it is the oldest and largest pyramid in this group, it is hard to avoid some statistics. Cheops' pyramid is built with around 2.3 million limestone blocks, each weighing an average 2.5 tonnes – 6.18 million tonnes in all. Originally 147m high, the loss of its shiny outer casing has lowered it to 137m. From the entrance, a long, narrow and low corridor descends into an unfinished room (sometimes closed), probably intended as a burial chamber. It is not clear why this chamber was abandoned. An ascending corridor leads to another unfinished room known as the Queen's Chamber and through the magnifi-

56

Getting in
You need a separate ticket to explore the secrets inside the Great Pyramid. It is a hot and exhausting business, so take water and wear comfortable clothing: for much of the climb you will be bent double or crawling on hands and knees.

The Pyramids of Giza (from left to right): Menkaure, Chephren and Cheops

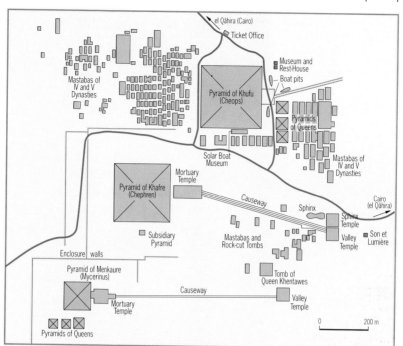

el Qâhira (Cairo)
Ticket Office
Museum and Rest-House
Boat pits
Pyramid of Khufu (Cheops)
Mastabas of IV and V Dynasties
Pyramids of Queens
Solar Boat Museum
Mastabas of IV and V Dynasties
Mortuary Temple
Pyramid of Khafre (Chephren)
Causeway
Sphinx
Cairo (el Qâhira)
Sphinx Temple
Son et Lumière
Subsidiary Pyramid
Mastabas and Rock-cut Tombs
Valley Temple
Enclosure walls
Pyramid of Menkaure (Mycerinus)
Tomb of Queen Khentawes
Causeway
Valley Temple
Mortuary Temple
0   200 m
Pyramids of Queens

cent 47m-long Great Gallery to the main burial chamber. In the undecorated King's Chamber, built in red granite, the sarcophagus is empty, the mummy never found.

Surrounding the pyramid, only fragments of paving from Cheops' mortuary temple were found, while the causeway and valley temple are buried under the village of Nazlet el-Simman, making excavation difficult. The three smaller neighbouring pyramids belonged to Cheops' queens or sisters. Five boat pits have also been found, of which three were empty and one contained a dismantled solar boat, now housed in the specially constructed Solar Boat Museum. In 1987 another boat was found, perfectly preserved under a canopy of limestone blocks. It has been left under the sand.

The Sphinx▶▶▶ is called *Abu 'l-Hol* (the Father of Terror) in Arabic, which sums up the mysterious aura surrounding this strange figure with a lion's body, a human face and a royal beard. Tradition suggests that Chephren found an outcrop of soft limestone where his father Cheops had quarried stone for his pyramid and had the Sphinx carved on it, in his own image. Recently, however, some archaeologists have claimed that the Sphinx was built by people of a lost civilisation who lived more than 2,600 years before Chephren. Herodotus, who visited the pyramids around 460BC, doesn't mention the Sphinx, probably because it was already buried in the sand. A stele (memorial stone) between the two

The enigma of the sands: who built the Sphinx, when and why? The answers to these questions are still unresolved

CAIRO

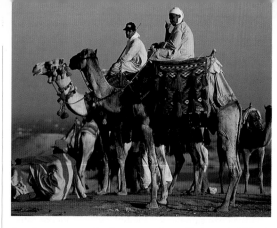

Another Great Wall
Napoleon Bonaparte is reported to have calculated that with the stones of these three pyramids, a wall 3m high and 0.3m thick could be built the whole way around France.

The unavoidable, ever-present camel drivers

58

Sound and Light
After sunset, the pyramids plateau is cleared for the Sound and Light show. From a terrace in front of the Sphinx, the story of the pyramids is told by the 'Father of Terror' in a quirky, mysterious voice and although the text can seem a little kitsch, the setting is always spectacular. There are two shows every night in different languages. Information is published in the daily *Egyptian Gazette* or you can call (02) 385 2880; there is an admission fee. The temperature drops considerably after dark, and although blankets are provided, a sweater might be necessary. Mosquito repellent is essential in summer.

two front paws tells the story of how Tuthmosis IV (18th Dynasty) dreamed that if he cleared away the sand he would become pharaoh, a dream which came true. The Sphinx's nose fell off after Turkish and French troops used the face for target practice. Today all the sand has been cleared away, but the Sphinx is threatened by incompetent restoration, rising ground water and pollution.

The Pyramid Complex of Khafre (Chephren)▶▶▶ (4th Dynasty) is well preserved as it was partly buried under the sand until 1853, when the French archaeologist, Mariette, started excavating. The exceptional diorite statue of the pharaoh (Egyptian Museum, Room 42) came from the limestone and granite valley temple just behind the Sphinx. Some believe that the pharaoh's corpse was brought to the valley temple to be mummified, while others believe that it was mummified in Memphis and brought here for the 'Opening of Mouth' ceremony. Mourners carried the mummy along the causeway, still partly visible, to the mortuary temple at the foot of the pyramid. Among the stones used for this temple, the largest was 13.4m long and weighed 163 tonnes.

Originally both the Pyramid of Chephren and the Great Pyramid were covered with polished limestone, but only the upper part of Chephren's retains traces. Perhaps because of this, and because it stands higher on the plateau, Chephren's pyramid looks taller than the Great Pyramid, although at 136.4m (originally 143m), it is slightly smaller. The pyramid has two entrances, both closed to the public. In the undecorated burial chamber an empty sarcophagus was found.

The Pyramid Complex of Menkaure (Mycerinus)▶▶▶ (4th Dynasty) is the smallest of the group. The 62m-high pyramid marks the decline of centralised power and the end of the great pyramid-building era. The pyramid was started by Mycerinus, Chephren's successor, and finished by his son. This is often called the Red Pyramid because of its red Aswan granite casing. The interior, recently opened to the public, contains an unfinished chamber, probably used for storing the royal canopic jars (which held the mummified viscera), and an underground burial chamber where human remains were found in a basalt sarcophagus, which are now believed to belong to a 26th-Dynasty king. The pyramid is flanked by three smaller subsidiary pyramids and, to the east, the remains of the funerary temple.

GIZA PYRAMIDS

5 L.E.

١٧٤٠٢

Ride **A desert ride**

One of the most pleasant ways to experience the desert and see some rarely visited monuments is to ride by horse or camel from Giza to Saqqara. The ride takes around three hours, one way, and is best started early in the morning to avoid the midday sun. Beware of the desert wind in winter. You can hire camels near the Sphinx, but they are usually more expensive and less comfortable than horses from the stables nearby (MG and AA stables are recommended). Make it clear from the start that you want to take the desert route past Zawiyet el-Aryan. As you head for the desert leaving the green cultivated land to your left, there are marvellous views of the Giza pyramids behind you.

After little more than an hour, you reach the **Zawiyet el-Aryan pyramids▶**. The 4th-Dynasty Unfinished Pyramid never made it beyond its granite foundations while the Layer Pyramid (probably 3rd Dynasty), with layers of small blocks, looks as though it was intended to form a step pyramid. After half an hour, the twin **Sun Temples of Abu Ghurab▶**, dedicated to Ra, the sun god of Heliopolis, stand at the edge of agricultural land. The courtyard of the Sun Temple of Nyuserre (5th Dynasty) contains an alabaster altar where cattle were sacrificed and the base of a solar obelisk. Beyond the ruined Sun Temple of Userkaf are the four 5th-Dynasty pyramid complexes of Abusir. Although the **Pyramid of Sahure▶** is badly damaged, it is possible to crawl through a narrow passage to the burial chamber.

Further along are the pyramid complexes of Nyuserre, Neferikare and Neferefre; the first and the last were never finished as the pharaohs died young. The Step Pyramid of Saqqara is now in front of you, half an hour away. Beyond Saqqara are the rarely visited Pyramids of Dahshur.

Riding round 40 centuries of Egyptian history

59

The Pyramids

■ **The Great Pyramid in Giza is one of the world's most famous monuments, but few realise that it was surrounded by more than 80 others along the Nile near Cairo. Until recently, little was known about the way pyramids were built and there are still disagreements as to what purpose they were intended to fulfil.....■**

Pyramidamania
More than 80 pyramids were built between Giza and el-Faiyum. Many of them have crumbled, but for the dedicated it is still possible to visit others, including: the Pyramids of Zawiyet el-Aryan (see page 59), pyramids in North and South Saqqara (pages 63–65), the Pyramids of Dahshur (page 59), and the Pyramids of Hawara, Lahun, Lisht and Maidum (Meidum) all near el-Faiyum (page 117).

Each limestone block of the Pyramid of Cheops was precisely placed to prevent pressure building up at any one point

Houses of Eternity A 12th-century Arab historian wrote that 'All things fear time, but time fears the Pyramids.' That is how the pyramid builders wanted it because they believed that the well-being of their *ka* (soul) in the afterlife depended on their corpses being preserved intact. The accepted theory is that the Houses of Eternity, as the pyramids were called, were built as enormous, impregnable tombs designed to protect the body and provide accommodation for the visiting *ka* (often represented in paintings and sculpture as a bird). Pyramids were served by temples at which rituals and offerings were made for the dead.

How to build a pyramid The perfect triangular form of the Giza pyramids evolved during the 3rd Dynasty. Earlier dynasties built tombs below ground and covered them with *mastabas* (mounds of mud-brick and plaster). The 3rd-Dynasty architect Imhotep had the means and the inspiration to build his *mastabas* in stone and then to mount them one on top of the other, creating the Step Pyramid at Saqqara. His master stroke is the earliest known, large stone building. From there, it was just a short step to the smooth-surfaced, gilt-capped pyramids at Giza: it took less than 200 years to perfect the pyramid form.

Statistics continue to astound admirers of the pyramids.

A design fault in the structure of the 'Collapsed Pyramid' of Maidum sent stresses outwards rather than inwards

The Great Pyramid, 137m high, was built out of 2.3 million stone blocks which are estimated to weigh 6.18 million tonnes. Recent excavations have produced an even more impressive fact: the pyramids were built not by slaves, as was previously thought, but by willing peasants, paid with lentils, onions and leeks and led by a few thousand skilled craftsmen. Only periods of wealth and stability could provide the necessary authority and administration for such an undertaking; it is not by chance that pyramids were first built when Egypt was newly unified, nor that building stopped when centralised power broke down at the end of the 6th Dynasty. Perhaps the act of building pyramids was itself a unifying factor, a visible symbol of a common goal, an expression of a hierarchy: pharaoh up on top, a broad base of peasants supporting him from below.

Costly Business
Now, the sum that was spent on radishes, onions and garlic for the workmen, is marked in Egyptian characters on the Pyramid... If these things be so, how much besides may we calculate was spent on the iron with which they worked, and on bread and clothes for the workmen...
Herodotus (c.460BC)
The Histories

The enormity of the building task at Giza is awe-inspiring

Of stars and staircases The perfection of the pyramids' construction begs the question which has yet to be answered conclusively: what purpose do they serve? This enigma continues to exercise imaginations and intellects around the world. Archaeologists are almost united in accepting that pyramids were built as tombs, and as homes for the pharaoh's *ka*, his living soul in the afterlife. But they disagree about other functions they might have served.

Some have loaded the pyramids with symbolism, claiming that their sides represent the sun's rays and that the steps of the Saqqara pyramid represent a staircase to heaven. Earlier Arab travellers thought they were filled with treasure while 18th-century Europeans, remembering Bible stories, believed they were the ancient granaries in which Joseph stored the corn which saved Egypt from famine. A modern theory suggests that the layout of the pyramids mirrors stars in the Orion constellation and that the size of the pyramids reflects the brightness of the stars to which they refer, all of this being an attempt to unite the dead pharaohs with Orion, the constellation of Osiris, the god of the afterlife.

CAIRO

Picnic in the desert
The Tent-Rest-House in North Saqqara offers a limited choice of foods. As it takes at least a day to visit the highlights of Saqqara, it's a good idea to take a picnic along with you. Egyptians often like to eat in the ruins of the 6th-century Monastery of Jeremiah, just off the car park, but if it's not too hot then an even better picnicking spot is available in the desert beyond Zoser's mortuary temple. From there you can admire Imhotep's genius while having lunch and then, as a sweet dessert, visit some exquisite *mastabas*.

The forever-young king, Ramses II, resting in Memphis

▶▶ **Memphis**   52B1

Open daily 9–4. Admission fee.

The ruins of Memphis, in the sleepy village of Mit Rahina, give little idea of the glory of the world's first imperial city, but still make a pleasant excursion into the countryside.

The legendary King Menes (c.3100BC), who united the southern valley and the northern delta, was the first pharaoh to wear the double crown of Upper and Lower Egypt. Symbolically, on the exact spot where the valley met the delta, he founded his new capital. Memphis became a magnificent city and its importance as a commercial centre and as the cult-centre for the God Ptah (the creator of the gods and the world) helped it retain its importance, even after the capital was moved to Thebes and later to Alexandria. The temple of Ptah was the city's most impressive building, but like the other temples and public places it was destroyed long ago. Memphis's houses and palaces, built like so many village houses today in mud brick, have also disappeared.

The site of Memphis is now a pleasant open-air museum. A limestone colossus of Ramses II as a young king, housed in a concrete pavilion, and a fine New Kingdom sphinx are the star exhibits. Both of them probably stood in front of the temple of Ptah. Other sculptures found on the site lie scattered around the garden, but the more important pieces are displayed in the Egyptian Museum (see pages 88–91).

▶▶▶ **Saqqara**   52B1

Open daily 9–5. Admission fee.

The necropolis of Saqqara, on a desert plateau 2km to the west of the ancient capital of Memphis, contains the tombs of Old Kingdom royalty and nobility. The burial site, about 7km long and 1,500m wide, was one of the largest

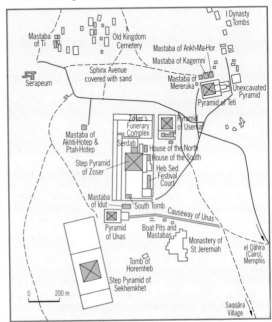

The first large stone building in the world: the Step Pyramid of Saqqara

and most important in Egypt and remained in use for more than 3,000 years, but much of it has still to be excavated. The necropolis is divided into two main areas, North and South Saqqara. As the most interesting monuments are in the northern part, only visitors with time and dedication go further afield to see the collapsed pyramids.

The **Step Pyramid Complex of Zoser▶▶▶** is the largest funerary complex in the necropolis. The Step Pyramid was constructed for King Zoser around 2650BC by the architect Imhotep, who was later deified for his achievements. This was not only the first pyramid to be built, but also the world's first large stone building and therefore a starting point for architecture. Imhotep began by building a single stone *mastaba*, the traditional funerary monument, and then added four and then another six smaller *mastabas*, one on top of the other. The finished structure, a stepped pyramid covered in a shiny white limestone, stood 60m high and measured 118m by 140m around its base. Inside, a 28m-deep shaft lead to the burial chamber and several galleries. The original entrance is now blocked and access is only possible through a later forced entrance (and with special permission from the Department of Antiquities).

The pyramid is surrounded by a vast funerary complex, which was enclosed by a limestone wall. Little of the wall is visible today, apart from the reconstructed entrance gate. From the gate, a colonnade leads to a wide court-

Early graffiti
Inside the corridor of the House of the South is some of the world's earliest graffiti, dating back to the New Kingdom. The visitors, who were scribes writing in a cursive hieroglyphic script, scribbled their admiration of Zoser's achievements.

Ptah-Hotep inspects the gifts and tributes that are brought by the estates from the North and the South

The Heb Sed festival
Traditionally this five-day festival was held in Memphis after 30 years of a king's reign; occasionally it took place more frequently as a symbolical renewal of the king's vitality. All the rituals had to be performed twice, once as the King of the South and once as the King of the North. In one ceremony the king ran between the two altars representing each region in a symbolic reunion of the country. Officials came from all over Egypt to witness the festival and renew their allegiance.

yard with the Step Pyramid in the north. Ahead is the South Tomb, a deep vertical shaft that may have stored the king's viscera. To the right of the colonnade is the Heb Sed Court, seen nowhere else in Egypt and now completely rebuilt. Inside the court, site of the Heb Sed festival, a double row of dummy chapels represents the shrines of Upper Egypt and Lower Egypt. Further north are the House of the South and the House of the North, which are thought to represent the archaic shrines of Upper and Lower Egypt. Nearby is the Serdab, containing a copy of a statue of King Zoser.

The **Pyramid of Unas▶▶**, the last king of the 5th Dynasty, is small and badly preserved, but on the walls of the burial chamber, made of alabaster and limestone, are some fine hieroglyphic inscriptions. These are known as the Pyramid Texts, a collection of the first written versions of the ancient ritual chants, from which the much later Book of the Dead derived. The mortuary temple is badly ruined but the causeway, a 1km-long covered corridor which runs from the mortuary temple to the pyramid, is one of the best preserved in Egypt. The pyramid is surrounded by *mastabas* (tombs) of the king's relatives; the Mastaba of Idut, his daughter, has some of the finest reliefs.

The **Mastaba of Mereruka▶▶** (6th Dynasty) is the largest *mastaba* in Saqqara and contains 32 rooms. Mereruka was a vizier (high official) to King Teti and married the king's daughter, who is also buried here with their son, Meri-Teti. Among the decorations there are lively scenes of Mereruka painting on an easel, of hunting, farming and dancing. The chapel in the middle has a fine statue of the tomb's owner and beautifully carved reliefs of funerary scenes and, to the left, of domestication of animals. Near by are the tombs of two other viziers to King Teti; the Mastaba of Kagemni, with decoration very similar to Mereruka's, and the Mastaba of Ankh-Ma-Hor, with the famous depictions of toe surgery, circumcision and a variety of craftsmen at work.

The **Double Mastaba of Akhti-Hotep and Ptah-Hotep▶▶▶** (5th Dynasty) is of interest for the way that it shows the different stages in the decoration of a tomb. In the corridor when you enter you can see how, before the reliefs were carved, the red drawings were first corrected in black by a master artist. The tomb chamber of the priest Ptah-Hotep has some of the most exquisite Old Kingdom reliefs, with very detailed depictions of children's games and Ptah-Hotep being manicured while surrounded by musicians. It is interesting to note that one of the games shown here, a jumping game called *Khaki el-Wizza*, is still played by Nubian children today. The tomb chamber of the priest's father, the vizier Akhti-Hotep, has similar but less refined decorations.

The **Mastaba of Ti**►►►, a 5th-Dynasty royal hairdresser who through marriage became overseer of the royal farms and mortuary temples, has an amazing variety of detailed scenes depicting life in ancient Egypt. The most famous relief is an unusual allegorical version of a traditional scene in which Ti and his wife go sailing in the marshes while hunting hippos (who here represent Evil) and fishes and birds (here representing Chaos). There are also fine reliefs of servants feeding cranes, of craftsmen and of musicians cheering Ti at his offering table.

The **Serapeum**►► is without doubt the eeriest place in Saqqara. It was discovered by the French archaeologist Mariette in 1851. In these cool, dark, underground rock-cut galleries, mummified Apis bulls were buried like royalty because the people of Memphis believed them to be reincarnations of their god Ptah and identified them with Osiris. The oldest gallery, now closed, dates back to the 19th Dynasty, the second to the 26th Dynasty, while the main chamber is Ptolemaic.

65

Above: the ubiquitous camel driver of the pyramids

Left: Ti, the royal hairdresser who climbed up the social ladder

Untouched Tomb
Mariette discovered only one chamber in the Serapeum that had escaped plundering. It was walled up during the reign of Ramses II (19th Dynasty), and after 3,700 years nothing had been disturbed. Not only was the mummy of the bull found, but there were also footprints left in the sand and a finger mark left in the mortar when the ancient workman put the last stone in the wall. The tomb is now closed again.

Trip on the river
Avoid traffic jams and take a cheap riverbus to Old Cairo, leaving from Maspero station, across the road from the Television Building. When the air isn't too thick and the windows not too dirty, it is a pleasure to zigzag across the river, passing an obelisk on the embankment, then fishing boats, yacht clubs, a fountain in mid-river, Qasr el-Aini Hospital, Manyal Palace, the Nilometer, feluccas (sailing boats) and then the high-rises of Maadi where the landscape opens up. Get out at Misr Qadima station and ask directions to Mari Girgis, a five-minute walk.

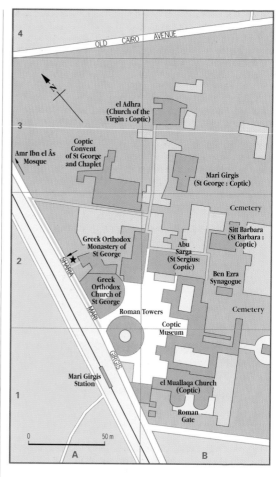

The architectural details of the mosque, synagogue and churches in this area show many similarities

Old Cairo

▶▶　**Abu Sarga (St Sergius Church)**　66B2

St Sergius is probably the oldest of the churches in the Coptic enclave, dated to the 5th century and typical in having 12 columns (one for each Apostle) separating the nave from the aisles. It was restored, along with several other buildings in the area, in the 12th century. To the right of the altar, steps lead down to the crypt where Coptic tradition claims the Holy Family rested after fleeing from Herod.

▶▶　**el-Muallaqa Church**　66B1

Sharia Mari Girgis. Donations welcomed.

This church, dedicated to the Virgin Mary, is called the 'Hanging Church' because of its position, built over the bastions of a Roman gate. It is reached from the stairway at the end of a pleasant courtyard, passing through a vestibule where videotapes of papal sermons and liturgies, crosses and plastic shrines to the Virgin Mary are on sale. Copts claim that the church dates back to the 4th century but the present building is unlikely to be older than the 7th century.

The interior, with the ceiling resembling an ark, is intricately decorated with cedar panels. The three *haikals* (altars) are hidden behind beautiful screens inlaid with bone and ivory. The carved marble pulpit, supported by 12 columns representing the Apostles, is the finest in Egypt. To the right of the entrance is a 10th-century icon of the Virgin and Child with Egyptian features. Coptic masses are held on Fridays (8–11am) and Sundays (7–10am).

▶▶ Amr Ibn el-As Mosque   66A3

Sharia Sidi Hasan el-Anwar. Admission fee.

This was the first mosque in Egypt, built in AD641 by the Muslim general Amr ibn el-As after he conquered Babylon-in-Egypt. The mosque provided the foundation of Fustat, the first Arab city in Egypt, which quickly became one of the wealthiest cities in the world. Fustat was burned by its own inhabitants when threatened by the Christian king of Jerusalem in 1168. Whatever is left now lies among the rubble behind Amr's mosque.

The mosque was originally a simple, mud-brick building, but it was enlarged as Islam became more established in Egypt and in 827 it was doubled to the present size. Later embellishments and restorations have left none of the original building intact. The façade was most recently rebuilt in 1977. The oldest part is to the right of the sanctuary. To the left is the tomb of Abdallah, Amr's son, buried in their house which was later incorporated into the mosque. The columns in the *qibla* (prayer niche) hall have been salvaged from various neighbourhood churches.

▶▶ Ben Ezra Synagogue   66B2

Egypt's oldest synagogue has been restored in all its splendour, but nothing can bring back its Jewish community. Old 'Rabbi' Cohen, selling Andy Warhol-style souvenir postcards, is the only Jew left here.

The Copts sold the 4th-century Church of St Michael to the Jews in the 11th century and it was restored in the 12th century by Abraham Ben Ezra, the rabbi of

The last Jew
Egypt's Jewish community is disappearing. Most Jews left for Israel long ago and the ones who stayed behind are old and usually poor; often there are not enough people to hold a service. 'Rabbi' Cohen saved the Ben Ezra Synagogue from falling down, and for 20 years he has overcharged visitors for his wacky postcards so that he could keep up the repair work. God must have heard his prayers as, a few years ago, big money was spent by the American Jewish Congress and the Egyptian government to restore the synagogue to its former glory. 'Rabbi' Cohen still potters around and, fortunately, still sells his postcards.

67

Ben Ezra Synagogue restored to its former glory

Hell on earth

Between the mosque of Amr and the cemetery walls is a bizarre sight: a moonscape where hovels made out of clay and recycled rubbish lie under a cloud of black smoke. It looks like hell on earth and it is hard to imagine any human life in this strange place, but as you walk in, treading carefully, you will be welcomed and shown around by brightly dressed children. This back end of the city is home to an interesting community of potters who burn rubbish in their ovens to fire everything from water-pipe stems and kitchenware to sewage pipes.

Artefacts such as this Coptic papyrus show how early Copts used the techniques and traditions of the ancient Egyptians to express their faith

Jerusalem. The synagogue resembles an early basilican church and its decoration would not be out of place in one of the nearby churches or mosques. Jews claim that this is where Jeremiah preached in the 6th century BC, while Copts believe Moses was found here in the bulrushes.

▶▶▶ Coptic Museum   66B2

Sharia Mari Girgis. Admission fee.

The two Roman towers and the sections of wall built around AD130, to the right of the garden of the Coptic Museum, are all that remains of Babylon-in-Egypt. At the end of the garden is the elegant building which, since 1908, has served as a museum of religious and secular Coptic artefacts. Coptic art flourished in the period between the Graeco-Romans and the arrival of Islam (AD300–1000).

The ground floor, in the New Wing, is arranged chronologically. Starting on the left of the entrance hall (Room 2), early Christian reliefs suggest how the pharaonic *ankh* (looped cross) evolved into the cross. Room 3 contains excellent frescoes; one from el-Bawit monastery (6th century) shows Christ ascending to heaven in a chariot and the Virgin and Child with the Apostles.

In Room 6, amid the fine artefacts from the 6th century Monastery of Jeremiah in Saqqara, is the earliest known stone pulpit, probably influenced by the Heb-Sed throne in Saqqara. Room 8 contains a splendid wooden screen from St Barbara's Church, reminiscent of Fatimid woodwork. A 10th-century fresco in Room 9 shows Adam blaming Eve for the Fall.

On the upper floor, Room 10 contains *ostraca* (flat pottery fragments used as writing tablets), manuscripts and the papyri (text written on papyrus) from the Gnostic Gospels of Nag Hammadi. Some fine examples of Coptic textiles are found in Rooms 10–12, including a 4th-century towel and a tapestry showing joyous musicians (Room 10), a linen cloth decorated with Isaac's sacrifice in cartoon style (Room 11) and a fine silk robe embroidered with images of the Apostles (Room 12). Room 13 contains icons and fine Alexandrian-style carved ivories. Among the artefacts in the last rooms are Nubian paintings salvaged from the villages now flooded by Lake Nasser.

Back in the courtyard, you can see part of the Roman wall and gate from Babylon. Steps lead down to the level of the Nile and to vaulted corridors, once used as prisons and stables. The Old Wing, which contains beautiful *mashrabiya* (carved wood) work with Christian motifs, pottery and glass, is closed for extensive restoration.

▶ Sitt Barbara (St Barbara Church)   66B2

This church was dedicated to St Cyrus and St John in AD684, but it is now known for the saint whose 3rd-century relics are held in the sanctuary to the right of the altar. Legend has it that Barbara's pagan father denounced his beautiful daughter when she chose to become a nun, after which she was tortured and executed by the Romans. Skylights give the church a lighter feel.

Walk Enclave of devotion

This is a two-hour walk through the narrow streets of Coptic Cairo. Although the area is usually quieter than an Egyptian village, on Sundays and Coptic holidays the streets are crowded with worshippers. See the map on page 66.

Start at Mari Girgis (the Monastery of St George), the seat of the Greek patriarch and scene of one of Cairo's largest Coptic celebrations, the *moulid* (festival) of Mari Girgis. Although it is closed to the public, you can visit the round Greek Orthodox **Church of St George►**, a modern building that sits over a Roman tower, which can be reached from the steps just outside the church. Downstairs in the chapel, priests wrap a heavy chain around the heads and waists of believers while they chant prayers in memory of the persecution of St George by the Romans.

Returning to Sharia Mari Girgis, take the steps to the right, through a passageway and out on to an old cobbled

The Chaplet of the Convent of St George

street. To your left is the Coptic **Convent of St George,** closed to visitors except for the **Chaplet►**, which is full of icons, heavy incense fumes and people chanting. In a side room, the nuns offer chain-wrapping and moral guidance. Continue to the end of the street, noticing the old houses, and turn left into a narrow lane. A woman often offers bunches of basil, as the **Church of the Virgin** here is known as Kasriyat el-Rihan (Pot of Basil). Walk back and follow the arrow to **Abu Sarga** (the Coptic Church of St Sergius, see page 66), with a crypt where the Holy Family is believed to have stayed during their flight into Egypt.

Continue along the street, with the **Ben Ezra Synagogue** (see page 67) on the right and **Sitt Barbara** (see page 68) on the left. Walk until the end of the street and stroll around the peaceful Christian cemetery.

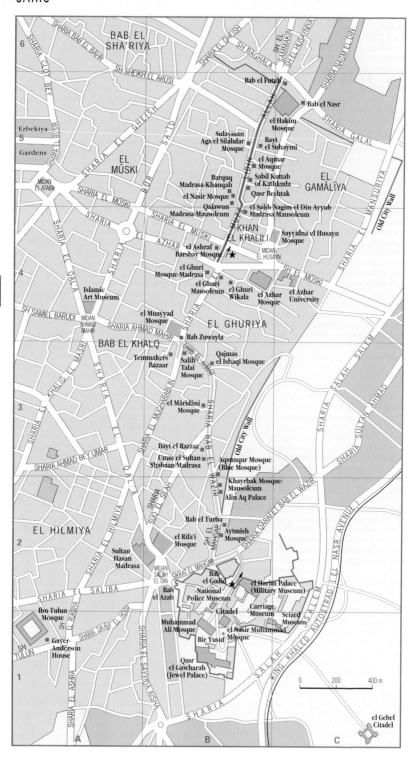

Students in the court-
yard of el-Azhar
Mosque

71

Islamic Cairo

►► el-Azhar Mosque and Madrasa 70B4

Sharia el-Azhar. Admission fee.

El-Azhar (the most blooming), founded in AD970, was the first mosque of the Fatimid city of el-Qahira and claims to be the oldest university in the world. As the foremost centre of Islamic theology, and with its sheikh the highest theological authority for Egyptian Muslims, el-Azhar also plays an important role in the country's politics.

The mosque is a confusing but harmonious blend of periods and styles. It is entered through the Barber's Gate, where students had their heads shaved. To the right of the central courtyard is a 14th-century *madrasa* (theological college) with a beautiful *mihrab* (prayer niche), and *riwaq* (free apartments) for students. The sanctuary hall original-ly contained only five rows of columns and the old *mihrab* is still there. It is here that students memorise the Quran, sitting in a circle round their sheikh. To the east is the Chapel of the Blind, whose blind students were always notorious for their religious fervour.

►► Bab el-Futuh, Bab el-Nasr and the city wall 70C5

Admission fee.

The monumental gates (AD1087), along with the remain-ing city walls, are a masterpiece of Islamic military archi-tecture. Bab el-Futuh (Gate of Conquests), with its twin oval towers, marks the northern end of the Fatimid city. Upon its annual return from Mecca, the Mahmal (see panel) entered the city through this gate in an impressive parade. You may need to look for the gate's custodian, but he is never far from the entrance. Inside is a huge vaulted room with stairs leading up to the wall, which has good views over the Bab el-Nasr cemetery. Inside the wall is a 200m tunnel with fine masonry, which allowed covered passage from one gate to the other. Bab el-Nasr (Gate of Victory) was built to a similar plan as Bab el-Futuh and is decorated with shields, the symbols of victory.

The Mahmal
Shagar el-Durr, 13th-century queen of Egypt, travelled to Mecca in a richly decorated howdah (canopied seat) or *mahmal*. Unable to make the pilgrimage the following year, she sent the empty *mahmal*, an act which subsequent rulers continued, making the annual departure of the *mahmal* the rallying point of Egyptian pilgrims.

Metropolis of the universe
'He who hasn't seen Cairo cannot know the grandeur of Islam. It is the metropo-lis of the universe, the gar-den of the world, the nest of human species, the gateway to Islam, the throne of royalty: it is a city embellished with castles and palaces and adorned with monasteries and dervishes, and with colleges lit by the moons and stars of erudition.'
Ibn Khaldun, 14th-century Arab historian

■ **Muslims are required to pray five times a day, but they don't have to go to a mosque to do it, which is why some mosques function as more than mere prayer halls.....**■

Until recently, muezzins called for prayer from the top of the minarets, but now a tape recorder does the job

Mosques closed to non-Muslims
Outside prayer time, all Cairene mosques are open to non-Muslims (sometimes for a fee and a tip) with the exception of the mosques of Sayyidna el-Husayn and Sayyida Zeinab, which will only admit Muslims.

Essential mosque glossary
Liwan – a hall opening on to a courtyard
Qibla – direction of prayer towards Mecca
Mihrab – an alcove or niche indicating the qibla
Minaret – thin tower above a mosque from which the muezzin used to call
Minbar – a stepped chair or pulpit from which sermons are delivered
Muezzins – men who call to prayer

The religious obligation Muslims are allowed to perform their prayers wherever they happen to be when they hear the *muezzin*. When they pray they should be in a state of purity (all mosques have some sort of washing facilities) and should pray on clean ground, facing Mecca. Egyptian hotel bedrooms usually have an arrow facing east, but mosques make the point more strongly with a *mihrab* to indicate the *qibla*.

Early mosques The world's first mosque was in the courtyard of the Prophet's house in Medina and offered nothing more than some shade. Early Egyptian mosques were rarely more elaborate, but they were larger. Ibn Tulun's 9th-century mosque is perfect in its simplicity, but its decoration is elaborate. It was intended as a congregational mosque, for social and administrative use.

Conflicting traditions Sunni Islam forbids the representation of the human form, which is why Egypt's mosques don't contain many pictures, though they make up for it in the variety of decoration. Islam also discourages the cult of the dead, but many rulers, from a companion of the Prophet to the last Shah of Iran, are buried in Cairo's mosques and their tombs attract worshippers.

A quiet corner Egyptian mosques are often used for more than just prayer. Although they are crowded and noisy at prayer times, at other times they are quiet enough for people to lie down and sleep. They offer a spot for meditation away from the bustle of the city.

An elaborate domed ceiling, Muhammad Ali Mosque

▶▶ Bab Zuwayla 70B4

Sharia Darb el-Ahmar. Admission fee for the mosque.
From the platform between the twin towers of Bab
Zuwayla (AD1092), which marked the southern end of the
Fatimid city, Mamluk sultans watched the departure of
the annual *mahmal* (pilgrimage). In the 19th century it
became known as the Bab el-Mitwalli, after a saint called
Mitwalli el-Qutb performed miracles near the gate. It was
then also a place of execution.

The two minarets rising above the towers belong to the
Mosque of el-Muayyad (AD1420), which contains the
mausoleum of Sultan el-Muayyad and his son. The courtyard contains a garden with palm trees, a good place to
rest after seeing the spectacular view from the minaret.

*The busy and crowd-
ed area around Bab
Zuwayla accentuates
the peace of the
courtyard of the
Mosque el-Muayyad*

▶▶▶ Bayt el-Suhaymi 70B5

19, Haret Darb el-Asfar. Admission fee.
This splendid and remarkably well-preserved merchant's
house offers a rare insight into the sumptuous lifestyle of
the 16th and 17th centuries. Behind the plain façade, the
cool, peaceful courtyard comes as a surprise after the
street. The house is a labyrinth of rooms on different levels
and, although one just wants to get lost, it is obligatory to
follow the guided tour included in the ticket price. As in all
Islamic houses of the period, there is a strict division
between the male, public areas and the female, private and
'forbidden' areas. Male guests were entertained with
music and dancers in the grand, ground-floor reception
room. The richly decorated, first-floor reception room of the
harem has beautiful *mashrabiya* (carved wooden) screens
which overlook the courtyard and the terrace opposite,
where men gathered on summer evenings. Beside the
private bathroom (rare at that time) is a room containing a
whalebone, believed to make barren women fertile.

1001 Nights
Cairo, as one of the cities
of the *Thousand and One
Nights*, has preserved
many of its medieval buildings. It is exciting to wander off into the narrow
lanes and stumble upon a
crumbling palace or a
small mosque, which can
be explored at the cost of a
small *baksheesh* (tip) to
the guard. Take time to
stroll around, sipping tea
and listening to stories
wherever they are on offer,
and you might find yourself
slipping back in time to a
world of fairy tales.

City of the Dead

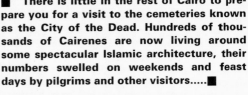

■ **There is little in the rest of Cairo to prepare you for a visit to the cemeteries known as the City of the Dead. Hundreds of thousands of Cairenes are now living around some spectacular Islamic architecture, their numbers swelled on weekends and feast days by pilgrims and other visitors.....■**

Ancient motifs
Even in so revered a place as the Imam el-Shafi'i's tomb, ancient Egyptian traditions mix with Islamic practice: the dome above the tomb is topped with a pharaonic boat, familiar from ancient tombs as the transport of the soul on its final journey. The Imam's boat used to be filled with grain to attract birds – which, to ancient Egyptians, represented a man's soul – but the present-day guardians are now loath to climb up there to fill it.

74

Pharaonic traditions Egyptians were traditionally buried in the west, towards the sunset, but Islam shifted the focus of devotion eastwards towards Mecca, and the conquering Arabs buried their dead in the desert to the east. As their settlements spread further north, forming what is now the older part of Cairo, the cemetery grew around its eastern edge. Muslims believe that the soul is independent of the body and the corpse need not be cared for, but Egyptians are traditionalists and, as in ancient Egypt, guardians and prayer reciters live in the cemeteries to ensure the spiritual and physical welfare of the deceased.

Growth of the cemetery The cemetery grew quickly after 1399, when Sultan Barquq chose to be buried not in the palace grounds but in the desert near some pious sheikhs. His son built schools, mills and bakeries, baths, rooms for merchants and a market around the tomb. Barquq's example was followed by Sultan Qaytbay and the cemetery soon developed into a suburb, a place of commerce and a retreat from the city. In recent times, Cairo's population explosion has increased the numbers living in and around the tombs, estimated at up to half a million people.

The great are buried beside the unknown in the City of the Dead

Important monuments The cemeteries' most important monuments are found in two groups. Barquq's complex, in the northern cemetery, was built between 1400 and 1411 and is known as a *khanqah*, an institution for mys-

tics and holy men. Barquq and his son, Farag, lie in one tomb chamber, and in another are two of Barquq's daughters. They rest beneath Cairo's earliest large stone domes. Nearby, Qaytbay's complex (1472–4) is a perfect example of late Mamluk architecture, elaborately decorated in stone, marble, glass and wood. Even the outside of the dome over Qaytbay's tomb is beautifully carved.

The southern cemetery is older and larger, and hidden among its new apartment buildings are some of the earliest Muslim graves in Egypt. The most important – and the largest – Islamic mortuary complex in Egypt is that of the Imam el-Shafi'i, descendant of the Prophet and founder of one of the four rites of Sunni Islam. The complex, enlarged and restored several times since his death in 820, is seen as a place of *baraka* (blessing) and Muslims from around the world come to pray at his tomb, kiss the sandalwood screen and an ancient marble pillar, and leave written requests for the saint. Behind the Imam's complex is the Hosh el-Basha, the kitsch resting place of some of Egypt's 19th-century royal family and of the Mamluks who were killed in 1811 to secure the family's position.

The dome of Qaytbay's Mausoleum, among the finest of Mamluk masonry

The living cemetery Tomb squatters now cover all of the cemeteries and have made them into crowded suburbs. On Fridays and holidays (particularly the Aid el-Fitr at the end of Ramadan), people from elsewhere in the city come to spend time at the graves of family or friends, reward the guardians and enjoy themselves. As there are many saints buried in the cemeteries, *moulids* – the feasts on saints' days (see pages 146–7) – are frequent. The Imam el-Shafi'i's at the beginning of the Muslim month of Sha'ban is one of the largest and most colourful. People come from across the city to shop at the weekly Friday market on and around Sharia el-Imam el-Shafi'i.

Walk with care
The best way to see the City of the Dead is to walk, but as the cemeteries are difficult to police, they are hiding places for criminals and deserters. Beware of straying too far from the main streets. Also, the earthquake of 1992 left many tomb chambers in a precarious state, and some graves are in danger of collapsing underfoot.

CAIRO

The Citadel

Oriental inhospitality
One evening in 1811, Muhammad Ali invited more than 400 Mamluks for dinner and, breaching the conventions of hospitality, locked the gate of Bab el-Azab and had them shot as they tried to leave. The victims were buried in the Hosh el-Basha, the crypt of Muhammad Ali's own family, near the Mosque of Imam el-Shafi, and Muhammad Ali became the sole master of Egypt.

General view
The best view of the Citadel's imposing walls and towers, built with limestone from the Muqattam quarries and with blocks taken from the Giza pyramids, is from Sharia Salah Salem.

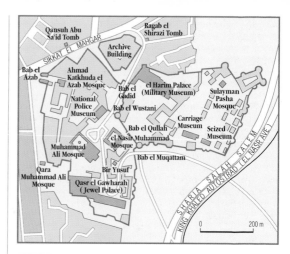

Many Cairenes are still bitter about the fact that they gave the French an ancient obelisk for a clock that never worked

▶▶ **Aqsunqur Mosque (Blue Mosque)** 70B3
Bab el-Wazir. Admission fee.
The Blue Mosque (AD1347) contains the mausoleum of its builder, Amir Aqsunqur, to the left of the pleasant courtyard. Beside it stands the mausoleum of his brother-in-law, Sultan el-Ashraf Kuchuk (the Little One), who ruled for five months before being assassinated at the age of six. To the right is the tomb of Ibrahim Aga, who added the beautiful panels of blue tiles in 1650. The *qibla* (direction of Mecca) hall has a fine marble *mihrab* (prayer niche) and one of Cairo's oldest surviving *minbars* (pulpits).

▶▶▶ **Citadel (el-Qal'a)** 70B2
Bab el-Gadid. Admission fee.
The Citadel and the minarets of Muhammad Ali's mosque tower high above Cairo's skyline. The original buildings, started in 1176 as part of Salah ad-Din's grand fortification plan, were torn down by Sultan el-Nasir and by Muhammad Ali to make way for their own mosques and palaces.
The **Mosque of Muhammad Ali▶▶** looks spectacular from anywhere in Cairo, but on closer inspection it is often disappointing. Although modelled on the Blue Mosque in Istanbul, it misses the integrity and simplicity of Cairo's great mosques. Its enormous dome, supported by four semi-domes, gives a sense of space but the decoration inside is kitsch and overdone. Muhammad Ali is buried under a marble cenotaph to the right of the entrance. The alabaster courtyard is overlooked by a French clock given by Louis Philippe (in exchange for the obelisk now adorning Paris's Place de la Concorde) and from the terrace beyond there are magnificent views over the city and the pyramids.
To the south is what remains of Muhammad Ali's **Qasr el-Gawharah (Jewel Palace)▶**, damaged by fire in 1972. It was Sultan el-Nasir who made the Citadel the seat of power, and it remained so for 700 years, but the striped **Mosque of el-Nasir Muhammad▶** (1318–35), with its faience minarets, is all that survives from his reign. Behind the mosque is Bir **Yusuf's Well▶**, 97m deep, which was linked to the Nile through natural channels. Muhammad Ali's Harim Palace has been turned into the uninteresting Military Museum. Further north is the

Carriage Museum▶, formerly in Bulaq, with royal carriages on show and the curious **Seized Museum**▶, displaying antiquities seized from people who tried to smuggle them out of Egypt. Back towards the entrance is the bizarre **National Police Museum**▶, providing information on a range of topics about criminality.

▶▶▶ Gayer-Anderson House (Bayt el-Kritliya)

70A1

4, Midan Ahmed Ibn Tulun. Admission fee.

The entrance to the Bayt el-Kritliya (the House of the Cretan woman) is to the left of Ibn Tulun's Mosque (see page 80). It is now part of the Islamic Art Museum and the ticket price includes a guided tour around the house. The Englishman Gayer-Anderson, a doctor to the royal family, lived here from 1935 to 1942. He restored the house – originally two houses, built in the 16th and 17th centuries and joined by a passage – and furnished it with oriental objects he collected on his travels. The *haremlek* (women's quarters) are 17th-century, with a beautiful reception room, several private rooms and a roof terrace where the women went to catch the breeze. A passage leads to the *salamlek* (men's quarters). The richly decorated reception room on the ground floor is one of the finest in Cairo. The names of other rooms – the Queen Anne Room, the Damascus Room with splendid wood panelling, the Persian Room, etc. – are the fantasies of an English Orientalist and have little to do with how the houses were originally used.

As in Bayt el-Suhaymi, the house suggests that wealthy Cairenes were able to enjoy a far more luxurious lifestyle than their 16th- and 17th-century European contemporaries.

No effort was spared in the baroque decoration of Muhammad Ali's Mosque

77

The Gayer-Anderson House; women from the harem watched the men from behind the first floor screens

The silhouette of the Sultan Hasan Mosque pagoda at dusk

into the tree-lined Sikket el-Mahgar. The **Mosque of Aytmish el-Bagasi** (AD1383) is 200 yards down on the right, with a *sabil-kuttab* (fountain and school) on the corner. The alley to the right leads to **Bab el-Turba,** an old gate to the Bab el-Wazir cemetery and the **Mausoleum of Tarabay el-Sharifi** (AD1503).

Return to the main street (now called Bab el-Wazir). The ruins to the right were once the imposing **Palace of Alin Aq** (AD1293), later occupied by Khayrbak (AD1502–1520) who built his **mosque-mausoleum** next to it. Farther down is the **Blue Mosque** (see page 76), while on the left, beyond the **Madrasa of Umm el-Sultan Shabaan** (AD1368), is **Bayt el-Razzaz,** a 15th-century palace with splendid *mashrabiya* (carved wood) screens on the third floor.

Past the small square, on the left, is the **Mosque of el-Maridani** (AD1339–1340) whose peaceful courtyard encourages a rest. The *qibla* hall, behind the beautiful *mashrabiya* screens, is said to have treasure hidden in the right-hand corner, to rebuild the mosque when it falls down. The **Mosque of Qajmas el-Ishaqi** (AD1481), to the right where the street becomes Sharia Darb el-Ahmar, is richly decorated with magnificent stained-glass windows and colored marble. Opposite **Bab Zuwayla** (see page 73) is the **Mosque of Salih Talai** (AD1160), attractive for its simplicity, and the entrance to the **Suq el-Khiyamiyyah,** or Tentmakers Bazaar (AD1650), a covered market where men make elaborately appliquéd tents.

Walk

From the Citadel to Bab Zuwayla

This 2-hour walk from the Citadel to Bab Zuwayla follows a street that changes its name several times. Formerly a cemetery outside the Fatimid city, then a pleasure garden in the reign of Salah ad-Din, the area prospered when the Citadel became the seat of power in the 14th century. See the map on page 70.

Leave the Citadel along Sharia Bab el-Gadid and turn right at the post office

Walk To the Northern Gates

Sharia el-Muizz li-Din Allah was originally called the Qasaba, which ran through the heart of the Fatimid city. It would take days to see every monument en route, but an afternoon will do to get the feel of it. See the map on page 70.

Start on the Khan el-Khalili (the bazaar) side of Sharia el-Azhar and walk along Sharia el-Muizz. The alley to the left, before the Mosque of el-Ashraf Barsbay (AD1425), leads to the **Spice and Perfume Bazaars.** Cross the crowded Sharia el-Muski to the **Goldsmiths' Bazaar,** with hundreds of jewelry workshops behind the shopfronts. Above an entrance to Khan el Khalili, where the street changes its name to **Suq el-Nahhasin** (Coppersmiths' Bazaar), is the **Madrasa-Mausoleum of el-Salih Nagm el-Din Ayyub** (AD1250), with Cairo's only surviving Ayyubid minaret. From here you get a magnificent view of the imposing Mamluk complexes of Qalawun, el-Nasir and Barquq (see page 84).

This part of the Qasaba is still known as **Bayn el-Qasrayn**

Making the tarbouche

(Between the Two Palaces), although nothing remains of the fabled Eastern and Western Palaces that stood at the city center. Before the road forks, the little alley to the right leads to **Qasr Bashtak** (AD1339), which once had five floors, with running water on each one. On the fork is the **Sabil-Kuttab of Kathkuda** (AD1744) with a tiled *sabil* (fountain) on the ground floor and a Quran school on top of it. Take the street to the left. Farther along on the right is the **Mosque of el-Aqmar** (the moonlit), built in 1122, the first with a decorated stone façade. On the left beyond the Darb el-Asfar is the **Mosque of Sulayman Aga el-Silahdar** (AD1839), with a blend of Mamluk style and European baroque and rococo. Farther north the street widens into the lemon, garlic, and onion market, ending at the **Mosque of el-Hakim** (see page 80) and the **Bab el-Futuh** (see page 71).

79

Fine plasterwork in the Ibn Tulun Mosque

Over the years the fabric merchants have expanded their shops into the foundations of the Madrasa el-Ghuri, making it a safety hazard

►► Ghuriya Complex 70B4

Sharia el-Azhar. Admission fee for wikala.

Getting out of a taxi at the pedestrian bridge over Sharia el-Azhar, you can't miss the Ghuriya, a complex built by Sultan el-Ghuri, the Mamluk sultan whose defeat began 400 years of Ottoman domination. Both the striped mosque-*madrasa* (AD1505) to the right and the domed mausoleum are supported by scaffolding, some say because of the 1992 earthquake, others because adjacent shops have weakened their foundations. The *wikala*, in the small street around the corner from the mausoleum, is the best preserved of Cairo's *caravanserais* (caravan hostels). Now converted into artists' studios, it is an oasis of peace and quiet, but imagine it in its heyday full of animals stabled on the ground floor and traders bargaining loudly with their clients above.

► el-Hakim Mosque 70C5

Sharia el-Muizz li-Din Allah. Admission fee.

The notorious Fatimid caliph, el-Hakim bi-Amr Allah (Ruler by God's Command), built his mosque between 990 and 1013, but the two unusual minarets and some Quranic inscriptions are all that remain of the original construction. Over the years it has been used as a prison, a stable, a museum and, under Nasser, a school. It has recently been restored beyond recognition, with the addition of shiny marble and gilt, by the Bohras, an Ismaili sect originating in Bombay who claim to be the true descendants of el-Hakim. During his life el-Hakim declared himself divine while his disciple el-Darazi, founder of the Druze sect, preached that el-Hakim was the Messiah.

►►► Ibn Tulun Mosque 70A1

Sharia el-Salibah. Admission fee.

If there is only time to see one mosque in Cairo, it should be this one. Ahmed ibn Tulun built his mosque near the Muqattam hills between 877 and 879. It is the oldest intact mosque in the city, impressive both for its grand

scale and its extreme simplicity, and a rare survivor of the classical period (9th and 10th centuries) of Islamic architecture. The entrance, through a *ziyada* (enclosure) later used as a bazaar, leads to a vast courtyard 92m square and simply covered with pebbles. The pointed arches are of red brickwork and stucco. Below the ceiling of the mosque runs a 2km-long sycamore-wood frieze which is inscribed with one fifteenth of the Quran. The strange spiral minaret was probably inspired by the minaret of Samarra in Iraq, where ibn Tulun grew up, although romantics prefer the story that he absent-mindedly rolled up a piece of paper and used it as the design for a minaret.

▶▶   Islamic Art Museum   70A4
Midan Ahmad Mahir (Bab el-Khalq). Admission fee.
The museum's collection of Islamic art from the 7th to the 19th centuries is the most extensive of its kind in Egypt, its exhibits saved from mosques and mausoleums in danger of collapse. The new entrance, through a garden at the side, leads to Room 7, but as most of the 23 rooms are arranged chronologically you should start with Room 1, opposite the old entrance. Note the lack of representations of animals or humans – no statues, for instance – which Sunni Muslims consider idolatry. The Fatimids, who were Shi'a Muslims, had no such restrictions and freely used birds, animals and scenes from daily life to decorate stucco and woodwork (Room 4).

In the archway between Rooms 4 and 5, note the Ottoman coloured windows in plaster frames (ask the attendant to illuminate them). Room 5 (Mamluk period) contains a finely worked, 14th-century mosaic fountain. Another fountain, this one a marble column, in Room 10 sits beneath a domed wooden ceiling whose windows would have allowed women to watch entertainment below. In the Room of Masterpieces (Room 13), linger over the decorated door from the mosque of Sayyida Zaynab. In Room 21 are glass lamps from mosques, with some fine ones taken from the Madrasa of Sultan Hasan.

Traders in the grain market, Islamic Cairo

Ask the guard
The Islamic Art Museum is under-visited so not all the exhibits are lit, but the guards will switch on lights when asked. Note that tips are not allowed here.

The city of el-Qitai
Ibn Tulun, remembering the grandeur of his home town Samarra, built his new capital, el-Qitai, on a spur of the Muqattam hills. The Tulunid dynasty only lasted from 868 to 905, and of Ibn Tulun's extravagant pleasure palaces, lavish gardens, enormous mosque and *maidan* (square) in the middle of the city, where he played polo with his captains, only the mosque has survived.

■ **Sufi mystics imported the coffee bean from Yemen long before the 16th century, after finding that the presence of the stimulant caffeine helped them to prolong their recitations. Since then** *qahwa* **(the Arabic word for coffee and café) has been an essential and fascinating part of life in Cairo.....**■

Welcome to women
It is possible that foreign women will feel uncomfortable in some of Cairo's cafés, but there are some atmospheric places which are particularly female-friendly. These include: el-Fishawi, el-Sukkariya, and Naguib Mahfouz, all in Khan el-Khalili; Mahran, in the alley beside 6 Qasr en-Nil St, downtown; Musicians Café, Muhammad Ali St, behind Ataba Market, downtown.

The flexible forum There are cafés which have remained intact over the past 200 years and are monuments in themselves, but even they will confound the expectations of visitors hoping to find grand European-style coffee-houses. The Cairene café is a much more flexible place, often starting out as nothing more than a bench or two, a water heater, a charcoal burner, a radio and fluorescent lighting, but capable of spreading chairs and thin copper-topped tables across pavements and around buildings in search of space or shade.

Much more than coffee Some cafés will stay open until the early hours of the morning, so it's not surprising that they offer a range of drinks to satisfy the needs of different times of day or night. Besides coffee and *shay* (tea, served strong and sweet) there are thick hot drinks for winter nights, but food cannot be counted on and alcohol is never served. (For more details on café drinks, see page 103.)

The men's room Most of Cairo's cafés are frequented by men only, some of whom are looking for things that are missing at home, like the companionship of a game of cards or *tawla* (backgammon) and the heady pleasures of a *sheesha* (water-pipe). Cafés are also the hunting grounds of hawkers selling everything from wallets, sunglasses and shoeshines to a chance of paradise if you buy a Quran. They used to be the stage of professional storytellers who retold legends as old as the *Thousand and One Nights*, but they and the musicians who accompanied them lost their places to radio and television. Nowadays the most compelling stories are usually enacted among the audience.

▶▶▶ Khan el-Khalili 70B4

This maze of bazaars is squeezed into a small area between Husayn's mosque (see page 85), Sharia el-Muizz and Sharia el-Muski. Amir Jarkas el-Khalil, a horse-master, built it in 1382 as a *khan* (caravanserai) and Sultan Qansuh reconstructed most of it in the 16th century, leaving a façade and an original gate, the Bab el-Badistan towards the middle of Sikket el-Badistan. It used to attract foreign merchants, but most of the Jews, Greeks and Armenians have left and nowadays you are most likely to bargain with Egyptians.

The main artery, Sikket el-Badistan begins with souvenir shops but there are antique and jewellery shops past the Bab el-Badistan. Gold is sold by the weight in the Goldsmiths' Bazaar in Sharia el-Muizz where it borders Khan el-Khalili. Although the price for gold is fixed, just watch the Egyptian women bargain as they buy their wedding dowry. You may do the same. Haret Khan el-Khalili is the place for silver and leather work. In the narrow alley off Haret and Sharia Khan el-Khalili a few shops sell the famous Muski glass.

Sharia Khan el-Khalili, with good carpet shops, leads to the end of Sharia el-Muski where the clothes for belly dancers glitter in the afternoon sun. In Sharia el-Muizz, left of the mosque of Barsbay, a tiny alley leads to the Perfume Bazaar. Remember that it is all part of the experience to be tempted into buying the essential oils of jasmine, amber, Opium and Chanel No 5 and to feel a little sheepish when your great bargain leaves marks on your clothes. Cairenes come here for cotton sheets, towels and fabrics. Further down the alley, your nose will lead you to a wonderful covered spice market. If you want to equip an Egyptian café, or just buy a water-pipe, take a look on Sharia el-Muizz past Barquq's Madrasa.

Above: Spice shops sell spices used in cooking and a wide array of herbal remedies

Opposite: almost every street in Cairo has its own café where locals meet for business during the day and for a game or a chat after work

Walk in al-Muski
Almost everything is sold on Sharia el-Muski, the street that starts to the east of Midan el-Ataba and runs parallel to Sharia el-Azhar, to Midan el-Husayn. Cars seemed to be banned in this street, more by the crowds than by law, but occasionally a pushcart will endanger your safety. It is a real bazaar and it is wonderful to get lost in the crowds of women and Upper-Egyptians who buy here for their small shops back home. It makes a pleasant stroll in the late afternoon.

CAIRO

By night
To appreciate the grandeur
of the Islamic buildings,
walk on Sharia el-Muizz
late at night. The sight of
the minarets rising up from
the deserted streets, lit by
the moon, is truly moving. It
is quite safe to roam the
main streets at night, and
people always return
greetings when you say
'Salaam alay-kum'.

*The rebuilt
façade of
the
Mosque of
el-Husayn,
central
landmark
of Islamic
Cairo*

84

► ► ►   **Qalawun, el-Nasir
            and Barquq complex**   *70B5*

Bayn el-Qasrayn on Sharia el-Muizz. Admission fee.
The 185m façade of this complex, built by three of the
most important Mamluk sultans, is a spectacular sight
both for its grandeur and harmony. The first building in the
complex that you come to from el-Azhar was built in 1285
by Sultan Qalawun. The original *maristan* (hospital), which
served as a lunatic asylum until the 1850s, is now partly
beneath and beside the new eye hospital. A second
entrance further on leads to a corridor with the badly damaged *madrasa* (theology school) to the left and, to the
right, his mausoleum, a rarely visited jewel of Mamluk
architecture. The tomb chamber, reached through a little
courtyard and an intricately carved stucco arch, is sump-
tuously decorated and overwhelmingly grand. It is hard to
imagine that all this was built in only 13 months.

The second part of the complex, begun in 1296 by
Sultan Kitbugha, was finished in 1304 by one of
Qalawun's sons, el-Nasir Muhammad. El-Nasir was an
obsessive builder, with 30 mosques, a canal north of
Cairo and an aqueduct from the Nile to the Citadel to his
credit. His *madrasa* and mausoleum, following the plan of
his father's, is under restoration, but you can admire the
delicate stucco work on the elegant minaret. El-Nasir
is buried in his father's mausoleum; his own son is
buried here.

Next door are a *madrasa* and *khanqah* (religious hostel)
built in 1384–6 by Sultan Barquq, the first Circassian
Mamluk sultan. The heavy bronze-plated doors, with
silver inlay under a panel of black and white marble, lead to a cruciform *madrasa*. Behind
the doors in the corners are stairs leading to living quarters (*khanqah*) for
Sufis and students. The
beautiful ceiling in the
qibla liwan (vault-
ed hall facing
Mecca)
to

Sultan Barquq's tomb, a masterpiece of Mamluk architecture

One of the surviving minarets decorating the Sultan Hasan Mosque-Madrasa

the right, is supported by pharaonic porphyry columns. Barquq is buried in the City of the Dead, while his daughter Fatima is buried in this splendid tomb chamber.

▶ Sayyidna el-Husayn Mosque 70C4
Midan el-Husayn.
The mosque of el-Husayn is closed to non-Muslims, but as it is one of the most sacred mosques in Cairo there is always plenty of activity outside it. Husayn, grandson of the Prophet Muhammad, was killed in 680 in Iraq. His head is believed to be buried here, although this is disputed. Muslims from all over the world come to pray. The mosque is so sacred that alcohol cannot be served in the area, and bread baked nearby is believed to be blessed. The *moulid* of el-Husayn, celebrated for two weeks in the Islamic month of Rabi el-Tani, is one of Egypt's greatest festivals and attracts up to 1 million Egyptians.

▶▶▶ Sultan Hasan Mosque-Madrasa 70A2
Sharia el-Qal'a. Admission fee.
The scale of this architectural masterpiece was unprecedented when Sultan Hasan started work in 1356 and it is still one of world's largest mosques. The vast complex, covering 7,906sqm, includes a cruciform mosque, a tomb and *madrasas* (theology colleges) for the four Quranic schools, as well as a market, a well and apartments.

The mosque is best visited in the morning, when the sun brightens up the dark mausoleum. Beyond the huge entrance portal and dark corridor, the magnificent space and light of the open courtyard are dazzling. The height of the vaults, already overwhelming, is emphasised by low-hung mosque lamps. Huge doors either side of the *mihrab* (prayer niche) lead to the sombre mausoleum; the original door to the right is made of bronze and inlaid with gold and silver. The mausoleum was placed here so that it would receive blessings from Mecca and overlook the Citadel. Sultan Hasan was never buried here; his body went missing after he was assassinated, two years before the mosque was completed. The guard often demonstrates the fine acoustics by chanting 'Allahu akbar' (God is the Greatest).

The Cairo World Trade Centre is a world apart from the relatively poor neighbourhood of Bulaq

Despair and frustration
If you need to register your passport or extend your visa (see Travel Facts, pages 254–5), you can join the stream of people going through the right-hand door of the Mugamma, up the right-hand stairs, asking at which of the 1001 windows they should queue and then hearing that it might be better to come back on another day, or week, or with another photograph. And you're the lucky ones, because recently things have become much easier for foreigners. Egyptians suffer more and the spiral staircase has witnessed more than one suicide out of total despair and frustration.

Shoe shops abound in downtown Cairo

Modern Cairo

► **Bulaq** 87A2

Bulaq was once an island cut off from the city, but accumulated Nile silt connected the island to the land by the 15th century, when Bulaq became an important port and industrial centre. Two mosques have survived that era: the **Mosque of Qadi Yahya►** (AD1489) and the **Mosque of Abu el-Ala►** (AD1485), of which only the minaret and the mausoleum are original. The rest is 19th century, but well worth visiting for its beautiful *minbar* (pulpit) and *mihrab* (prayer niche). Under the Ottomans commerce began to flourish in Bulaq, which is why Sinan Pasha chose it as the site of his **Mosque of Sinan Pasha►►** (AD1571). It boasts the largest stone dome in Cairo, but nowadays it lies somewhat forlorn between workshops. Although Port Said and Suez took over as ports after the opening of the Suez Canal, Bulaq is still bustling with trade, especially second-hand car parts and clothes and fabrics. The recent **Cairo World Trade Centre►** on the Corniche focuses its attention on expatriates and wealthy Cairenes on the island of Zamalek.

►►► **Downtown (Wust el-Balad)** 87A1

This is the centre of Cairo, enclosed by the Nile, Garden City, Bulaq and the Ataba-district. Khedive Ismail had the area rebuilt in the 1860s for the inauguration of the Suez Canal. The once-elegant shopping streets (see page 87) are no longer tree-lined. The main square, Midan el-Tahrir (Liberation Square), has some imposing landmarks: the **Museum of Egyptian Antiquities►►►**; the Nile Hilton, Cairo's first modern five-star hotel, built on the site of the British barracks after the 1952 revolution (the barracks had formerly been the royal Qasr en-Nil, palace of the Nile); the **Mosque of Umar Makram►** where funerals of important people are held; the **Mugamma►**, the Kafkaesque temple of Egyptian bureaucracy, and the **American University►**, an island for wealthy young Egyptians.

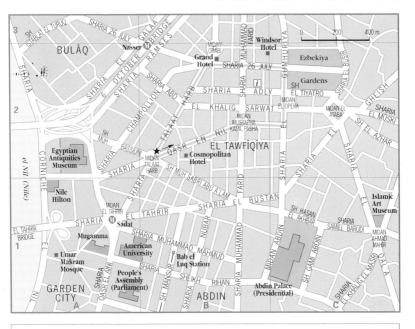

Walk Along 1001 shoe shops

This 2-hour walk in downtown Cairo is ideal for getting accustomed to Cairene crowds and noise, before the inevitable cultural shock that comes with getting lost in the medieval part of town.

Start from the heart of the city centre, Midan Talaat Harb, better known by its pre-revolution name, Midan Sulayman Pasha. **Groppi**, the famous coffee-house, still stands out as a reminder that 40 years ago these were elegant streets with café-terraces under the trees. The façades are rapidly crumbling, but it's still worth looking up for their neo-classical and neo-pharaonic details.

On Sharia Qasr en-Nil, newly planted trees disappear among shoppers, office workers, beggars and touts. Most of the shops here have European names. The **Cosmopolitan Hotel**, an art nouveau beauty, is down the second street on the right. To the left is **Sharia Shawarbi**, a popular pedestrian precinct with good music shops. Cross Sharia Sherif and

walk up to the elegant square of **Mustapha Kamil Pasha**. Look back towards the Nile Hilton for the Haussmann-esque long views. Continue along to Midan el-Opera where a modern car park has replaced the opera house, built for the inauguration of the Suez Canal and burned down in 1971. In the centre of the square are the once magnificent **Ezbekiya Gardens**. At the junction with Sharia Adly, the old Continental Savoy Hotel has been reduced to offices and a vaccination centre. Turn left into 26th-of-July Street and in the second street on the right is the **Windsor Hotel** ,with an old-fashioned bar and the el-Hati restaurant where Nasser once ate kebabs. Return to the main street until you reach Sharia Emad el-Din, with cinemas and theatres. Continue on to the Grand Hotel, have a look across the street at charming **Tawfiqiya market** and then turn left into Sharia Talaat Harb, with more cinemas, many more shoe shops and the square from which you started.

■ The Egyptian Museum was founded in Bulaq in 1858 by the French archaeologist Mariette and moved to this neo-classical building on Midan el-Tahrir in 1902. In spite of dust and old-fashioned displays, it contains some of the world's most extraordinary antiquities. The ground floor is arranged chronologically, moving clockwise.....■

The last great dig
The museum's basement has been called the last great archaeological dig in the Middle East. Overwhelmed by the wealth of antiquities excavated this century, curators have resorted to piling treasures – many of them uncatalogued – into the dark basement. The government has plans to build a new antiquities museum out near the pyramids and perhaps then the last great dig will take place.

Old and Middle Kingdom The Narmer Palette (left of the entrance in Room 47) marks the beginning of Egyptian art and history and records the unification of Upper and Lower Egypt by King Menes (c 3100BC). Among Old Kingdom masterpieces (Rooms 46 and 47) are statues of King Zoser, the first pyramid builder, and of King Mycerinus, from his valley temple in Giza; a panel from Userkaf's temple showing birds in the marshes (2475BC) (back wall); statuettes of scribes (Case C) and the hunchbacked gnome Khnum-Hotep (Case B).

The 'Sole Companion and Master of the Secrets of the House of the Toilet', Tepem-Ankh (5th Dynasty), is on guard in Room 41, near the Maidum reliefs. Some of the most striking figures (Room 42) are the 5th-Dynasty, painted limestone scribe; the wooden Sheikh el-Balad, with rock crystal and alabaster eyes, and a diorite King Chephren (4th Dynasty), protected by Horus. Six wooden panels (Room 31) come from the tomb of the earliest-known dentist, Hesire (3rd Dynasty). Room 32 contains the lifelike geese of Maidum, painted on plaster (4th Dynasty); the perfect statues of Prince Rahotep and his wife Nofret (4th Dynasty) and, more unusual, the happy family group of the dwarf Seneb.

New Kingdom The painted head of Hatshepsut (Room 11) and masterpieces of the 18th Dynasty (Room 12) reflect the power and energy of a period of imperial expansion. Tuthmosis III' s sandstone chapel from Deir el-Bahri was dedicated to Hathor and an enormous gilded statue of the cow goddess stands in front of it, suckled by Tuthmosis's son Amenophis II. Amenhoptep, the man responsible for building the Colossi of Memnon at Thebes (Room 12) is shown in youth as a fat scribe and later as a mystical, skinny octogenarian. The long gallery (Room 7) contains granite sphinxes of Hatshepsut, damaged by her stepson Tuthmosis III.

Top and right: the Geese of Maidum, often copied on papyri sold to tourists

Amarna period A model of an Amarna house (Room 8) gives a rare insight into ancient Egyptian

domestic architecture, while the four massive statues of Akhenaton (18th Dynasty) in Room 3 reveal a revolution in art, as there had been in politics and religion. The informality of the stele (inscribed stone) showing Akhenaton and Nefertiti playing with their children is unlike anything else produced in ancient Egypt, while cuneiform tablets – 'the Amarna letters' – and several busts give a wider but incomplete picture of this remarkable period, which lasted just a lifetime and came to an end with the accession of Tutankhamun.

Detail from one of the many sarcophagi displayed in the museum

89

Later periods In the Late Dynastic and Late periods, Egypt was often controlled by foreign rulers and King Taharqa (Room 25) was clearly a Nubian from the Sudan. Beyond Room 30, Graeco-Roman influences create a strange hybrid art, most typically (Rooms 49 and 50) with the bust of Serapis; the sarcophagus of Petosiris (4th century BC), inlaid with glass mosaics, and the Persian-period dwarf, a dancer at the Serapeum Apis ceremony.

The Atrium From the stairway, the scale and magnificence of this group of larger objects from all periods is striking. The 17th-Dynasty group of Amenophis III, his wife Tiy and their three daughters appears soft and sensual in spite of the statues' size. At the centre is part of a painted floor from Akhenaton's palace in Tell el-Amarna. Egyptians from all periods loved embellishment and decorations; even pyramidions (pyramid capstones) were carved and inscribed. These pyramidions from Dahshur are probably similar to the ones that sat on top of the Giza pyramids.

Opening times
The Egyptian Museum is open daily 8–5. On Fridays it is closed for prayers from 12–2pm.

Left: ground floor plan

If time is short
It is said that if you allowed one minute for each exhibit, it would take nine months to see every object in the museum. Most package tourists are allowed two hours, but if you have the time, two or three half days would be more useful. If you don't, a minimal tour should include the following: On the ground floor, Old Kingdom masterpieces (Rooms 48, 47, 46, 42, 32), Hathor Shrine and New Kingdom statues (Room 12), the Amarna gallery (Room 3), large stonework (the Atrium); on the upper floor, Tutankhamun's treasures and the mummy room.

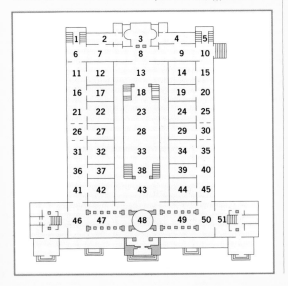

■ Most of the exhibits on the upper floor have come from tombs. There are always crowds to see the famous Tutankhamun collection, but most of this floor is under-visited, which makes it pleasant to browse around if you have the time. The exhibits are arranged more or less chronologically, starting with Room 43 and moving in a clockwise direction.....■

The blue faïence hippopotamus seems to strike a chord in most visitors' hearts

The face of eternity
'The more I walk along, the more I listen, the more I move around the columns, the more I experience the feeling of a dark world which fastens on to ours and which will not loosen the suckers through which it takes its life. Whatever it may cost, they find it necessary to confirm their existence, to perpetuate themselves, to incarnate, to reincarnate, to hypnotise nothingness and to vanquish it. Fists closed, eyes wide open and fixed, the Pharaohs march against the void, put it to sleep, braving its powers.'
Jean Cocteau, 1949

Old and Middle Kingdom Room 43 has a very fine wooden head of a woman from Lisht, the much-copied blue-faïence hippopotamus and, just outside Room 42, a striking panel of faïence from Zoser's pyramid in Saqqara. The alabaster vase in Room 42 is exquisite and the black Palermo Stone yielded important knowledge of the Old Kingdom as it contains a list of pharaohs from the 1st to the mid-5th dynasties and the main events of that period. Wooden Middle Kingdom sarcophagi fill Room 37; the finest ones belong to Sepi, decorated inside with images of his favourite objects, and to General Mesah, including his neck pillow, sandals and his model army. Room 32 and 27 have wonderful models of sacred boats and scenes of daily life in ancient Egypt.

Mummy Room There is an additional fee for the Mummy Room (Room 52), which opened in 1994 after many years under lock and key. It contains the mummies of some of the mightiest pharaohs in history. The mummies on display, all found in a cache in Deir el-Bahri in 1875, include great 18th-Dynasty pharaohs like Amenophis I and Tuthmosis IV, and the 19th-Dynasty Seti I and Ramses II.

New Kingdom Room 22 contains interesting artefacts from New Kingdom tombs including *ushabtis* (small tomb figures), scarabs, painted linen cloth and headrests. The

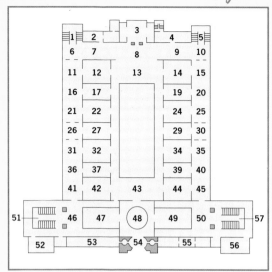

Collections abroad
European and American involvement in the rediscovery of ancient Egypt, particularly the activities of early 'entrepreneurs' such as the 19th-century rivals Giovanni Belzoni and Bernadino Drovetti, who exported sculpture, paintings, papyri and even small monuments, made possible the creation of important collections of antiquities outside Egypt. Museums in Berlin, London, New York, Paris and Turin today house remarkable treasures and are well worth a visit.

Left: first floor plan

91

papyri in Room 17 are from the Book of the Dead. The artefacts found in royal tombs in the Valley of the Kings (Room 12), including a case of wigs for priests, suggest how grand the tombs and their contents must have been before they were robbed. The corridor from Room 41 to Room 11 features mainly New Kingdom sarcophagi, many of which still contain their mummies.

Tutankhamun Collection This collection of 1,700 objects found in the small tomb of the boy-king Tutankhamun is overwhelming. Every item is a highlight and even the smallest objects are finely and delicately executed. Rooms 7 and 8 contain four gilded shrines which fitted one inside the other, enclosing the sarcophagus with the mummy (still in his tomb in Thebes) and a canopic chest (Room 9) with jars for the king's viscera. The golden funerary mask (Room 3), inlaid with semi-precious stones, is startlingly beautiful and incredibly perfect, as is the golden coffin. The rest of the room and part of Room 9 are filled with the fine jewellery, sandals, socks, sequins and other objects that covered Tutankhamun's mummy. Other rooms are filled with exquisite funerary furniture, games, hunting bows and arrows and, in front of Room 45, the two *ka* (soul) statues of the king who guarded his tomb for more than 3,000 years.

And more Rooms 53 and 54 contain prehistoric and pre-dynastic artefacts, with a collection of dusty, mummified animals. Rooms 24 and 29 contain painted *ostraca* (pottery fragments) with scenes of the Book of the Dead and depictions of daily life. The household objects in Room 49 look amazingly like objects on sale in the *souks* (markets) today. Room 4 has a dazzling collection of jewellery from the 1st Dynasty to the Byzantine era, among which is a divine 6th-Dynasty golden head of a falcon. Last but not least are the beautiful, almost photographic Faiyum Portraits (Room 14), made of pigment mixed into molten wax, which were strapped on to mummies (AD100–250).

Goddesses protect the golden canopic chest which contains Tutankhamun's viscera

A night at the opera
Information about performances at the Cairo Opera House is available at the Opera House itself, and is published in *Egypt Today* and the *Middle East Times*. You can call the Opera House on (02) 341 2926. Note that there is a dress code: men are expected to wear a jacket and tie to evening performances.

Cairo Tower, a symbol of the success of modern Egypt

▶▶▶ Gezira   52B2

Gezira (Arabic for island) is the largest and most exclusive island in Cairo. It is split into two distinctive parts by the 6th of October Bridge: Gezira proper and Zamalek (see page 95). The first landmark beyond the Qasr en-Nil Bridge (el-Tahrir Bridge) is the **Opera House▶▶**, a US$30 million dollar gift from Japan. It was built in 1988, in a daring combination of oriental and western styles, to replace the opera house which burned down in 1971. The complex houses the **Museum of Modern Art▶**, devoted to works by Egyptian artists since 1908.

Further along Sharia el-Tahrir are the **Gezira Exhibition Grounds▶**, which contain the Gezira Museum, Museum of Egyptian Civilisation (both closed for restoration) and the Planetarium. Across the street is the **Mohtar Museum▶**, devoted to the works of the sculptor Mohtar (1891–1934) whose monument, *The Renaissance of Egypt*, stands at the entrance to Dokki. The 187m-high **Cairo Tower▶▶** was built between 1957 and 1962 with Soviet help. A lift takes you to a lacklustre restaurant (it revolves only by popular demand), cafeteria and viewing platform, with spectacular views over the vastness of Cairo.

▶▶ Giza   52A1

Giza, in ancient times a stopover between Memphis and Heliopolis, is now a rapidly expanding governorate between the Nile and the pyramids. In the 1860s the area affected by the Nile floods was drained, and Khedive Ismail built his hunting palace (now the Mena House Hotel) and the Pyramids Road, now infamous for its sleazy nightclubs which are popular with visiting Gulf Arabs. The land which now contains el-**Urman Gardens▶** and the **Zoological Gardens▶▶** once formed the khedival gardens, laid out by the Frenchman Deschamps. The avenue between them leads to Cairo University, founded in 1908 as a counterpart to el-Azhar University, but nowadays the site of just as much fundamentalist fervour as the latter. Wagons-Lits night trains leave from Giza Railway Station for Upper Egypt.

▶▶ Heliopolis (Masr el-Gadida)   53E4

At the end of the 19th century, as Cairo became too small for its fast-growing population, the Belgian Baron Empain had the idea of building a garden city in the desert, connected to Cairo by a tram line. Baron Empain's empty villa, designed by the French architect Marcel as a Cambodian temple, with a revolving tower to follow the sun, stands abandoned along the main road to the airport. Marcel also designed the 300-room Heliopolis Palace Hotel in a traditional Islamic style; it is now the official presidential residence. Nowadays the desert is nowhere near, but the elegant avenues with Moorish buildings are still there, mainly around Sharia Marghani and Sharia el-Ahram. The centre of Heliopolis has become the playground for foreigners and wealthy Cairenes, while low-rent housing pushes further and further into the desert. To the north is Merryland, one of the first and biggest funfairs in Cairo, to be avoided over the weekends.

▶▶ **Imbaba** *52B3*

Imbaba, the site of the 1798 Battle of the Pyramids where Napoleon defeated the Mamluks, is now a popular and fast-expanding suburb north of Cairo. On Fridays it becomes even more crowded with both tourists and journalists. The tourists come for the **Suq el-Gimal**, a daily camel market which is particularly lively early Friday morning. After their 40-day walk from the Sudan to Aswan (see Daraw page 177), the camels are put on the overnight train or on trucks to be sold in this market. The bargaining and trading is fascinating to watch and often looks like a cockfight.

Imbaba was also a stronghold of the fundamentalist group Gamaa el-Muslimeen. Journalists came to the Friday noon sermon to hear the group's thoughts and its intended actions. The group also provided free veils and Islamic clothing in the market. The situation is calmer but foreigners should still be cautious about visiting the area around the mosque at this time on Fridays.

Ancient Heliopolis
The City of the Sun, called On by the ancient Egyptians, was the most important theological centre of the Old Kingdom, dedicated to the sun god Ra. During the New Kingdom Karnak became pre-eminent and when Alexandria became the new intellectual centre in the 3rd century BC, the glorious city of On more or less disappeared. After centuries of pillaging, nothing is left beyond the Obelisk of Senusert I on a square in Matariya.

Imbaba camel market

■ **The Metro in Cairo, the first in the Arab world, is unlike anything else in the city: it works, it is unnervingly clean, it is easy to use, well organised, quick and rarely crowded. So if the hustle and bustle of Cairo gets on top of you, look for the 'M' signs and go underground.....■**

A pleasure garden
'On the bank of the Nile opposite Cairo is the place known as el-Rawda (the Garden), which is a pleasure park and promenade, containing many beautiful gardens. The people of Cairo are fond of pleasure and amusement. I once witnessed a fête there which was held for el-Malik el-Nasir's recovery of a fracture which he had suffered in his hand. All the merchants decorated their bazaars and had rich stuffs, ornaments, and silken fabrics hung up in their shops for several days.'
Ibn Battuta, *Travels*, 1326

94

The route The existing line runs from the northern to the southern suburbs and two more lines are planned to connect the other parts of the city. The first carriage of every train is reserved for women only. Hang on to your ticket, as you will need it to exit the station. Here are a few interesting stops along the way:

Ain Shams► (Spring of the Sun) provides water for the Virgin's Tree under which the Holy Family allegedly rested on their flight into Egypt. It used to be a popular spot for Christian pilgrims, but recently it became another stronghold of Islamic fundamentalism.

El-Matariya► was the site of the ancient temple of the sun god Ra, but all that is left is the Obelisk of Senusert I on Midan el-Misallah.

Mubarak► is the stop for Ramses (Cairo Central) railway station.

Sadat►► is Midan el-Tahrir (see page 86).

Mari Girgis►►► is for Old Cairo (see page 66)

El-Maadi► is a wonderful place for an afternoon stroll amid the old villas set in lush gardens.

Ain Helwan► leads to a wax museum with a strange selection of the biggest moments in Egyptian history, a Japanese Garden and a spa with sulphurous baths which was extremely fashionable as a winter resort in the 1920s.

▶▶   Roda   52B1

The 'Garden Island' was rural until the 1950s but has rapidly become yet another crowded residential area. The Meridien Hotel on the northern tip of the island has beautiful views over the Nile and the centre of Cairo. Further south is the **Manyal Palace▶▶**, built in 1903 in a charming blend of oriental and occidental styles by Prince Muhammad Ali, King Farouk's uncle. The palace is now an excellent museum displaying the private possessions of the prince. Part of the vast gardens are now occupied by a hotel. There has probably always been a **Nilometer▶▶** on the southern tip of the island to measure the rise and fall of the river, but the one which stands there now dates back to 861. The kiosk is a modern reconstruction of a Turkish original. The Centre for Art and Life is housed in the *salamlek* (men's quarters) of the former Monastirli Palace, which was built in 1830.

▶▶   Zamalek   52B3

Zamalek, on the northern tip of the Gezira Island (see page 92), is often called the Manhattan of Cairo. Many old villas and luxurious flats in this exclusive, tree-lined residential area are occupied by diplomats, wealthy Egyptians and expatriates. Zamalek is now bisected by 26th-of-July Street, around which most of the shops are concentrated, and a large part is taken up by the Gezira Sporting Club, founded in the 1880s by the British Army. Although there are heavy restrictions on membership, more and more people fight for a chair and a breath of fresh air in what is still central Cairo's largest patch of green. Opposite the club is the old Gezira Palace, built in 1869 for Empress Eugenie and now incorporated into the Marriott Hotel. Next door, in an elegant 19th-century villa, is the **Mahmud Khalil Museum▶▶▶**, home to an extraordinary collection of important European Impressionist and oriental paintings, which are periodically threatened with removal elsewhere. Many of Cairo's trendy restaurants and bars are in this part of town (see pages 271–83).

This complex, geometrically patterned screen is typical of the eclectic architecture lavished upon the Manyal Palace

A late afternoon walk
Starting at the Mahmud Khalil Museum, turn right into Sharia Marsaf, pass the square and at the British School take a left and then a right. On 26th-of-July Street, turn left and stop for a juice or cappuccino in Simmonds. At the lights outside Simmonds, turn right into Sharia Brazil and continue straight on (it becomes Sharia Muhammad Mazhar). At the Iraqi Embassy, turn left into Sharia Marashli, then take the first right into Sharia Ahmad Hishmat, then turn right again until you reach the Nile. Walk to the left along Sharia Abu el-Feda, where the river is lined with houseboats, and take a left at the flyover to return to 26th-of-July Street.

Europeans in Cairo

■ **Europeans came to Cairo as traders in the 13th and 14th centuries because Egypt, along with Venice, controlled one of the principal routes to the East. As Europeans built their own empires beyond the Red Sea, they fought for influence in the city to gain political and financial rewards.....■**

Hotel company
William Thackeray wrote of an evening in Cairo's Hotel d'Orient (long since gone): 'One of the Indians offers a bundle of Bengal cheroots and we make acquaintance with these honest bearded white-jacketed Majors and military commanders, finding England here in a French hotel kept by an Italian, at the city of Grand Cairo, in Africa.' *Notes of a Journey from Cornhill to Grand Cairo* (1846)

Right: James Bruce, who went in search of the source of the Nile in 1768. Below: picnicking on the Great Pyramid, now a forbidden pleasure

Explorers and travellers When the Scottish explorer James Bruce visited Cairo in the 1760s he was forced to stay in a religious house in Old Cairo. Napoleon Bonaparte, who landed on a beach outside Alexandria in 1798, declared that the conquest of Egypt would have an incalculable effect on the world's civilisation and trade. It also affected Egypt, and by the 1850s visitors like Lady Lucie Duff Gordon were able to live wherever they chose.

At that time, attention was focused on Egypt's present possibilities as well as its past wonders. The overland route between Alexandria and Suez, via Cairo, which was developed in the early 19th century under

Muhammad Ali, gave Europeans a faster passage to India and the Far East than the old route via South Africa. In 1839, 275 passengers crossed between the Mediterranean and the Red Sea. Within eight years there were over 3,000 of them and, by then, there was also a sizeable European community offering hotels and other services for travellers.

A city of Europe, not Africa Europe had a great influence on the development of 19th-century Egypt. At the opening of the French-inspired Suez Canal in 1869, Khedive Ismail wanted to show Europe's rulers that Cairo belonged to Europe, not Africa. He initiated a building boom which defined the face of modern Cairo. Streets were laid out by European architects along European lines and the narrow alleys of the old Arab city were avoided by fashionable Cairenes, though not by romantic foreigners. At Abdin, in the centre of the growing metropolis, the khedive built himself a grand palace fit for a European monarch.

The veiled protectorate After Ismail's abdication in 1879, Britain controlled Egypt by influence and, on occasion, as in 1884, by military intervention. Though the British were loath to annex the country, they nevertheless established in Cairo many familiar colonial institutions. In the British Agency (now the embassy, which retains Queen Victoria's initials on the gates) there were grand balls with dancing on what was regarded as 'the finest sprung dance-floor in the East'. There were horse and flower shows in the Gezira Club, golf drives and hunts elsewhere. The exclusive apartment buildings around the Gezira Club in Zamalek, with names like Park Lane and Dorchester, and the remaining hotels (the Windsor with its colonial-style bar, the Mena House Oberoi, the Cairo Marriott – formerly the Gezirah Palace Hotel – and the Heliopolis Palace Hotel, now used as the president's official residence) are part of the surviving legacy of that time of European dominance.

Revolutionary activities The 1952 revolution which overthrew Egypt's monarchy was also an attempt to free the country from foreign control. More than 2 million Allied troops are reckoned to have passed through Egypt between 1939 and 1945, and there were almost 90,000 British troops stationed along the Suez Canal when Cairo's Shepheard's Hotel was burned in 1952. The crisis brought about by the nationalising of foreign interests, including the Suez Canal Company, and the British-Israeli invasion of 1956 saw Europeans fleeing the city. But they were soon back – the Russians in particular – and many of the buildings of the late 1950s and early 1960s, like the monolithic Mugamma in Midan el-Tahrir, reflect the era of Soviet influence.

Modern Cairo Cairo is now host to nationals from many countries around the world. The many Europeans among them have opened clubs and centres to encourage an understanding of their cultures, while many of the older European-style institutions, like the Gezira Club in Zamalek, are enjoyed principally by better-off Cairenes.

Western cultural centres in Cairo
American Cultural Centre: 4 Sharia Ahmad Raghed, Garden City (tel: 354 9601).
British Council: 192 Sharia Qasr en-Nil, Aguza (tel: 345 3281).
French Cultural Centre: 1 Sharia Madrasa el-Huqquq el-Faransia, Munira (tel: 355 3725).
German Cultural Centre (Goethe Institute): 5 Sharia Abd el-Salam Aref, downtown (tel: 575 9877).
Greek Cultural Centre: 14 Sharia Emad el-Din, downtown (tel: 575 3962).
Italian Cultural Centre: 3 Sharia Sheikh el-Marsafi, Zamalek (tel: 340 8791).
Netherlands Institute of Archaeological and Arabic Studies: 1 Sharia Mahmud Azmi, Zamalek (tel: 340 0076).

The ornate garden entrance to the Gezira Palace, now the Cairo Marriott Hotel

Shopping

Fixed prices and a bargain Egyptians love to shop, as do visitors. There are three different places to do it but remember, whichever way you choose, you'll need time. Bazaars and markets are the most enjoyable, but also the most time-consuming and nerve-racking. The rule is to bargain, and bargain hard. Start by halving the asking price, unless it seems ridiculously high, in which case start lower. To get a feel for prices, look around first and decide what an item is worth to you. Always bear in mind that bargaining is a game and Egyptians are wonderful players – an invitation to drink tea is often one of their finest opening moves, though it is certainly not an obligation to buy.

Secondly, there are small retail shops with fixed prices (usually written in Arabic, so learn those numerals!). Lastly, there are department stores which also have fixed prices and credit card facilities. Even this easier option takes time: choose what you want, take the invoice to the cashier and then go to yet another desk to collect your purchase.

Handicrafts Egypt has always been famous for its handicrafts, but unfortunately the quality has deteriorated as many products are now made to be sold cheaply. The main crafts to look out for are *mashrabiya* (carved woodwork), mother-of-pearl inlay work, pottery, alabaster (cheapest in Luxor), brass and copper ware, handmade glass and the obligatory painted papyrus. The best place to shop is in the bazaars at **Khan el-Khalili** (see page 83) or, if you have time, in the workshops around el-Azhar.

Antiquities Most antiquities offered to tourists are fakes, which is just as well because genuine antiquities can only be exported with a licence from the Department of Antiquities. There are a few antique shops and auction houses on Sharia Qasr en-Nil (downtown), around the Marriott Hotel in Zamalek and in Sikket el-Badistan at the Khan el-Khalili, but things are often overpriced.

Carpets and appliqué work Carpets are not an Egyptian speciality, but the camel-hair rugs are cheap and colourful. The best place to look is the alley of **Haret el-Fakhamin**, behind the Mosque of el-Ghuri (see page 80). The **Tentmakers' Bazaar** outside Bab Zuwayla is a must. The appliqué tents are typically Cairene, used for weddings and funerals, and you don't have to buy a whole tent as appliqué comes as cushion covers as well. Copts were once famous for their weavings and the tradition has been continued in the **Wissa-Wasif School** in Haraniya, a village near the pyramids. A good place to find them and other textiles is **Senouhi**, 5th floor, 54 Sharia Abd el-Khaled Sarwat, downtown.

Jewellery If you are on an organised tour you will be offered *cartouches* with your name in hieroglyphics, but Cairo has more than that to offer. Shops in the **Goldsmiths' Bazaar** in the Khan al-Khalili and jewellers in the five-star hotels are the obvious places to look for serious jewellery. Shops like **Senouhi** (above) and **Nomad** in the Marriott Hotel sell interesting silver Bedouin jewellery.

Arabic numerals
It is very useful to recognise Arabic numerals, especially when reading prices and bus numbers.

1 = ١	8 = ٨
2 = ٢	9 = ٩
3 = ٣	10 = ١٠
4 = ٤	20 = ٢٠
5 = ٥	100 = ١٠٠
6 = ٦	1001 = ١٠٠١
7 = ٧	

Papyrus
Ancient Egyptians wrote on sheets of papyrus, but the craft of making it disappeared in the 10th century. Dr Ragab rediscovered the ancient technique and is, in a way, responsible for the millions of papyrus sheets that are thrown at you wherever you go in Egypt. His Papyrus Institute, on a houseboat between Cairo's Gezira Sheraton and University Bridge, shows how papyrus is produced and sells papyri at high but fixed prices. Cheap papyri bought in the street are often made from banana leaves.

Clothes and fabrics International chains like Benetton, New Man, and Naf Naf have recently opened shops in Cairo and sell good-quality cotton clothes made in Egypt. You can find them all together downtown or at the **World Trade Center**, 1191 Corniche el-Nil in Bulaq. **On Safari**, in the World Trade Center or in the Marriott, is an Egyptian chain selling good-quality, locally styled clothes. Their shirts (also in the Shirt Shop) are a good deal. For traditional Egyptian clothes like *gallabiyas* (men's long robes) look in Khan el-Khalili or Nomad (Marriott Hotel). **Atlas,** in Sikket el-Badistan in the Khan el-Khalili or in the Semiramis Hotel, sells excellent hand-woven silk, cotton and moiré fabrics as well as tailor-made clothes. **Salon Vert,** on Sharia Qasr en-Nil, downtown, and the government-owned **Ouf,** in the alley beside the Madrasa of Barsbay on Sharia el-Muizz, are the best places to buy cotton sheets, towels and fabrics.

A man working appliqué in the Tentmakers' bazaar

Food

Hotel restaurants in Egypt, as elsewhere, cater for tourists and the result is often bland and uninspiring cooking. The choice of restaurants outside Cairo and Alexandria is often limited, but if you know where to go, in Cairo the whole world is at your palate.

Street food All over the city you will be assaulted by smells coming from colourful food carts and corner stalls. Unfortunately, most of them don't have running water and, however tempting the food, it is only recommended for the adventurous or the hardened of stomach. If you feel confident about this (after all, Egyptians eat at these stalls all the time), then the delights awaiting you include sandwiches with fried shrimps, stewed liver or brain, and the more obvious *fuul* and *taamiya* (see page 102) or *shawarma* (pressed lamb kebabs roasted on a spit).

Egyptian fast food Many Cairenes eat lunch in small local restaurants that will often specialise in just one particular dish. Men are always in the majority in these places, but one part of the restaurant is often reserved for families or women. Among the typical Egyptian dishes these places serve you might find *kushari*, *fuul* and *taamiya* served with eggs or *torshi* (see page102) and, less common, *fateer* (a light pizza made of filo pastry topped with eggs, minced meat, peppers and cheese or the sweet version with raisins, jam and sugar). Other places sell roasted chicken, kebabs or fried fish. Most of these restaurants are far from luxurious, but they are usually cheap, clean – with sawdust on the floor to confirm it – and definitely worth trying out.

Restaurants Cairo is one of the Middle East's main meeting places and in all areas of the city frequented by foreigners, there is a wide range of restaurants, from simple Levantine to superb Lebanese cuisine, from bland, internationalised French to exquisite nouvelle cuisine and Far Eastern delicacies. Downtown has more middle-priced restaurants, while the more expensive places are in the five-star hotels and in Zamalek and Mohandeseen. In the more upmarket establishments it is worth noting that a service tax will be added to your bill, sometimes up to 22 per cent.

Basic rules Tap water is heavily chlorinated and safe to drink, but plastic bottles of mineral water are widely available. Baraka (blessing) is the most widely available brand. When buying water, check that the plastic seal is intact: unsuspecting tourists have been sold bottles refilled with tap water.

As most places have running water and hygiene standards are improving, there should be no reason not to indulge your culinary fantasies, as long as you bear in mind some basic rules. Go easy on your stomach for the first few days and avoid eating raw salads, ice creams, unpeeled fruit and food that has been stewing for several hours, like *shawarma* and cheap buffet meals. Try to make sure the food has been properly washed, drink plenty of water and fresh juices to replace fluids and, if you can resist, try not to eat too much if you are not used to the climate.

A place to rest and watch the world go by in the middle of Khan el-Khalili

Food markets Most fruit and vegetables are locally grown, always fresh and full of flavour. Although fruit is not often found on the menu in restaurants, don't miss out – it's cheap and plentiful. The best places to shop for fruit are at the food markets like the covered **Ataba market** (off Midan Ataba) and **Tawfiqiya market** (off 26th-of-July Street, downtown). Loud salesmen sell pyramids of lemons, oranges, very red tomatoes, artichokes, mangoes and strawberries, their stalls standing between entire cow carcasses dangling from hooks, cages of pigeons and hens which are slaughtered by order, and women coming from the outskirts of Cairo selling home-grown lettuces and herbs while nursing babies. In Zamalek, 26th-of-July Street has upmarket fruit and vegetable stores, where of all things you may well find imported bananas and apples.

Oranges are plentiful in Egypt and very sweet

Egyptian food

■ The influences of Greece, Turkey, Lebanon, Syria and France reflect Egypt's long history, but Egyptian cuisine does have its own character, so *bon appetit* or, as Egyptians say, *Bi-l-Hana wash-Shiffa* (with pleasure and health).....■

Traditional Egyptian mezze and salads served in a Cairo restaurant

Sweets and pastries are always a welcome present when visiting an Egyptian family

Beans, beans, beans Egypt's staple diet is bread and boiled fava beans (*fuul*). The bread is either *aish shami*, a white pitta bread, or wholewheat *aish baladi*. *Fuul* are often eaten mashed with lemon juice and cumin. *Taamiya* are deep-fried fava-bean balls, often served with *torshi* (pickled vegetables) and *tahina* (sesame paste). *Kushari* (a mixture of macaroni, rice, lentils, chickpeas and fried onions) makes a cheap lunch or dinner, served with a spicy tomato sauce.

A table of mezze When Egyptians eat together they often share a selection of *mezze* (small dishes), eaten with bread. The most popular dips are *tahina* (pureed sesame seeds), *baba ghanoug* (aubergine puree with tahina) and *hummus* (mashed chickpeas). *Salata baladi* (country-style salad) has finely chopped tomatoes, parsley, cucumber and lettuce with cumin and lime. There are some excellent vegetable dishes like *shakshuka* (Egyptian ratatouille with eggs) or the more elaborate *waraa aynab* (stuffed vine leaves) and *mahshi* (cabbage or courgettes stuffed with rice). Meat is often grilled (*mashwi*) like *kebab* (of lamb or beef) or *kofta* (meatballs). *Hamam* (pigeon), considered a delicacy and aphrodisiac, comes grilled or in a stew, stuffed with wheat.

Sweet delights *Umm Ali* is a traditional dessert of cracker bread, raisins, nuts, coconut and cream, soaked in hot milk. *Roz bi-laban* (rice pudding), *mahallabiya* (cornflour pudding) and the ubiquitous *creme caramel* are more plain. The most popular oriental pastries are *basbusa* (semolina cake dripping in honey and nuts), *baklawa* (filo pastry, honey and nuts) and drier *kunafa* (angel hair with cream or nuts).

■ 'Once you drink water from the Nile,' Egyptians will tell you, 'you will always come back to Egypt.' Most tourists stick to their bottles of mineral water, but if you want a taste of the country, try out the wide variety of hot and cold drinks.....■

Hot drinks *Shay* (tea) is drunk with heaps of sugar, *bi 'l-naana* (with mint) or *bi-laban* (with milk), while *qahwa* (Turkish coffee) has varying levels of sweetness: *saada* (without sugar), *ariha* (little sugar), *mazbut* (medium) and *ziyada* (syrupy). Western-style coffee is called French or American; instant coffee is always called Nescafé. *Sahlab*, delicious on a cold winter evening, is a thick milky drink of arrowroot, cinnamon and nuts. *Karkadeh*, a red infusion of hibiscus flowers, is available hot or cold in Cairo but is more popular in Aswan and the Sudan. Most cafés will serve herbal infusions like '*irfa* (cinnamon), *yan-sun* (anis) and the bitter *helba* (fenugreek).

Fruit juices *Asir* (fruit juice) is sold in colourfully tiled juice bars – the pyramids of fruits on the counter tell you what's in season. There is usually *asir burtuqan* (orange juice), *moz* (banana), *manga* (mango), *farawla* (strawberry), *gazar* (carrot), *asab* (sugar-cane), *gawafa* (guava) and the delicious *asir ruman* (pomegranate). To be reck-less, try the juices sold by street vendors with enormous jugs, *asir laymun* (lemon), *tamar hindi* (tamarind) or *er soos* (liquorice).

Forbidden pleasures The local-ly brewed Stella beer is usually enjoyable, though the quality varies. The Stella Export is stronger, sweeter, more reliable and also more expensive. Egyptian wine has never been famous, but the quality nowadays varies from drinkable to dangerous. The com-mon red wine is called Omar Khayyam; Cru des Ptolemees is a dry white wine. Local spirits, apart from the often excellent Zibeeb (Egyptian Ouzo), should only be bought for the labels. Resembling well-known brands, with such names as Dry Din, Johnny Talker, Marcel Horse and Ricardo, their contents can be lethal.

Alcohol in Egypt
Religious tension is making much of Egypt dry, but while you may not be offered them, it is usually possible to get alcoholic drinks in hotels and restaurants if you ask for them specifically. During Ramadan it is illegal to serve alcohol to Egyptians, be they Copts or Muslims, and you may be asked for your passport in some establishments. Many bars close for the month.

Nightlife

104

Small nightclubs with popular singers and belly dancers abound on and around 26th-of-July Street in downtown Cairo

Most tourists are too exhausted to enjoy Cairo's nightlife. Neither Arabian dream nor nightmare, there are plenty of possibilities to fill your evenings. Cairenes come out after sunset to catch the Nile breeze which usually refreshes the city on summer evenings. There is entertainment until the early hours, and it is a special pleasure at the end of a long night out to see the sun come up while the call for dawn prayers echoes across the city.

Watering holes There are plenty of bars around 26th-of-July Street and Sharia Alfi in downtown Cairo for some *couleur locale* (local colour). The trendiest bar in town is **Piano Piano** in the World Trade Centre (Corniche en-Nil, Bulaq). **Harry's Pub** in the Marriott Hotel in Zamalek is popular with expatriates, as is **Pub 28** (28 Sharia Shagaret el-Durr, Zamalek). The top-floor bar in the **Ramses Hilton** has expensive cocktails and wonderful views over Cairo. Downtown, foreign correspondents favour the roof terrace of the **Odeon Palace Hotel** (6 Sharia Abd el-Hamid Said) and Egyptian actors and intellectuals meet on the terrace of the **Le Grillon Restaurant** (8 Sharia Qasr en-Nil, tel: 578 3114).

Discos and nightclubs Nightclubs often offer an early evening programme of oriental dance for tourists and a late-night one for Egyptians and Gulf Arabs (see page 106). Discos in some five-star hotels, like **Jackie's** in the Nile Hilton and **Regina** in the Gezira Sheraton, only admit members and residents. Others, like the popular **Tamango** on top of the Atlas Zamalek Hotel (Sharia Gama'a el-Duwal el-Arabiya in Muhandeseen), only accept couples and sometimes single women. A lot of discos are quite strict about dress code and often don't admit people in jeans. The **Club Med** disco is more excit-

Up to date
For listings of events, especially in foreign languages, look in the daily *Egyptian Gazette* or the government-run English *Al-Ahram Weekly* and the *Middle East Times*. The magazine *Egypt Today* lists events all over Egypt as well as reviews and articles on the performances. They also list occasional lectures at the American University or the weekly lecture (every Thursday at 6pm) at the Nederlands Instituut in Zamalek.

ing and buzzing on Thursdays and Saturdays. If you really want to dance, without restrictions, look for the seedier venues, often much more fun, like **Borsalino** (on Sharia Rustum, Garden City) or **Ondine** (Corniche el-Nil, Maadi).

Film and theatre Cairo is the centre of Arab film and theatre and there is a wide variety of shows. Most theatre is in Arabic, although it is often easy to follow the story; occasional performances in English are announced in the *Egyptian Gazette*. Going to see a film in a downtown cinema can be an interesting experience, with a mostly male audience eating, drinking tea and cheering or insulting the main characters. It can be frustrating to watch a foreign film, censored and subtitled in Arabic, because the audience will chat through it. Foreign cultural centres show uncensored movies, usually classics to be enjoyed in quieter surroundings. Check the *Egyptian Gazette* for addresses and programmes.

Concerts The main venue for musical events is the prestigious **Cairo Opera House** on Gezira (tel: 341 2926 or 342 0589), with performances by the Cairo Symphony Orchestra as well as foreign artists, often sponsored by embassies. Programmes for the Opera House and for concerts in the cultural centres are published in *Cairo Today* and the English-language newspapers. Tickets for the Opera House should be bought a few days in advance. Jacket and tie are compulsory for men. Classical Arab music is performed most Thursdays at the **Gumhuriya Theatre** (Sharia el-Gumhuriya, downtown, tel: 578 2864).

Nile-side attractions On a hot summer night the only place to be is by or on the river. Boats for hire are moored in front of the Nile Hilton and on the opposite bank, and *feluccas* (sailing boats) are best taken from beside the Meridien Hotel in Garden City. Along the Nile, there are cafeterias called 'casinos' serving food, beer and ice-cream. But in the evening it can be most pleasant just to walk along the Corniche from the Ramses Hilton to the Meridien Hotel on Gezira Island, or among the Cairene families having a picnic on 6th-of-October Bridge.

Whirling dervishes
The Mawliyya are Egyptian members of a Turkish Sufi sect founded in the 13th century, who whirl and dance in order to lose their worldly ties and become one with God. In Cairo they perform at the Ghuriyya Cultural Centre, housed in the Mausoleum of el-Ghuri (see page 80) on Wednesday and Saturday evenings, starting around 8pm (tel: 909146).

105

A last coffee
The cafés around Midan el-Husayn are open until early in the morning and some even claim that they never close. If everything else has closed, head for this square to relax with a strong coffee and a water-pipe, and watch Cairo wake up.

Lovers meet secretly in 'casinos' beside the Nile to discuss their future over a cold drink

Belly dancing

■ **Belly dancing in its many forms occupies a central place in Egyptian culture and is as much a part of its traditions as telling stories and smoking water-pipes. In spite of this, some groups are calling for its abolition on grounds of indecency.....■**

The Bee
Gustave Flaubert's account of a Syrian dancer in Esna did much to encourage sexual fantasies about belly dancing, but nothing like this is on show in Egypt: 'Kuchuk dances the Bee... A black veil is tied around the eyes of the child, and a fold of his blue turban is lowered over those of the old man. Kuchuk shed her clothing as she danced. Finally she was naked except for a *fichu* which she held in her hands and behind which she pretended to hide, and at the end she threw down the *fichu*. That was the Bee.'

Female dancers and and musicians were a popular entertainment in ancient Egypt

A long tradition Egyptians claim that oriental dance – of which the belly or *baladi* dance is one form – began in ancient Egypt and there are tomb paintings to support the claim. So perhaps it was from Egyptian dancers that Salome learned her trade. According to the Bible story, her fame was so widespread that King Herod told her to name her price to dance for him: she demanded the head of John the Baptist.

Natural rhythm Although connected to death in Salome's story, oriental dance probably has its origins in instinctive dances that were part of primitive fertility rituals. Much of it certainly comes naturally and if you hear music playing in a Cairene street, it won't be long before you see a child raise its arms, lean back and start to swing its hips. Egypt's greatest dancers all claim to have started like this, dancing with other children, only later learning how to refine impulses which other people often suppress. The more skilful dancers can be remarkably expressive, suggesting not just sexuality, but tenderness, vitality and grace. Modern demands for spectacle have added large numbers of musicians to the original two- or three-member bands while dancers now wear extravagant glittering costumes to exaggerate their curves.

Today's stars Egypt's most famous dancers enjoy the same status as film or pop stars in the Arab world and are just as highly paid. Although much of their dancing takes

place at private parties, most of them also have contracts to dance at the hotel clubs. Stars like Fifi Abduh, Lucy and Dina have their own individual styles and a devoted body of fans, although many dancers go in and out of fashion. Recently, with the threat of violence from reactionary Islamist groups, some dancers have announced their retirement and made a point of being seen in public wearing a veil. Others, like Fifi Abduh, have been more defiant and insist on their right to perform.

Spectacular entertainment Stories of dancers being flown off to Riyad or Amman for a night's work have made oriental dance sound exclusive – and some of it is – but the image is misleading. There is nothing as pervasive in the West to compare it with, and you are just as likely to see a dancer in the poorest slums as in the president's palace. Because it cuts across social strata, you can see dancers in some very different venues. Most of Cairo's big hotels have early evening shows for foreign tourists who want to get up early the following morning, although these are often bland affairs. The star dancers often don't appear until late-night shows, which are more popular with Arab audiences.

Cheaper clubs Many of today's stars started out in nightclubs like Palmyra and its neighbours on 26th-of-July Street, or in the many clubs in Giza along Pyramids Road. In these cheaper, less sophisticated clubs, the show usually starts in the middle of the evening and continues until 3am or later, but individual dancers will perform only for as long as they please the audience. The test of this is how much money admirers are prepared to throw on the stage: when the bank notes stop falling, the next act is brought on. In these clubs, foreigners, not being used to this habit, are rarely seated near the stage.

Dancers will also perform at weddings and Cairo's wealthier families pay well over the odds to persuade one of the stars to make a brief appearance at their reception. At other weddings, guests themselves will dance and if you are lucky enough to be invited this will certainly be expected of you.

Dance of Life
Life is like a *ghaziya* (an Egyptian dancer), she dances just briefly for each.

Egyptian proverb, quoted in *Serpent of the Nile: Women and Dance in the Arab World*

Vitality and sensuality are at the heart of oriental dance

107

Accommodation

Touts upon arrival
You might be offered assistance with booking a room when you arrive in Cairo by people who are not tourism officials, who will make the call for you and then tell you that the hotel of your choice is fully booked. He will offer you an alternative – 'just the place for you' – and his friend the taxi driver will offer to take you there for a 'friendly price'. Decline, unless you're desperate!

The main tourist areas offer accommodation for everyone's wallet, everything from bottom-end flea pits to sumptuous old palaces. The choice will be much more limited elsewhere and if, for instance, you decide to spend the night in the Delta, the oases or Middle Egypt, you will have to put up with more basic accommodation. Most hotels are classified with star ratings from one to deluxe five stars and, while these do not conform to international ratings, it is quite obvious why most of the unclassified pensions missed their star.

Old glamour which is no more The opening of a hotel for Europeans in Cairo in 1841 by an Englishman, Samuel Shepheard, started a tradition of hostelry which has been continued until this day. By the turn of the century, Cairo boasted a handful of first-class hotels, and a couple still offer rewarding glimpses of the past. The cosmopolitan Shepheard's Hotel burned down in the riots of 1952, while the Continental Savoy now stands empty on Midan Opera. The Semiramis, once known for its weekly society dances, was pulled down and rebuilt in the 1980s as the Semiramis InterContinental. But all is not lost: the Gezira Palace, with two towers added, is now the Cairo Marriott Hotel, still with notable gardens, casino and architecture, while the Mena House remains well appointed with a golf course and swimming pool overlooked by the pyramids.

Luxury palaces Most of the international chains have opened five-star hotels in Cairo. They are invariably modern, offer every imaginable facility and service, and often succeed in making you feel as though you could be anywhere in the world. But these hotels are also popular venues for wealthy Cairenes who come to stroll in the gardens, socialise on the terrace and throw expensive wedding parties on weekends. Cairo's luxury hotels are

The old khedival hunting lodge, with excellent views over the Giza Pyramids, is now the luxurious Mena House Hotel

Pension exotique
One of the cheapest and most colourful hotels in town is the Pension Oxford (32 Sharia Talaat Harb). The Oxford has become a backpackers' institution. It is wonderfully cosmopolitan, with cool Sudani receptionists, a punk Italian hairdresser in residence, an American lady praying naked to Allah on her balcony, a Syrian belly dancer waiting for fame, all blended in with jaded backpackers relaxing after too many months in Africa. No need to book in advance, there is always room on the floor.

The sumptuous palace built to house the Empress Eugenie for the opening of the Suez Canal is now part of the Cairo Marriott Hotel

Swimming pools
Looking to cool off in a pool? You can use the pools of hotels like the Nile Hilton, Marriott, Gezira Sheraton and Meridien at a considerable day-fee or, more cheaply, at the Atlas Zamalek Hotel. But the best offer is the Manyal Palace Club Med, where the day-fee includes a delicious buffet with wine, and an after-lunch nap under the banyan trees.

mostly clustered in four main areas: at the airport, along the river near Tahrir Square (good for the Egyptian Museum and downtown), in the quieter and more sophisticated area of Zamalek and out near the Pyramids, an hour's ride back into town if the traffic is bad. Avoid turning up individually at these hotels; a more favourable rate is always to be had if you book through the chain's central office or, even better, as part of a package tour.

Mid-range and mediocre Cairo's three- and four-star hotels miss out on the ambience of the cheaper ones and never even closely achieve the facilities and service of the upmarket places. Many hotels in this range, scattered across the city, are in modern concrete buildings with dodgy plumbing and without character. Fortunately there are exceptions. Zamalek has some excellent modern hotels, the President Hotel among them, which have the advantage of a quiet location close to shopping and restaurants. The Victoria, Windsor and Cosmopolitan hotels have kept much of their old-style aura and are much recommended if you don't mind the unstoppable hubbub of downtown as a background.

Cheap and sometimes cheerful Cairo is also famous for its wonderful cheap pensions. Most are in Mohandiseen, around Ramses Station and Midan Talaat Harb; opt for the latter area if you want some character. Some, like Pensione Roma, are in 19th-century buildings with spacious rooms and ceiling fans, while others thrive on cheap tattiness. The better pensions are clean, good value for money and popular, so booking is recommended.

Transport

Jump on the bus
Buses don't stop, they merely slow down, so people have to jump on and off at speed. After football, it is probably the favourite and most spectacular Cairene sport: you see the bus arriving, wait for the people to get off, let the bus go on a little bit further, sprint through the traffic and, often with the helping hand of someone hanging out of the door, you jump... and you're off!

Wagon-Lit trains
Wagon-Lits runs a daily sleeper service to Aswan and Luxor, the excellent Turbeen trains to Alexandria (2 hours) and in summer, three trains a day to Mersa Matruh. Wagons-Lits' main office is in Ramses Station, but it is much easier to use their office in Shepheard's Hotel at Garden City (8:30am–4:30pm). Take your passport with you to book sleepers.

Nile barrages
Around Maspero on a Friday there are boats loaded with dressed-up Cairene families out for a good time. They are heading for the Nile barrages – ornate, brightly painted dams where the river divides in two. At the fork there is a pleasant park with boats and bikes for rent, carriage rides and shady picnic spots. The outing is much recommended.

Public transport is quite well organised in Egypt. If you can't be bothered with the crowds and waiting times for buses, taxis are cheap and abundant, and don't forget the Metro (see page 94).

Buses The cheapest transport in Cairo is on the battered red buses which run along fixed routes from 5.30am until midnight. Numbers and routes are indicated in Arabic. Apart from the main ones on Midan el-Tahrir, most bus stops are only vaguely signposted. Because they are cheap they are also crowded, with passengers hanging out of the doors. It is pickpocket and bottom-pincher territory and best avoided. More expensive orange and white minibuses are a good alternative as no standing passengers are allowed. They will only stop when requested to do so. The main terminals are on Midan el-Tahrir and Midan el-Ataba. River buses operating on the Nile leave hourly from Maspero opposite the Television Building and go to Giza and Old Cairo, or to the Nile barrage at Qanatir.

Taxis Taxis are easy to find and reasonably cheap if you choose the right one. Look out for four-seater, black-and-white taxis, which you stop by holding out your hand and shouting your destination. If there is someone in it and they are going your way the driver will usually take you, too. The meter may work, but doesn't actually indicate the fare: Cairenes know the going rate, so either ask someone in the hotel how much you should pay or decide on a price in advance with the driver. As a tourist, you will usually pay a little bit more because the drivers expect that you can afford it. It is best to avoid black-and-white, seven-seater Peugeot taxis, whose drivers prey on innocent tourists and often charge considerably more than the going rate. If you don't want the hassle, book a limousine

in any five-star hotel for a higher, fixed price. It can be a good deal if you take it for a whole or half-day excursion.

Trains Most trains leave from Ramses Station. Buy your tickets well in advance. It is best to take express trains for longer distances, as the local trains are incredibly slow and often unreliable. Finding the right window to buy your tickets is not always easy, but you can usually pay *baksheesh* (a tip) to someone in your hotel who can do it for you. Or opt for a comfortable Wagons-Lits sleeper and buy your ticket from their offices at Shepheard's Hotel.

Long-distances buses There is a good network of air-conditioned, inter-city buses which are often faster and more reliable than the train. Tickets should preferably be bought one or two days in advance from the appropriate bus terminal. Buses for Alexandria, Mersa Matruh and Libya leave from the Abd el-Muneem Riyad Terminal, outside the Ramses Hilton Hotel. Buses for Hurghada, Upper and Middle Egypt and el-Faiyum leave from the Ahmad Hilmi Terminal behind Ramses Station. Buses for Sinai leave from the Sinai Terminal in Abbasiya, past the Misr Travel Tower. Buses for the Western Desert oases leave from the dusty el-Azhar Terminal on Sharia el-Azhar in the Ataba area and buses for the Canal Zone and the Delta go from Kulali Terminal in Abbasiya.

Planes The fastest way to go is to fly. The national airline, Egypt Air, has offices just about everywhere. Air Sinai flies to Sinai and Hurghada and has an office in the Nile Hilton, and ZAS, for Sinai, Hurghada, Luxor and Aswan, has an office in the Novotel by the airport. American Express, Thomas Cook and other agents can buy and reconfirm tickets on all flights for you.

Amidst a spaghetti of fly-overs stands the beautiful, pseudo-Moorish Ramses Railway Station

The traffic in Cairo is usually chaotic, and crossing a main street can seem like a serious suicide attempt

Useful bus numbers
From the Nile Hilton on Midan el-Tahrir: Red buses No 66 Khan el-Khalili; No 173 camel market in Imbaba; No 400 Cairo Airport Terminal 1 and No 949 Cairo Airport Terminal 2.
From the Mugamma on Midan el-Tahrir: Red buses No 174 Ibn Tulun Mosque and Citadel; No 900 Mena House and the pyramids; No 913 Sphinx and Sound and Light show; Minibuses No 24 Heliopolis; No 82 and No 83 the pyramids.

LOWER NILE VALLEY

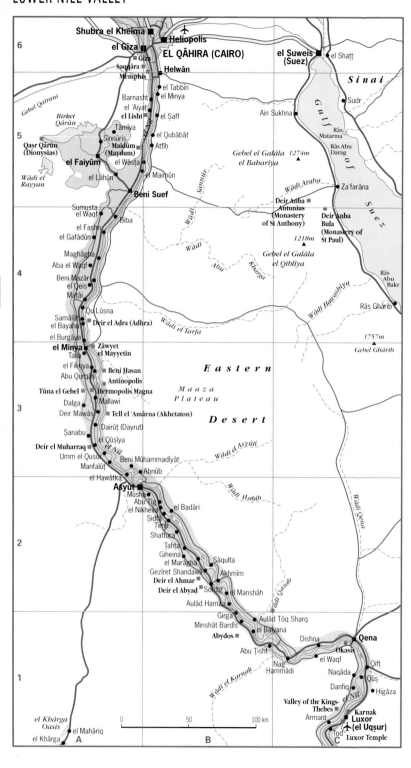

The Lower Nile Valley This region offered 19th-century tourists a first taste of adventure as they sailed along in their *dahabiehs* (large sailing boats), heading for Luxor and Aswan. Today, it still offers an excellent introduction to the splendours of the south and some surprises of its own.

The land Egypt, as has often been observed, is a country of contrasts and some of them become apparent as soon as you leave Cairo. Even from the window of a train or Egypt Air jet, after the overcrowding and industrialisation of the capital, the countryside to the south looks different, composed of a string of small villages and larger towns separated by lush farmland. The valley here is much broader and far less dramatic than it is further south. El-Faiyum, often visited as a day-trip from Cairo, shares not only the Nile water, but also the appearance of the lower Nile Valley and the character of its people.

Rarely visited tombs It is easy to travel through from Cairo to Luxor and as a result the antiquities of the lower Nile Valley are often overlooked. But just as the country-side and its people are a vital link between the north and south, so some of the ruins are crucial for an understanding of Egyptian history. The Middle Kingdom tombs at Beni Hasan, for instance, and the Middle Kingdom pyra-

Above: local man
Above left: the Nile is the river of life for many rural communities

Relief carving of Isis

The fellaheen, *Egypt's peasantry, depend on farming for their livelihood and agriculture remains the basis of the country's economy*

LOWER NILE VALLEY

mids outside el-Faiyum make the shift from the Old Kingdom pyramids at Giza to the New Kingdom tombs in Luxor's Valley of the Kings all the more understandable.

Beautiful temples The lower Nile Valley also contains the ruins of two contrasting settlements. The radical pharaoh Akhenaton built his new capital, Akhetaton (modern el-Amarna), halfway between the modern towns of Minya and Asyut and worshipped the sun-god Aton there. Some 50 years after Akhenaton's death, the pharaoh Seti I built a magnificently preserved temple complex at Abydos, south of Akhetaton to confirm the restoration of the old regime that Akhenaton had tried to overthrow.

In Jesus's footsteps Coptic tradition claims that Joseph, Mary and the infant Jesus travelled through Egypt to escape Herod. St Matthew reported that an angel told Joseph, 'Arise, and take the young child and his mother, and flee into Egypt.' Many sites along the Nile, from churches in the Coptic quarter of Cairo to the Deir el-Adhra north of Minya, lay claim to having accommodated the family.

The modern valley Here, more than in the upper valley, you can see an Egypt that is not geared to tourism. The hotels and restaurants in towns and villages of this region are generally basic, if they exist at all, but in return for discomfort and for overcoming the difficulties of communicating across languages, you might find a welcome from people whose lives, for thousands of years, have been regulated by the same forces: the rise and fall of the river, the need to sow and harvest crops and the adherence to religious calendars, now Coptic and Muslim.

Changing character Like the landscape, the *fellaheen* (peasant farmers) of the lower valley were once characterised as gentle, and less explosive than their brothers fur-

Living side by side in Asyut, the crescent-topped minarets of a mosque and the cross-capped towers of a Coptic church

On the Nile
'... and when the wind freshens, you see a fleet of little cangias coming out, like water lilies, upon the river (you don't know from where), or like fairy boats, a fleet of Efreets [spirits] coming up the Nile, doubling a cape, cutting in among each other. There are islands and headlands and creeks, just like at sea, and sometimes, when the wind blows against the current, he is no longer the solemn Nile, but a most tempestuous lake, with white horses, and turbulent little waves. But he is always beautiful.'
Florence Nightingale, *Letters from Egypt* (1849–50)

ther south. One fifth of the population were Copts – many more than elsewhere – and their cohabitation with Muslims was a source of pride to Egyptians. But population growth, lack of work and other social problems have shattered the calm. Fundamentalist Muslims have attacked Copts, government representatives and tourists, killing many people and making a visit to the area around Asyut particularly inadvisable (see pages 126–7). Throughout the region, Christians and Muslims have built new churches and mosques, their belfries and minarets reaching higher and higher above the palm trees, trying to get the better of each other and changing the look of the land in the process.

Sunset on the Nile
'We watch the banks glide past us as in a dream. With the drawing on of evening a glory of colours comes out in the light of the setting sun... The reds and greys of sandstone, granite, and limestone cliffs blend exquisitely with the tawny yellow of the desert, the rich green of the banks, and the blue of the river, giving combinations and contrast of colour in which the artist revels... This is the most fairy-like and magical effect of colour I have ever seen.'
Samuel Manning, 1875

LOWER NILE VALLEY

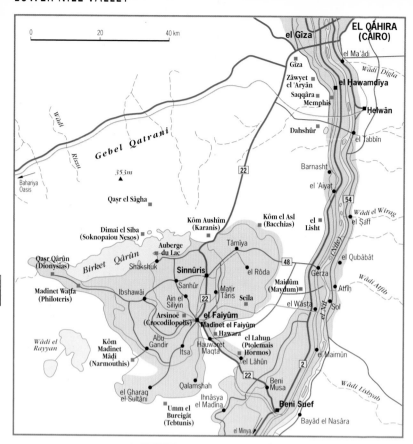

►► el-Faiyum

112A5

El-Faiyum, 100km southwest of Cairo, can be reached by bus. It is surrounded by the Western Desert but it is not a true oasis, for it depends on a branch of the Nile, the Bahr Yusuf, for its water. The marshes of el-Faiyum were popular hunting and fishing grounds until the 4th century BC, when the Ptolemies drained the land and created the 'Garden of Egypt'. Today el-Faiyum produces cotton, clover, tomatoes and an abundance of fruit and vegetables. Its chickens are considered to be the best in Egypt.

Walk along the waterwheels
Following the Bahr Sinuris canal northwards out of town, first on the west bank, then on the east, and passing the Governorate Club, you will reach one wheel and then beyond the weeping willows, a group of four. Further along the canal (about half an hour's walk) are the famous Seven Waterwheels, set in beautiful countryside.

►► Madinet el-Faiyum (Faiyum City)

The 12th-Dynasty Obelisk of Senusert I stands at the entrance to the governorate capital. Tour buses stop at the Four Waterwheels, by the cafeteria in the middle of the town, but the **Seven Waterwheels►**, north of the centre, are more interesting. The **Mosque of Qaytbay►**, the oldest in town (1499), is said to have been built for the sultan's favourite concubine. The mosque has a beautifully carved *minbar* (pulpit) inlaid with ivory and ancient columns taken from Kiman Faris. Qaytbay also built the two-arched bridge near by, now known as the Bridge of Farewells because it leads to the cemetery. The white-domed **Mausoleum of Ali ar-Rubi►**, the favourite local holy man, is also nearby. (Continued on page 118.)

■ **Most visitors come to enjoy the serenity of lake and countryside, all easily accessible by public transport. Some of the rarely visited ancient sites on the outskirts of the oasis can only be reached by four-wheel drive, but their isolation adds a sense of discovery to the visit.....■**

Birket Qarun (Lake Qarun), a salt lake 45m below sea level, is all that remains of the fabled Great Lake. Swimming is not recommended as many drainage canals pollute the *birka* (lake), but it is possible to rent boats to row across it, or to enjoy the sun on its beaches. Bird-watchers are attracted by the variety of migratory species, as are hunters who come to shoot the wintering ducks, geese and quails. The spring of Ain el-Siliyin, en route to the lake, has been overly commercialised: spring water now comes out of metal pipes in a concrete wall.

Kom Aushim, the site of ancient Karanis, is easily accessible from the Cairo road. There is a museum (closed Monday) and the well-preserved ruins of the mud-brick Ptolemaic-Roman town (3rd century BC–5th century AD).

Dimai el-Siba and Qasr el-Sagha are difficult to reach, but are interesting for their history and their beautiful setting, overlooking the lake and the desert. The Qasr el-Sagha (Palace of Jewellers) is a small, Middle-Kingdom temple of irregularly shaped blocks, reminiscent of Inca architecture. The isolated ruins of Dimai el-Siba (Dimai of the Wolves), encircled by a thick wall and with a rough-hewn temple in the middle, can also be reached by boat.

Qasr Qarun is a well-preserved and easily accessible Ptolemaic temple 45km northwest of the city. There are also four pyramid sites around el-Faiyum, the 12th-Dynasty el-**Lahun and Hawara Pyramids** off the Beni Suef Road, the 12th-Dynasty and ruined el-**Lisht Pyramid** and the 3rd-Dynasty collapsed **Pyramid of Maidum**.

Legends of el-Faiyum
In ancient mythology the Great Lake of el-Faiyum was identified with Nun, the primeval ocean and origin of all life; the high land around Kiman Faris was seen as the primeval hill, where life first started. Diodorus records that Crocodilopolis (el-Faiyum) was built by King Menes, who united Upper and Lower Egypt, after a crocodile saved his life on the Great Lake. Modern Faiyumis claim that it took 1,000 days to build the city, and thus it was called Madinet Alf Yaum (City of a Thousand Days).

Lake Qarun is a favourite day-trip destination for Cairene families in need of some fresh air and quietude

The semi-oasis of el-Faiyum has a fertile soil irrigated by a branch of the Nile, the Bahr Yusuf

Getting around
As public transport to the ancient sites is limited and time consuming, it is advisable to hire a private taxi for a day excursion to Beni Hasan, Tuna el-Gebel and Hermopolis. The tourist office on the Corniche (off Sharia Abdel Monem) can give information about transport.

(*Continued from page 116.*) The **souk►**, in an area on the canal called el-Qantara, is a labyrinth of small alleys with shops that, for once, are not directed towards tourism. The beautiful Faiyumi baskets are sold around the water-wheels, and the best pottery is sold at the pottery market (Tuesday morning) in Sharia el-Mudarris.

►► el-Minya 112A3

This provincial capital, some 250km south of Cairo, can be reached by train from Cairo in 3–4 hours, or by bus (5 hours) from the Ahmad Hilmi terminal. There is also a direct train from Luxor, but by bus you will need to change in Asyut.

El-Minya is a pleasant, provincial town with worn-out colonial villas, once inhabited by Greek and Egyptian cotton barons, set in overgrown gardens. There is little to see in the town itself, but its relaxed atmosphere and good accommodation make an ideal base for discovering the region's archaeological sites. After sunset, the entire population seems to come out for an evening stroll along the breezy corniche (waterfront) or the busy streets between Midan el-Tahrir and Midan el-Saa. Minya has a large Christian community and occasionally its peace is disturbed by religious tension.

El-Minya's vast cemetery, the **Zawiyet el-Mayyetin (Corner of the Dead)►**, is on the east bank of the Nile, near the village of el-Sawada. Until recently the dead were transported by *feluccas* (sailing boats) to their final resting place, but a new bridge has changed the ancient tradition. It is a spectacular sight, with thousands of domed mausoleums in the Muslim cemetery and thousands of crosses defining the Coptic tombs. On 6 July, Copts camp here during the annual *moulid* (festival) of Aba Hur, whose subterranean, rock-cut church is nearby.

About 20km north of el-Minya, on the east bank, is the Gebel el-Teir (Bird Mountain) with the Coptic **Deir el-Adhra (Monastery of the Virgin)►** on its summit. The monastery was inhabited until the 19th century and is still a place of pilgrimage. The 4th-century Church of the Holy Virgin, partly cut out of the rock, is said to occupy a cave where the Holy Family took shelter and many miracles are ascribed to the picture of the Virgin that weeps holy oil.

▶▶ **Rock Tombs of Beni Hasan** 112A3

Tombs open: 8–4 daily. Admission fee.
Only 4 of the 39 11th- and 12th-Dynasty tombs are open. These tombs of local Middle Kingdom rulers represent a transition from the Old Kingdom pyramids in Giza to the tombs in the Valley of the Kings in Luxor. Although most were unfinished, the painting on stucco is excellent, with vivid depictions of everyday life of the period.

Tomb of Baqet III (No 15)▶▶ Baqet was the 11th-Dynasty monarch of Oryx. On the left wall there is a papyrus harvest, acrobats, women spinning and, above, a gazelle hunt in the desert. On the rear wall there is a catalogue of 200 wrestling positions, and on the right wall are scenes of Baqet's daily life.

Tomb of Kheti (No 17)▶▶ The 11th-Dynasty tomb of Kheti, son of Baqet, still has two of its six painted lotus columns. On the left and rear walls are figures in different stages of movement, like a film in slow motion. Paintings depict papyrus harvesting, weavers, hunters, dancers, musicians, wrestlers and a desert hunt. On the right wall, Kheti is overseeing various activities and receiving offerings.

Tomb of Amenemhet (No 2)▶▶ (12th Dynasty) Proto-Doric columns support the painted ceiling. The wall to the left has the customary hunting scenes as well as Amenemhet collecting tributes. On the rear wall the voyage to Abydos is depicted and in the niches are broken statues of the man himself between his mother and wife. On the right wall are scenes of harpooning fish, musicians, wrestlers and offerings.

Tomb of Khnumhotep (No 3)▶▶▶ This 12th-Dynasty tomb of Amenemhet's successor has the most beautiful paintings of hunting, fowling and fishing (rear wall). On the left wall, beneath a desert hunt, Khnumhotep receives eye paint from the Semites, meticulously depicted in their strange clothes. To the right, he sails to Abydos and inspects various artisans.

Death on the Nile
In AD30 Emperor Hadrian travelled with his lover, Antinous, through Egypt. After an oracle predicted a great calamity, the emperor's lover was drowned in the Nile. In his honour, Hadrian built the city of Antinopolis, the ruins of which are 10km south of Beni Hasan.

Below: wrestlers on the walls of Kheti's tomb (11th-Dynasty) in Beni Hasan Bottom: unassuming entrances to the Rock Tombs of Beni Hasan

119

■ **It is difficult to build a comprehensible image of religion in ancient Egypt. Most ancient literature in Egypt is concerned with some aspect of religion, which means there is very little secular writing to help put it into context. It was also a religion that evolved gradually over a period of many centuries, and a reasonable knowledge of how it developed is an important step towards understanding the subject....■**

Egyptian gods

Amun-Ra: Amun and Ra, from Thebes and Heliopolis, merged to form an important state god.

Anubis: the jackal-god of funerary matters.

Bastet: a cat-headed goddess of pleasure.

Bes: a grotesquely fat dwarf, god of childbirth and children.

Hathor: the cow goddess of pleasure and protector of women.

Horus: a falcon, popularly known as the young king who avenged his father Osiris.

Isis: Osiris' sister and wife, and Horus' mother, she epitomised female qualities and was represented with cow's horns and a solar disk, or with a throne on her head.

Khnum: human-headed ram, god of fertility who created men on a potter's wheel.

Maat: a woman with an ostrich feather, who symbolised justice and order.

Min: a god of fertility, usually with large phallus.

Nephthys: sister of Isis and Osiris, and sister and wife of Seth.

Nut: a naked female straddling the earth, she swallowed the sun at night and gave birth to it at dawn.

120

In the beginning Creation myths lay at the heart of Egyptian religious belief. There were several versions, the most widely accepted of which was developed at Heliopolis. Before the world was created, the only thing that existed was the water of Chaos. Eventually some ground began to emerge above the water and on it stood the sun-god Atum (later identified with Ra). Atum created air (Shu) and moisture (Tefnut), who in turn created the earth (Geb) and the sky (Nut) and from their union came Osiris and Isis, Seth and Nephthys. The similarity between this myth and the experience of Egyptians is striking: just as the first earth rose out of the waters of chaos, so Egyptians' fields emerged each year as the floodwaters of the Nile receded. The priests of Memphis preached that the god Ptah created heaven and earth by his command, a belief that also appears in the Old Testament account of Genesis.

Renewal through ritual Egyptians were uniquely dependent on hidden, natural cycles – it was of paramount importance that their river, with its hidden source, should flood with measured force and at just the right moment for the sowing of crops. So it's not surprising that their religious beliefs were intimately connected to the forces of nature and to the animals with whom they shared the valley. As their world was one of contrasts, epitomised by the fertile valley and the surrounding desert, so their pantheon divided into forces for good and evil. It was believed that good could only triumph and the well-being of the valley could only be ensured if the correct rituals were repeated. Thus the images of the gods were given fresh coverings each morning, food was offered morning and night, incense was burned at the right moment and all other observances were kept.

The development of state gods By the end of the Old Kingdom, rituals were fairly standardised throughout the country. Feasts were observed at all the great temples. Many of them connected myths of the gods with natural cycles so, for instance, the feast of the Coming-Forth of Min (a god associated with fertility) took place at the time of harvest. The king held the post of high priest, but in his absence priests performed the daily rituals in which the public took no part, being forbidden to enter the inner sanctums of temples. As temples grew rich on gifts of land and precious objects, so their political power increased, and during a weak monarchy and in the reign of a king like Tutankhamun, it was the priests who effectively ran the country. But although gods such as Osiris maintained their popularity, others came and went and the influence of their priesthood declined with them.

Graeco-Roman influences Osiris emerges as the most popular and enduring Egyptian deity, perhaps because he was seen as a victim of injustice and because he was intimately connected to the passage of the dead from this world to the next. After the conquest of the eastern Mediterranean by Alexander the Great, his successors, hoping to unite Greeks and Egyptians, encouraged the worship of a new god, Serapis, evolved from Osiris and the Greek god Dionysos. The Egyptians built sanctuaries for the god at Memphis and Alexandria, and the cult of Serapis spread to Athens, Rome and far into Asia. When the Roman emperor, Theodosius I, declared Christianity as the religion of the empire, he unleashed a wave of Christian fundamentalism in which tombs and temples were defiled; the Serapeum at Alexandria was destroyed and the ancient religion along with it.

Egyptian gods
Osiris: a mummified man, with false beard, crook and flail, associated with vegetation and regeneration (see p130–31).
Ptah: mummified man with tight cap, he was seen by some as the creator of the universe.
Sekhmet: the lioness goddess of war and wife of Ptah.
Seth: god with a dog's head who murdered his brother Osiris and epitomised chaos and destruction.
Thoth: ibis-headed god of wisdom and writing.

Relief carving inside the Temple of Seti I and Ramses II, Abydos

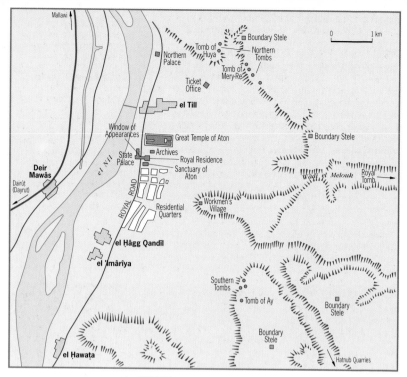

Tell el-Amarna

The god Thoth
Thoth was the god of wisdom and, more specifically, the god of science and medicine. The sun-god Ra appointed him as his assistant and gave him the moon. He usually appeared as a man with the head of an ibis, because Ra gave him an ibis as a helper, or as a baboon with a large erected phallus. Baboons were identified with the sun because they shriek at the crack of dawn.

▶ **Hermopolis Magna**   *112A3*

The ruins are near el-Ashmunayn, off the secondary road from el-Minya to Mallawi, about 6km before Tuna el-Gebel.

From early dynastic times Khmunu was an important cult centre devoted to the moon-god Thoth and was believed to be the site of the primeval hill where the sun-god Ra emerged to create the world out of chaos. The Ptolemies, identifying Thoth with the Greek god Hermes, called the city Hermopolis. The ruins seem still to be waiting for the Creation to happen: beyond two giant baboons and a 5th-century basilica built with columns of a Ptolemaic temple, mounds of rubble, potsherds and earth are all that remain of the temple of Thoth. But the site under the palm grove, with villagers walking through, is very picturesque.

▶ **Tuna el-Gebel**   *112A3*

Open: 9–5 daily. Admission fee.
Tuna el-Gebel was the necropolis of Hermopolis. On the road between the town and the site is a rock-cut boundary stela (inscribed stone) depicting Akhenaton and Nefertiti with their daughters, adoring the sun.

A path (right of the entrance) leads to the eerie catacombs where mummified ibises and baboons, sacred to Thoth, were buried. The most impressive building is the Tomb-chapel of Petosiris (c 300BC), the high priest of Thoth, whose exquisite coffin is in the Egyptian Museum in Cairo. Traditional Egyptian scenes of harvesting, sewing, wine-making and so forth on the vestibule walls show a Greek influence in the clothing and the perspective. The tomb contains brightly coloured scenes of the Book of the Dead and the Book of the Gates.

►► Tell el-Amarna (Akhetaton) 112A3

Open: 7–5 daily. Admission fee.

Tell el-Amarna can be reached by road from Mallawi (12km) and then by ferry to the villages of el-Till or el-Hagg Qandil on the east bank. From the ticket office there is basic transport to the Northern Tombs and the palace area. A car is necessary to see the rest of the site.

Around 1349BC Akhenaton founded his new capital, Akhetaton (Horizon of the Sun Disc), on an empty plain halfway between Memphis and Thebes. The city was abandoned soon after his death in 1336BC, when the court returned to Thebes. Little remains of the mud-brick city, the ruins of its palaces and temples are scattered across an arid plain, but realistic tomb paintings make it possible to imagine what the city might have looked like.

From the landing stage at el-Till a dirt track follows the Royal Road along the main axis through the centre of the city. It leads to the Muslim cemetery, once the Great Temple of Aton, and then to the archives where the Amarna Letters were found. Three rectangular markers identify the Royal Residence, which was decorated with colourful scenes of birds, flowers and fish. A walking bridge, with a window from which the royal family made public appearances, led over the Royal Road to the State Palace. Next door is the Sanctuary of Aton, and beyond it the residential quarters, mostly covered by sand. It was here in the workshop of the sculptor Tuthmosis that the bust of Nefertiti was found in 1912.

On the other side of el-Till is Nefertiti's Northern Palace, the best-preserved of Amarna's buildings. Amarna's necropolis is in the eastern cliffs. Of the Northern Tombs, the tombs of Huya (No 1), superintendent of the Royal Harem; Mery-Re (No 4), the high priest of Aton; and Panehesi (No 6), vizier of Lower Egypt, are most worth a visit. There are 19 Southern Tombs, but the tombs of Mahu (No 9), chief of police, and Ay (No 25), scribe and confidant to Akhenaton, are the finest and best-preserved.

Hymn to the Sun

'At dawn you rise shining in the horizon, you shine as Aton in the sky and drive away darkness by sending forth your rays. The Two Lands awake in festivity, and men stand on their feet, for you have raised them up. They wash their bodies, they take their garments, and their arms are raised to praise your rising. The whole world does its work.'

From Akhenaton's *Hymn of the Sun*

123

Light in the dark

Although guards will offer to reflect sunlight on a foil-covered board, it is recommended to take a torch to appreciate the delightful, unlit tombs.

Relief carvings in the rock tombs at Tell el-Amarna

■ **Early in his reign, around 1349BC, the pharaoh Akhenaton rejected the state god Amun and moved his capital north from Thebes to el-Amarna. Whatever the politics behind his break with the Theban priesthood, the move was a joyful liberation for his followers and this period produced Egypt's most radical art and some of its most enlightened thinking.....■**

Right: Akhenaton's queen, Nefertiti, still embodies our ideal of beauty (see below)

124

The face of Nefertiti
A 3,000-year-old bust of Nefertiti, one of the most famous images from ancient Egypt, was the prize discovery of an extraordinary dig during the winter of 1912 in the studio of Akhenaton's chief sculptor, Tuthmosis. The queen probably sat for this excellently preserved master portrait, on which all other images of her would have been based. The 50cm-high limestone bust, showing the beautiful queen wearing make-up, a flat-topped crown and necklace, officially belonged to James Simon, the Berlin merchant who held the licence to dig, but it is now on display in the Egyptian Museum in Berlin.

Akhenaton's rift It has been said that 'more ink has been spilt on the Amarna period than the whole of the rest of Egyptian history.' A slight exaggeration, perhaps, but there are good reasons why Akhenaton's actions – banning the worship of the state god Amun and raising Aton, the solar disc, previously a minor deity, to the status of the sole god of Egypt – have exercised the pens of theologians and Egyptologists alike. After all, to turn a well-established state religion on its head required an immense leap of the imagination, far greater, for instance, than the one which developed *mastabas* (tomb chambers) into pyramids. With Akhenaton's revolution, Egypt is seen to have been looking for a new direction. Its longing for spiritual and intellectual renewal is all the more poignant because it was so short-lived and because the reactionaries who succeeded to the throne – Tutankhamun among them –' were thorough in their restoration of the old way.

God or gods? Some consider that Akhenaton's rejection of all other gods in favour of Aton was the first known instance of monotheism. The mummified remains of Yuya, Akhenaton's grandfather and a high official of common birth, were found in the Valley of the Kings in Thebes; as they don't look particularly Egyptian, one recent theory suggests that Yuya was Joseph, the youngest son of the Canaanite patriarch Jacob (and owner of a technicolour coat). If true, then perhaps it was Joseph who inspired Akhenaton to break with the past.

The new capital Akhenaton's new capital was built in a hurry, which explains its mud-brick construction. There is less for the visitor to see, but the ruins have been of great value to archaeologists: because Akhenaton chose ground that had not previously been built upon and has not seen any major construction since, the ruins have afforded a privileged look at a New Kingdom community.

From what is known, the city covered 290sq km, facing the river and enclosed by a line of hills along its eastern edge. Its planning and decoration, its large palaces and comfortable houses, seem to have confirmed Akhenaton's emphasis on celebrating the living. The pavement from the palace at el-Amarna, painted with lush vegetation and flocks of birds (in Cairo's Egyptian Museum), and the other works that escaped the destructive hand of Akhenaton's enemies are further testimony to the beauty of the city.

The new art After centuries of increasingly stylised representations of Egypt's rulers, Akhenaton appears to us in an entirely different way. Here is a man we can understand: he plays with his children rather than staring into eternity, he has bodily imperfections which are shown and perhaps even exaggerated, he eats, drinks and clearly loves life. Identification is made even easier by the fact that his queen, Nefertiti, so closely adheres to our ideals of beauty. Much as we might like to see the beginnings of Judaism, Christianity and Islam in Akhenaton's revolution, the artistic expression he seems to have encouraged lasted only as long as he did.

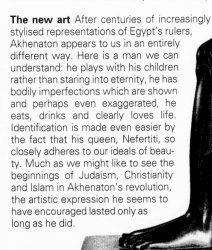

The awesome, demi-god image of Akhenaton staring into eternity, sculpted in the traditional manner prior to the advent of his new art

125

❑   The Islamic University in Asyut, associated with el-Azhar in Cairo, has long been a stronghold for fundamentalists in the region. The struggle between Islamist groups and the security forces escalated when President Sadat tried to suppress religious extremism, a conflict which culminated in his assassination in Cairo in 1981. Egyptians returning from the Afghan war and the estimated 1 million who lost jobs in the Gulf because of the Gulf War have provided the fundamentalists with a new base of support. Since 1992 several groups have become actively involved in terrorism, most noticeably the Gamaat Islammiya, who have called for the setting up of an Islamic republic and the deportation of foreigners. Tourists have been easy targets; night trains, cruise boats and tourist buses have been attacked, with some injuries and deaths to foreigners. As most incidents have occurred in the area around Asyut and Dayrut (Dairut), the majority of visitors to Egypt who avoid this area have experienced no security difficulties at all. The Asyut area is best avoided while violence continues. ❑

Pupils from Sohag attending the Coptic School at Deir el-Abyad (White Monastery)

▶ ▬▬ **Asyut**   *112A2*

Asyut, the largest and least pleasant town in the Lower Nile Valley, has few sights, bad accommodation and traffic congestion to offer visitors. Recent violence has added to the reasons to avoid it, unless you are determined to complete the Great Desert Circuit (see page 196). It lies 378km south of Cairo and can be reached by train or bus from Cairo, Luxor and el-Minya.

In the 19th century Asyut was the terminus of the Forty Days Road and its slave market, the biggest in Egypt, offered 'merchandise' from Sudan and the Libyan Desert.

The White Monastery, south of Sohag

A few decaying *khans* (merchant hostels) survive in the *souk* as well as the Hammam el-Qadim, an early Muslim public bath. At the canal end of Sharia Gumhuriya, there is a small **museum►** that displays local findings.

The large Coptic population ensures the survival of several fascinating monasteries in the area. **Deir el-Adhra (Monastery of the Virgin)►** (12km north of Asyut) is built around the caves of Dirunka, where the Holy Family is believed to have sheltered on their flight into Egypt. It is now a large commercial centre, accommodating more than 50,000 pilgrims who celebrate the Moulid of the Virgin (feast day) each August. **Deir el-Muharraq (Burnt Monastery)►** (42km north of Asyut, at el-Qusiya) is believed to be the southernmost point in Egypt where the Holy Family stayed. The monastery has a thriving theological college, graduating hundreds of monks each year. In the week of 21 June, over 50,000 pilgrims attend the Feast of the Consecration at the Church of the Virgin.

►   Sohag   *112B2*
Sohag lies 470km south of Cairo; you can get there by train from Cairo or Luxor, and by bus from Asyut. Monasteries can be reached by private or service taxi.

Unlike Asyut, Sohag is a pleasant rural town with a large Coptic community and a university. South of the town, on the edge of the desert, are two of Egypt's most celebrated monasteries. From a distance the **Deir el-Abyad (White Monastery)►►**, with its limestone walls, looks like a pharaonic temple. It is also called Deir Anba Shenuda, after St Shenute who founded it in the 5th century. The monastery once thrived with 2,000 monks, but only the Church of Shenuda and three or four monks remain, joined by thousands of pilgrims who visit on the Moulid of Shenuda (week of 14 July). The nearby **Deir el-Ahmar (Red Monastery)►** was founded by St Bishoi, a disciple of Shenuda. Although it resembles the White Monastery, it is smaller and less impressive.

Monasticism in Upper Egypt
Monasticism in Upper Egypt started around AD320 after Pachom, born in Esna, founded the first community. Pachom had served in the Roman Army until he converted to Christianity and the regime of the monk, influenced by the military life, was strictly disciplined and of service to the community. Pachom's rule served as a model for monasteries in the West. Shenute (end of 4th century AD), founder of Coptic Christianity, went further and introduced strict rules to regulate every segment of the monk's daily life.

Omm Sety

In her early childhood Dorothy Eady, born in 1904 in a London suburb, had visions that in her former life she was the mistress of Seti I. In 1933 she left for Egypt, married an Egyptian teacher and worked, in Giza and later in Abydos, as a respected Egyptologist. Soon divorced, she moved to the village of el-Araba el-Madfuna to be near her ancient lover, and revealed much about his temple. She had hoped to be buried in a tomb in her garden, but when she died in 1981 permission was refused. Turned away by Christian and Muslim cemeteries, she was eventually buried in the desert beyond the temple.

▶▶▶ Abydos   112B1

Open: 7am–6pm daily. Admission fee.

The town of el-Balyana, between Sohag and Qena, can be reached by road or train from Cairo or Luxor. From el-Balyana, private and service taxis run the 10km to the village of el-Araba el-Madfuna near the temple of Seti I.

Few tourists take the trouble to visit this New Kingdom temple, but it remains one of the finest and most astounding monuments in Egypt. Just as Muslims nowadays hope to visit Mecca at least once in their life, so ancient Egyptians aspired to make a pilgrimage to Osiris' cult centre at Abydos. Even before the Old Kingdom, when Abydos first became associated with Osiris, it was a desirable place for burial, as the ancient Egyptians believed that the afterworld began in the hills to the west of town.

The Temple of Seti I▶▶▶ Only 29 years after the collapse of the Amarna regime (see pages 123–5), Seti I (19th Dynasty) built this lavish temple in the cult centre of Abydos, hoping to reinforce his position by identifying his dynasty with Osiris and reconfirming his faith in the traditional pre-Amarna gods. The temple was built in the finest white limestone and its bas-reliefs are sublime. After Seti's death his son Ramses II continued the work, but with a less refined taste.

The pylon and the first and second forecourts have

After Seti's death, his son Ramses II finished the decoration of his mortuary temple but the later carvings are visibly inferior

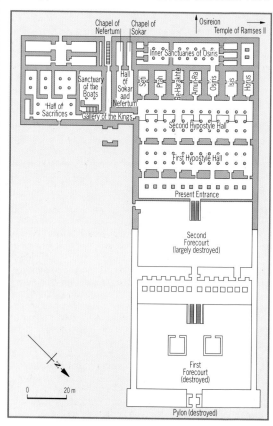

The greatest temple in Egypt
'To pass through the great central doorway and enter into the Temple of Seti I is like entering a "Time Machine" of science fiction. One leaves the modern world outside in the glare of the sunshine and, in the soft subdued light of the interior, enters the world of the past which for a time becomes the present...Every element in the scenes on the walls had a magical significance.'
Dorothy Eady (1956), quoted in *The Search for Omm Sety* by Jonathan Cott (widely available in Egypt).

Seti I wanted to forget about the Amarna interlude and led a renaissance of Old Kingdom styles in art

almost entirely disappeared and the temple is entered through the central of seven doors, leading to the seven sanctuaries. Reliefs in the First Hypostyle Hall, completed under Ramses II, are quite roughly executed. Some reliefs in the darker Second Hypostyle Hall were never finished, as Seti I died during the decoration of this part of the temple, but what is there is truly remarkable. On the right wall Seti is shown making offerings to Osiris, attended by several goddesses.

More fine bas-reliefs cover the walls of the seven sanctuaries and most have retained their original colouring. The sanctuaries are dedicated (right to left) to Horus, Isis, Osiris, Amun-Ra, Ra-Harakhte, Ptah and Seti himself. The Sanctuary of Osiris leads to the inner sanctuaries of Osiris, where Seti performed the daily offering ritual. The Sanctuary of Seti emphasises Seti's recognition by the gods, who lead him into the temple as the 'Uniter of the Two Lands'. A door near Seti's sanctuary leads into the Hall of Sokar and Nefertum, with two chapels. On the right in the Chapel of Sokar, Osiris is portrayed holding his penis, Isis hovering over him in the form of a hawk to conceive their son Horus. The other door leads to the Gallery of Kings where 76 *cartouches* (oval figures) trace Seti's descent from King Menes, omitting a few rulers like Akhenaton and Tutankhamun. Behind the temple, the Osireion or the Cenotaph of Seti I, is sunk within an artificial mound. The interior, with a beautiful ceiling, is now under water.

The Temple of Ramses II, 300m further up, is almost completely destroyed, but must have been a magnificent edifice. Funerary monuments from the Old, Middle and New Kingdoms are scattered across the area.

Voyage to Abydos
Tomb paintings all over Egypt depict the voyage to Abydos, where the body of the deceased was brought by boat. One of the biggest festivals at Abydos, an annual celebration of Osiris' resurrection which was tied in to the cycle of the moon, the seasons and the rising of the Nile, was attended by the pharaoh and thousands of pilgrims. The festival survived until Christians sacked the temple in AD395.

■ **Osiris was one of the most popular and powerful figures in ancient Egyptian mythology and religion. He was a king, assassinated by his jealous brother Seth and buried at Abydos by his sister-wife, Isis. His resurrection as the Lord and Judge of the Afterlife made him a figure of both fear and hope.....■**

Isis' lament
'I am seeking after love:
Behold me existing in the city, great are its walls:
I grieve for your love for me–
Come you only, now that you have departed!
Behold your son, who caused Seth to retreat from destruction!
Hidden am I among the plants, and concealed is your son that he cannot answer you, while this great calamity remains!
Yet concerning you–
There is no likeness of your flesh left:
I follow you alone and surround the plants, each of which holds danger for your son,–
Lo, I, a woman, in front of all.'
(From the laments that Isis sang for her murdered husband)

The story so far No complete version of Osiris' myth has survived from ancient Egypt, but in the 1st century AD the Greek historian Plutarch recorded it like this: Osiris, born a god, grew up as a man and is credited with civilising Egypt and organising agriculture and the cultivation of vines (he was believed to be the first person to drink wine). Osiris became king, his sister/wife Isis was his queen and everything in the valley blossomed until their brother Seth became jealous, trapped Osiris in a coffin and threw him into the Nile. The coffin floated into the Mediterranean and was washed up on the Syrian shore, where it was encircled by a tree which eventually became a pillar in the royal palace at Byblos. When Isis eventually found Osiris' body, she took him back to the Egyptian Delta, where she and their sister Nephthys mourned him. Images in temples at Abydos, Dendara and elsewhere show Isis as a bird, hovering over Osiris' erect penis: she was able to revive him long enough for their son Horus to be conceived.

The first mummy Seth hadn't finished with his brother and when he found the corpse, he cut it into 14 pieces and threw them into the Nile. Some 13 pieces were washed up at various places along the Nile, but his penis was eaten by fish. Wherever Isis found a part, she buried a wax copy to fool Seth (which explains why there are so many shrines to Osiris). With Horus, Anubis and Thoth, she reassembled his body at Abydos, adding a phallus, and wrapped it in bandages to make the first mummy.

Horus' revenge and Osiris' glory When Horus reached manhood, he avenged his father's death in an heroic struggle with his uncle for control of the kingdom on earth. He then guaranteed his father's immortality by feeding one of his own eyes to Osiris. A symbol of resurrection, it was appropriate that Osiris was chosen to judge dead mortals who wanted to follow him to heaven.

Osirian rites The rituals connected to Osiris were among the most complicated and secretive in ancient Egypt, touching on the mysteries of creation and the afterlife. Because he had died and been reborn, Egyptians who could afford it had their bodies sent to Abydos, where they were mummified and had the 'opening of the mouth' ceremony (whereby the ka entered the deceased's body) performed in an attempt to be united with Osiris in eternity. But there were many dangers and tests to be passed before that was possible. Some of them are represented in tomb and coffin decorations, along with spells to protect the deceased.

Heavy at heart The most difficult moment of all on the journey to heaven was the trial known as 'the weighing of the heart'. It was a final test of worthiness and, in tomb paintings, the dead often provided reminders of gifts and offerings they had made to the gods during their lives. But there was no way to buy themselves a happy verdict. Instead, Osiris sat in judgement as their heart was put in the balance against the feather of the goddess Maat, who stood for truth.

Echoes from the past The myth of Osiris, Isis and Horus, so central to life and death in ancient Egypt, hasn't entirely disappeared and there are many ways in which you confront their memory, most obviously in the depiction of Isis and Horus. Horus, the saviour of the world, is often shown suckling the good woman Isis's breast. The parallel with Jesus and Mary might explain why some aspects of Christianity were so readily accepted along the Nile.

A prayer to Osiris
Glory be to you, O Osiris... king of eternity and lord of everlastingness, the god who passed through millions of years in your existence... As prince of the gods and of men, you have received the crook and the whip and the dignity of your divine fathers. Let your heart which is in the mountain of [the underworld] be content, for your son Horus is established upon your throne.
(From the ancient *Book of the Dead*).

The Temple of Isis, Philae

Day excursion
The easiest way to visit Abydos and Dandara is on an all-day excursion from Luxor. Start early, visit Abydos in the morning and Dandara in the afternoon. An alternative is to stay overnight in Nag Hammadi, which offers basic accommodation between the two. A torch is necessary for exploring Dandara.

New Year festival
On the eve of the New Year, at the end of the inundation (flood) season when the waters of the Nile receded, the statues of Hathor and other gods were taken in a procession to the roof of the temple where they were united with the sun, who gave them power and strength for the coming year.

The Temple of Hathor

►►► Dandara   *112C1*

Open: 6am–7pm daily. Admission fee.
Dandara lies 4km across the Nile from Qena, which can be reached by trains and taxis from Cairo and Luxor. From Qena there are taxis and horse carriages to the temple.

There were shrines to the cow goddess Hathor here in pre-dynastic times and throughout the Old, Middle and New Kingdoms pilgrims were attracted by her healing powers. At the annual great festival, the statue of Hathor was taken from her sanctuary at Dandara and sailed to the temple at Idfu (Edfu) where, for two weeks, she was united with the statue of Horus. Mere mortals celebrated the divine union by copying the gods, or by getting drunk in the Festival of Drunkenness.

The present structure, built between 125BC and AD60, shows how the Ptolemies and Romans used their temples to emphasise their dedication to the main Egyptian gods – the Osirid trinity and the cow goddess Hathor – and also to legitimise their rule by proclaiming their divine birth and association with Horus, the deified king, as can be seen in the *mammisi* (birth houses).

The temple enclosure, surrounded by a well-preserved mud-brick wall, is entered from the monumental Roman gateway. To the right of the courtyard are the Roman Birth House, a 5th-century Coptic basilica and the Birth House of Nectanebo I. The **Roman Birth House►**, which was started by Augustus, has beautiful carvings on the south wall. To the left of the second birth house is a mud-brick sanatorium where sick pilgrims were treated, inspired by Hathor.

The **Temple of Hathor►►►**, although never completed, was covered in sand until the mid-19th century and has been well preserved. The pylon and forecourt were never built, so the visit starts in front of the First Hypostyle Hall. The façade, shaped like a pylon, with six

A Roman interpretation of the Hathor-headed column

Hathor-headed columns, was built during the reign of Tiberius. The carvings show Roman emperors making offerings to the gods. The central doorway leads into the Pronaos (or First Hypostyle Hall), its 24 Hathoric columns decorated with *ankhs* (looped crosses) and sceptres, symbols for life and prosperity. The ceiling preserves colourful astronomical scenes from the Egyptian zodiac, the hours of night and day, the planets and stars, and deities crossing the cosmos on their *felucca* (sailing boat).

The Ptolemaic part of the temple starts with the Hall of Appearances (or Second Hypostyle Hall), where Hathor consorted with the gods before going on her journey to Idfu (Edfu). The raised reliefs on the walls show the temple foundation rites. Daily offerings were made in the Hall of Offerings, while statues of the nine deities worshipped in the temple were stored in the Hall of the Gods. Hathor's statue and ceremonial boat were kept in the closed Sanctuary, the temple's most sacred place; only the pharaoh was permitted to enter and adore the goddess. These rituals are represented on the inner walls. Behind the Sanctuary are three chapels: the middle Per-Ur Chapel was where the New Year procession started and the Per-Nu Chapel to the left was the starting point of Hathor's journey to Idfu. Return to the Hall of the Gods, turn left and then right into the Pure Place (or New Year Chapel), where all the rituals were performed before the procession went on to the roof. On the ceiling is a magnificent relief of the sky goddess Nut giving birth to the sun which shines on Hathor.

Back in the Hall of Offerings a staircase, decorated with scenes of the New Year procession, leads to the roof. In the southwest corner of the roof is the Disc Chapel, an unroofed kiosk where the statue of Hathor resided during the New Year festival. On the north side of the roof are the twin Chapels of Osiris with scenes of the Mysteries of Osiris. In the eastern suite is a plaster cast of the famous Dandara Zodiac, the original of which was taken to the Louvre in Paris.

The Earth Mother

Hathor, the cow goddess, the goddess of love, joy and music, was one of the most ancient Egyptian gods. She was sometimes identified by the Greeks with Aphrodite. Her name, Hat-Hor, means 'House of Horus', but according to mythology she first suckled Horus and later became his wife. She is represented as a cow, as a woman with a cow's head, as a woman with horns holding a sun disc or, as in the Temple of Dandara, as a woman with cow's ears.

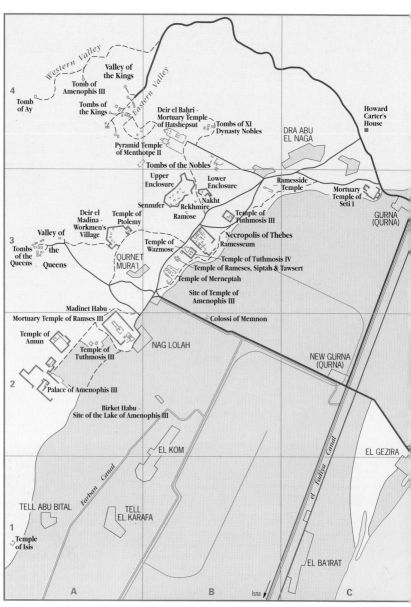

Right: crossing the Nile with animal feed

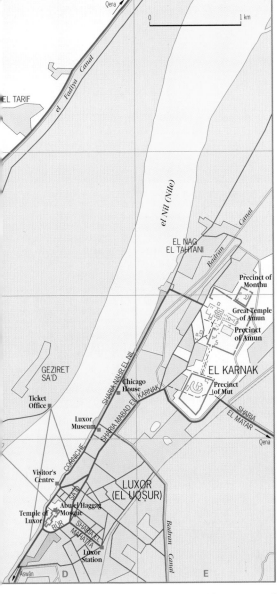

Luxor Luxor contains the crowning achievements of Egyptian architecture. It was the capital of the New Kingdom for 500 glorious years and remained the country's spiritual centre for much longer. Luxor's ruins are among the most extraordinary buildings ever constructed.

The ancient city Though there were settlements here from an early period, Luxor was an insignificant mud-brick village during the Old Kingdom. The kings who reunited Egypt under the Middle Kingdom came from nearby Armant but chose to be buried on the west bank of the Nile at Thebes.

LUXOR

Essentials
(Minimum two days)
East bank (one day):
Karnak Temple, Luxor
Temple, Luxor Museum
West bank (one day):
Valley of the Kings,
Deir al-Bahri, Tombs of
the Nobles

Luxor's other names
Ancient Egyptians knew it
as Waset and, as their
scribes claimed, it was 'the
pattern of every city' and
that 'mankind came into
being within her'. To the
Greek poet Homer, Waset
was the fabled 'hundred-
gated Thebes'. When the
Arabs came upon the
remains of the city in the
7th century AD, they called
it al-Uqsor (the Palaces),
the name which it retains
in Arabic and which has
been corrupted into Luxor.

Slowly power, both political and spiritual, shifted to the growing city until it became the capital of the kingdom.

Great temples Amun was a minor deity in Thebes, but he was the local god of the Middle Kingdom pharaohs. As they became more powerful, so their god's cult also gained ascendancy and, in a transformation lasting several centuries, he was united with the sun-god Ra and worshipped as Amun-Ra. By the start of the New Kingdom, Amun-Ra was worshipped as the most important state god. During this period of international conquest, when Egyptian armies fought in Africa and Asia, some of the immense wealth that poured into the imperial capital of Thebes was spent building or embellishing temples. The most magnificent of these was Amun's temple at Karnak, a perfect expression of religious devotion, and its sister temple at Luxor, devoted to another aspect of the god as Amun-Min. Over successive centuries, pharaohs added to the great state temples and built their own mortuary temples on the west bank.

Famous burials Among Luxor's most famous monuments are the tombs of Thebes, in what are known as the Valley of the Kings and Valley of the Queens. These predominantly New Kingdom royal burial sites contained extraordinary treasures, but so far only Tutankhamun's tomb has been found intact. Their decorations are among the finest surviving examples of ancient Egyptian art. Less well-known are Deir el-Madina's workers' tombs and the tombs of the nobles, decorated with less mysterious images than the royal tombs. Many show how the deceased lived on earth.

The decline of Thebes Such was the glory of Thebes that it remained the country's spiritual centre long after the end of the New Kingdom (1085BC), when political power shifted northwards to the Delta. The Nubian kings of the 25th Dynasty (747–656BC) restored the capital to Thebes, but imagine the shock to Egypt's stability when the city was sacked by an Assyrian army in 671BC, and again in 663BC. Vulnerable and strategically insignificant, Thebes' decline was inevitable and although Ptolemaic and Roman rulers continued to build in the city, when the Arabs conquered Egypt they abandoned Thebes to be buried by sand and silt.

The rise of Luxor Secular buildings in Thebes were constructed using mud bricks and these have either disintegrated under the onslaught of time and climate or been built over, but the great stone temples remain. They were used as churches and provided shelter for villagers for 200 years, and they have also been the object of a new kind of pilgrimage – tourism. Early tourists camped in or around the tombs and temples, or stayed on board their sailing boats, but for the opening of the Suez Canal in 1869 Thomas Cook arranged the first package tour. Egyptology and the city have grown hand in hand ever since: more tombs and temples uncovered, more tourists wanting to visit them, more hotels needed to accommodate them. Luxor today is a noisy, bustling city strung along the east bank of the Nile, but the temples remain at its centre, appropriate for a city that has been born of tourism.

After the sun sets, a gentle breeze blows away the heat of the day

137

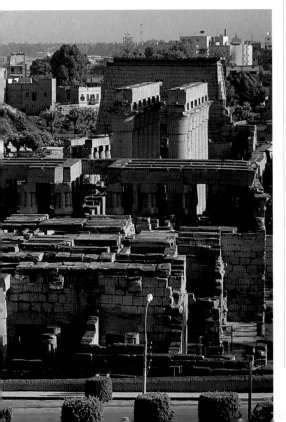

Brooke Hospital for Animals

In 1934 an Englishwoman, Dorothy Brooke, started an animal clinic in Cairo called the Hospital for Old War Horses. Run by a London-based charity, there are now Brooke hospitals providing free treatment to thousands of horses and donkeys in Cairo, Luxor, Edfu, Aswan and Alexandria. The hospitals survive on voluntary donations which can be made direct to the hospitals or via the headquarters in London (UK tel: 0171-930 0210).

The Temple of Luxor lies right in the heart of Luxor town and seems always within sight

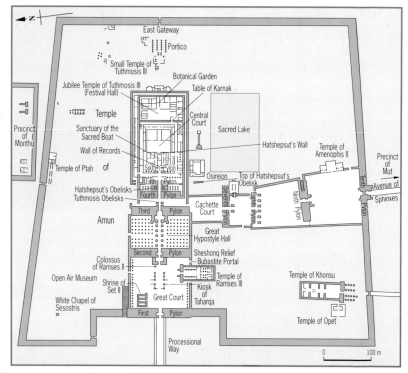

The processional avenue at Karnak

A ride to Karnak
You can take a taxi to Karnak but it's more pleasant to go by bike or *calèche* (horse-drawn carriage). *Calèches* can be hailed in the streets, but drivers in Luxor have got haggling down to an art. Discuss the price in advance and ask your driver to spare the horse, allowing you time to enjoy the Nile breeze.

East Bank

▶▶▶ **Karnak**   *135E2*

Open: 6am–5:30pm daily in winter and 6am–6:30pm daily in summer. Admission fee.

The scale of Karnak surpasses every other pharaonic temple, with over 100 acres devoted to the gods (enough land to accommodate ten large European cathedrals). For 13 centuries successive pharaohs added their share to make this the most magnificent temple complex in the country and in the entire ancient world. It is also the most complicated because Karnak, unlike other temples, was developed on a north–south as well as on an east–west axis. Known as 'The Most Select of Places', it was not only a religious capital but also one of the most important intellectual centres in antiquity. The names of pharaohs and the different dynasties responsible for Karnak can be overwhelming; in general, the deeper you penetrate into the temple the older the monuments are.

The local god Amun started to grow in importance from the early Middle Kingdom onwards and during the 12th Dynasty several temples were dedicated to him; their foundations were found under 18th-Dynasty structures in the Temple of Amun. During the 18th Dynasty, Amun was promoted to state god and Karnak soon became the most important religious centre in the country. Amenophis I built a chapel around the Middle Kingdom temple, and his son Tuthmosis I erected both the fourth and fifth pylons, and a pair of obelisks. Queen Hatshepsut started building south of the older temple and added another pair of obelisks. Tuthmosis III built the seventh and eighth pylons, and the impressive Festival Hall.

Amenophis III came to power when the empire was at its zenith. Egypt's wealth was phenomenal and this was reflected in the art and architecture of the time. Amenophis started the building of the Great Hypostyle Hall and erected the third pylon. Amenophis IV (Akhenaton) added his share before turning away from Amun and founding his new capital in Amarna, but most of his buildings were destroyed. Under his son-in-law Tutankhamun, Amun was soon reinstated as the national god and Thebes regained its importance.

Seti I (19th Dynasty) instituted a period of renaissance, an early classical revival, to ease the doubts and heal the rifts caused by the Amarna revolution. Together with his son Ramses II he completed the Hypostyle Hall, which was the largest of any temple in the world. By this time the hierarchy of the priesthood at Karnak owned great wealth and wielded much power: it was inevitable that they would also seek political power. During the 20th Dynasty it was the high priest of Karnak who collected the taxes and effectively ruled the country, the pharaoh being nothing more than his puppet. The first pylon and first court were added by the later 20th–30th Dynasties.

It would take weeks to explore every relief on every wall in Karnak, but you should reserve at least two half-days to explore it – the first morning to be overwhelmed by the sheer size of it all and then an afternoon to enjoy a more detailed view in the soft warm glow of the late-day sun. The whole complex can be divided into three main areas: the most important is the Precinct of Amun (page 142–3), with the Precinct of Mont to the north and the Precinct of Mut to the south, but the last two are rarely visited as they are badly ruined. (Continued on page 142.)

The colossal statue of Ramses II with one of his daughters guards the entrance to the Second Pylon

139

Temples

■ **Ancient Egyptians believed in the link between their own society and the universe around them: order, kept by the pharaoh and the gods, had to be maintained throughout the universe. Their temples stand as testaments to this belief.....■**

Egypt's finest
Earlier mortuary temples can be seen at Maidum (Meidum) and Dahshur. Idfu (Edfu) is the most perfect and complete state temple to have survived. Karnak's hypostyle hall was and still is the finest and the grandest. Dandara and Philae have the best-preserved roof temples. Abydos has the finest carvings.

The processional colonnade of Amenhotep III and the pylons of Ramses II, at the Temple of Luxor

Two types of temples Egyptian temples can be divided into two groups. State or cult temples, often built on the site of earlier shrines, were intended for the worship of local or state deities, whose images resided in the temple sanctuary and were attended to by the priesthood. They would have been enlarged or rebuilt at some time in history, particularly during the New Kingdom. Mortuary temples were built as a focus for continuing rites for dead pharaohs. They were originally built on to or near the pharaoh's tomb, as at Giza and Saqqara, but as pharaohs sought greater security for their remains, mortuary temples were built at some distance from the royal tombs, which were sealed and intended never to be visited.

Approaching a temple Temple design evolved early and soon began to follow a set pattern, although pharaohs often sought to innovate or to outdo their predecessors. Temples were usually built at the border between the agricultural land and the desert, so they would be above the level of the Nile's annual flooding. Some mortuary temples also had connecting valley temples, situated at the high water point, so that boats could approach it during the annual flood. Temples were often approached along a processional way, sometimes lined with sphinxes

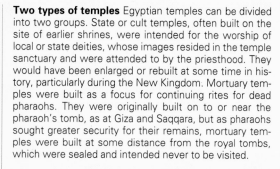

or other statuary, with the avenue usually ending at a gate in the temple wall. Except on certain holidays, this was as far as the public was allowed to go.

Interior design Enclosures often contained houses for priests, storerooms, a sacred lake, sometimes even a palace for the pharaoh or, in Ptolemaic and Roman times, a birth house, but the temple proper consisted of a series of courts. The first was the outer or peristyle court, usually open and pillared, which led into the hypostyle hall, with pillars supporting the roof and the ceiling decorated with sky motifs. Beyond the hypostyle hall lay the sanctuary, where the deities rested in state, and beyond that, some chapels. Some temple roofs contained shrines, often concerned with the Osiris cult and the New Year celebration.

Decoration Decoration was as important as the form the building took, and from the outer pylon to the innermost sanctuary temples were often heavily adorned with painted, raised or sunk reliefs. Even the pillars were carved as Osirid figures (the kings as Osiris), or their capitals shaped as deities. The decorations often indicate the use the temple was put to and there are many images of temple processions and festival offerings.

Message in the design Temples were built on rising ground so that if you had stood at the first pylon when the doors were open – they have disappeared so you can do so now – you could have looked up through the courts, each ceiling progressively lower, each door narrower, towards the sanctuary. There was a point to this staged effect, and the themes were plain to see: nothing less than heaven and earth. Temples performed crucial symbolic functions in the struggle to preserve order in the universe, and just as the pillars of the hypostyle hall represented papyri in the primeval marshes, so the sanctuary on higher ground represented the first primeval mound that rose above the waters of Chaos and the roof represented the vault of heaven. That, after all, was the place to which the pharaoh and his people aspired.

The Hypostyle Hall with Osirid statues of Ramses II, at his temple in Abu Simbel

Columns and pillars
In pre-dynastic Egypt people built with the available natural materials: mud, reeds and trunks of palm trees. The earliest type of stone columns reproduced bundled reeds as in the entrance hall of the Step Pyramid at Saqqara. From the Old Kingdom onwards there were different types of plant columns: a palm column with palm leaves tied on to a pole, or the lotus and papyrus-bundled columns. From the New Kingdom there are open papyrus columns and papyrus-bud columns. The columns in temples symbolised the plants of the primeval marshes: papyrus symbolised Lower Egypt and lotus and palms stood for Upper Egypt.

Above: ram-headed
sphinx, the Temple of
Amun
Far right: the high
and massive columns
of the Great
Hypostyle Hall never
fail to impress mere
mortals

(Continued from page 139.) With so many additions to
Karnak by various rulers, it is hard at first to understand the
vast main **Temple of Amun**▶▶▶. The easiest place to
start is at the Processional Way, with ram-headed sphinxes, and follow the east–west axis, walking straight through
to the Festival Hall. After that, time and energy allowing, it
is worth visiting the Open Air Museum, the Cachette Court
and the Sacred Lake which are off this axis.

The short Processional Way leads to the massive First
Pylon, which at 113m wide and 43m high is the largest
pylon in Egypt. It was built either during the 25th or the
30th Dynasty, but was never finished and was left undecorated (note the mud-brick ramp used in its construction).
Behind the pylon, the Great Court was another later addition (22nd Dynasty), built to enclose several earlier buildings which had previously been located outside the
temple proper. Immediately to the left is the Shrine of

Seti II, which held the sacred boats of Amun, Mut and Khonsu during the preparations of the Opet festival. In the centre of the court stands what is left of the Kiosk of Taharqa (25th Dynasty), one of the original ten open papyrus columns.

The small **Temple of Ramses III▶▶** (20th Dynasty), which served as another way station for the sacred *barques* (royal barges) during processions, stands to the right. The court of the temple is lined with Osirid columns, while reliefs on the walls depict scenes of the annual festival. The Bubastite Portal, a doorway between this temple and the Second Pylon, leads to the left to the fine Sheshonq relief depicting the victory of the biblical king, Shishak, over the son of Solomon. Back in the court, in front of the Second Pylon stands the granite Colossus of Ramses II with one of his daughters. The Second Pylon was built by Horemheb (18th dynasty) using blocks from several Aton-temples built by Akhenaton.

Behind the Second Pylon lies the most breathtaking sight in Egypt, the magnificent **Great Hypostyle Hall▶▶▶** (19th Dynasty), covering an area of 5,500sq m. It probably began as a processional way with the 12 columns with open papyrus capitals in the central nave. However, Seti I had grander plans and with his son Ramses II he added another 122 papyrus-bud columns, a roof and walls, forming an enclosed forest in stone. Seti I decorated the left wing with fine bas-reliefs of offerings and cult scenes on the inside walls and columns, and scenes of his victories on the outside wall, while in the right wing Ramses II used a less-refined sunk relief for similar scenes.

At the eastern end of the hall is the badly ruined Third Pylon, built by Amenophis III (18th Dynasty) on top of older Middle Kingdom structures. Between the Third and the Fourth Pylon, built by Tuthmosis I (18th Dynasty), only one of the original four obelisks has survived. Beyond the Fourth Pylon stands one of two obelisks erected by Queen Hatshepsut to mark the sixth year of her reign; the tip of the second, fallen obelisk lies on the way to the Sacred Lake, near the Osireion. The columns around Hatshepsut's obelisk suggest that there was another hypostyle hall here, perhaps built by Tuthmosis III in an attempt to hide his stepmother's monuments. The Fifth Pylon was also built by Tuthmosis I and is followed immediately by a ruined Sixth Pylon by Tuthmosis III, with the Wall of Records, a list of Nubian and Asian enemies conquered by Tuthmosis. In the court beyond are two pink granite pillars, one finely carved with three lotus flowers and the other with three papyrus flowers, symbols of Upper and Lower Egypt. Towards the north of the court are two large statues of Amun and Amonet, dedicated by and looking like Tutankhamun, while a statue of Amenophis II sits against the west wall.

At the end of the court is the granite Sanctuary of the Sacred Boat, built by the

144

The morning and evening play of light and shadow lends the Hypostyle Hall an air of even greater grandeur

Sound and light
If you only see one sound and light show in Egypt, this should be the one. There are two 90-minute shows per night, but check during your daytime visit for times and languages of the performances. Visitors first walk through the dramatically lit temple, while the story of Karnak is narrated. The second part is viewed from a grandstand behind the lake.

half-brother of Alexander the Great over a similar sanctuary by Tuthmosis III. In one of the rooms to the north is Hatshepsut's Wall with well-preserved reliefs.

Beyond the Central Court , the site of the original 12th-Dynasty temple of Amun, lies the **Jubilee Temple of Tuthmosis III▶▶**. The Festival Hall, unusual in its suggestion of the interior of a tent, has fine reliefs of the king celebrating his jubilee. In a chamber in the southwest corner the Table of Karnak, showing Tuthmosis making offerings to his predecessors, was found; it is now in the Louvre in Paris. Behind the hall in a small chamber with four papyrus columns, the Botanical Garden contains a splendid relief of plants and animals found in Syria.

On the north–south axis, next to the Hypostyle Hall, lies the Cachette Court where around 17,000 bronze and 800 stone statues were discovered. In front of the Seventh Pylon, built by Tuthmosis III and decorated during the 19th Dynasty, are seven statues from Middle Kingdom pharaohs. The Eighth Pylon, built by Hatshepsut, is flanked by four of the original six colossi. Between the Ninth and Tenth Pylons, built by Horemheb, is a small Temple of Amenophis II. Further south is the partly excavated Precinct of Mut.

To the south of the Cachette Court is the Osireion, built in the Late Period, a now-cemented Sacred Lake and a shaded café. To the north of Amun's Precinct is the Open Air Museum, with some reconstructed early buildings.

Walk Along the Corniche

Above: a calèche *on the Corniche*

Early 20th-century travellers describe the riverfront in Luxor, with colonial houses, gardens and hotel terraces as delightful. It is noisier today, lacking the romance of the past, but since the Corniche was restored in 1987 it makes a pleasant afternoon walk and the sun still sets magnificently behind the pink Theban Hills. See the map on pages 134–5.

Start at the **Old Winter Palace Hotel**, founded in 1887 and recently refurbished, trying hard to keep up the glory. The views across the Nile to Thebes from its front terrace are beautiful, while the garden, less grand than before, is still pleasant. Turn right before **Luxor Temple** (see page 149) and walk into the garden of the **Wena Hotel**, formerly the Luxor Hotel and the oldest in town, where a bronze plaque commemorates the British physician, Thomas Longmore (1864–98).

Past the Wena, the road forks, the widest street leading to the station.

To the left of it, Luxor's *souk* starts as a tourist bazaar before becoming a food market. Return to the Corniche and turn right at the temple past two 19th-century houses that once belonged to Europeans (one is now occupied by a political party). Below the Corniche, by the waterside, is the new shopping centre and, opposite the Mina Palace Hotel, the **visitor's centre**. In the street beside the Mina Palace is the **Brooke Hospital for Animals**, caring for Luxor's sick and abused horses and donkeys since 1963. Further along, past the ruin of the old Savoy Hotel, the modern Etap Hotel is popular for local wedding parties. To the right is the modern building of the **Luxor Museum** (see page 148) and further north is Luxor Hospital, originally supported by tourist donations. The walk ends at **Chicago House**, home of the Oriental Institute of the University of Chicago, which has been recording the monuments in Luxor since 1924. Its wonderful library can only be visited by prior appointment (tel: 095-372525).

Moulids

■ **Visitors rarely get to see *moulids* – the celebrations of saints' days – but they are well worth tracking down as they offer some of the most unique, interesting and ancient spectacles in Egypt. Festivals take place throughout the year and throughout the country.....■**

Moulids to watch out for
Most *moulids* are regulated by the lunar Islamic calendar. Some of the more notable ones in Egypt are: Abu Haggag, Luxor; Moulid el-Nabi, the Prophet's birthday (all over the country, especially Cairo); el-Husayn, Cairo; Sayyid el-Badawi, Tanta; Sayyida Zaynab, Cairo.

146

Ancient traditions There is one group of historians who argue that the pagan religion of ancient Egypt wasn't abandoned when Christianity was adopted as the state religion, but rather that its beliefs and rituals were merged with the new religion. When Islam came along in the 7th century AD, another merger took place. *Moulids* seem to confirm this theory. There is nothing in Islam to encourage the elevation or remembrance of holy men, but in Egypt almost every village, and every district in the big cities, has its 'saint' and their festivals are celebrated once a year, just as the local gods of ancient Egypt were fêted at their annual festivities. Some remain local events, lasting a few days and attended by no one beyond the village boundary, while others, like the *moulids* of Husayn in Cairo and Sayyid el-Badawi in Tanta, are national events, lasting more than a week and attracting millions for their blessing.

The programme of a *moulid* The programme of events is dictated by tradition, not by any religious obligation. The tomb of the saint is usually the focus of celebrations and prayers from different groups are said around it, increasing each day with the number of visitors, while loud speakers and lighting installations around the tomb become increasingly complex and insistent. The displays of *moulid* toys and hats, and the carts piled with nuts, boiled beans, chick peas or sweets also multiply each day until there is a crowd of traders waiting to serve the people who come to honour the saint. Often when the crowd is at its thickest, brotherhoods of Sufis or dervishes parade through the streets before beginning their prayers and *zikrs* (ritual dances). Their chanting lasts for hours and is usually amplified through the streets in competition with the chants of rival brotherhoods intent on filling the night with noise.

Above and top: the moulid at Siwa of Sidi Suleyman, a local holy man who is said to have once conjured up a sand-storm to defeat a band of Sudanese raiders

Far right: the popular moulid of el-Husayn, prophet Muhammad's grandson, in Cairo

A big night out The highlight of a *moulid* is the *layla kebira* or big night, the last one of the celebration. This is usually the best time to see a *moulid* if you don't mind crowds (they can be overwhelming, with more than a million people at the big *moulids*, and foreign women can feel very uncomfortable). The Sufis will be at their most energetic, their *zikrs* usually lasting till dawn.

The mawalidiya *Moulids*, like the ancient Egyptian festivals from which they are descended, are only partly to do with religion. As always when Egyptians get together, there is plenty of opportunity to do a little business or to sit and smoke with friends. The people who provide the more 'social' of the services are known as *mawalidiya*. Travelling from *moulid* to *moulid* they sing, offer blessings or 'medical' advice, and run food stalls, cafés, shooting ranges, swings and often a circumcision booth.

More unusual attractions There used to be a *moulid* procession through Cairo in which a naked boy, pulled on a float, carried a huge phallus which was swung from side to side with strings. That particular attraction disappeared earlier this century, but at the *moulid* of Abu Haggag in Luxor a boat is carried around the saint's mosque – and therefore also Luxor Temple – as it was several thousand years ago. At some *moulids* there are people who enact ceremonial fights with sticks, or joust on horseback, and among the more unusual spectacles in Cairo is a *moulid* near the cemetery which includes floats of transvestites.

Not just Muslims Although most *moulids* are Muslim, some Christian and Jewish saints are also honoured in their places. The Copts celebrate the *moulid* of St Damyanah in May and Jews from Israel and Europe come to honour Abu Khatzeira in June.

The language of love
Sufis often use the language of love when singing about the mysteries of religion, as in this verse:
'She swayed as she moved; and I imagined each side, as she swang it, a twig on a sand-hill, and, above it, a moon at the full; And my every member had, as it were, its several hearts, the one which as she glanced, was pierced by its showers of arrows.'
Nicolaas H Biegman's *Egypt: Moulids, Saints, Sufis* is an excellent introduction to *moulids*.

147

Tuthmosis III wearing the royal beard and the so-called atef-crown

148

The latest on excavations
Every Thursday afternoon at 3:30, Dr Elsayed Hegazy, director of Karnak and Luxor Temples, gives an interesting lecture about the latest findings in the recent excavations in both temples. The lectures are held in the Mövenpick Jolie Ville Hotel on Crocodile Island and are open to everyone. The Mövenpick has a complimentary shuttle bus (frequent departures from outside the Gaddis book-shop, Winter Palace Hotel) and a ferryboat (from the pier opposite the Winter Palace). Check beforehand with the hotel (tel: 374855) for the exact time of the lecture and transport, as it may vary.

▶▶▶ **Luxor Museum of Ancient Egyptian Art**   135D2

Open: winter 9–1 and 4–9 daily, summer 9–1 and 5–10 daily, in Ramadan 10–4. Admission fee for museum and separate fee for the New Hall.

This small, modern museum has an exquisite collection of statues and funerary objects found in temples and tombs in and around Luxor and is an absolute must. Every object is carefully chosen, well labelled, and both mounted and lit to bring out the best qualities.

On the ground floor there are masterpieces from the New Kingdom, including an exquisite bust of a young Tuthmosis III (No 61), a strange alabaster statue of the seated crocodile god Sobek holding Amenophis III (No 107, labelled as Amenhotep III), a brightly coloured wall painting of Amenophis III (No 101) and a finely carved relief of Tuthmosis III (No 64) – all from the18th Dynasty.

Upstairs there is a series of sunk reliefs from Akhenaton's temple in Karnak (18th Dynasty), with the king and his wife Nefertiti worshipping the sun god Aton and detailed scenes of Egyptian labourers at work (No 141). There are smaller relief fragments of the same temple, some representing Nefertiti praying and making offerings (Nos 165–8), and two fascinating sandstone heads of Akhenaton, from Osirid statues, in the typically realistic Amarna style (Nos 156 and 171).

In the glass case upstairs are a few objects from Tutankhamun's tomb (18th Dynasty): sandals (Nos 186–7), arrows (No 193), a fine wooden head of Hathor (No 196) and two beautiful funerary *barques* (Nos 199 and 200). The New Hall was specially designed to house the impressive cache of 26 statues discovered in Luxor Temple in 1989. Among the finest of the large statues are Ramses II, Queen Nefertari, Tutankhamun and Amenophis III.

Block statue of Yamu-Nedjeh, First Herald of King Tuthmosis III

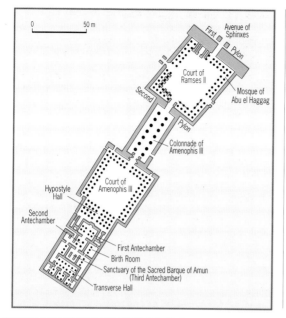

Court of Ramses II
Avenue of Sphinxes
First Pylon
Mosque of Abu el Haggag
Second Pylon
Colonnade of Amenophis III
Court of Amenophis III
Hypostyle Hall
Second Antechamber
First Antechamber
Birth Room
Sanctuary of the Sacred Barque of Amun (Third Antechamber)
Transverse Hall

0   50 m

Town within the temple
'...The next day we visit Luxor. The village can be divided into two parts, separated by the two pylons: the modern part, to the left, contains nothing old, whereas on the right the houses are on, in, or attached to the ruins. The houses are built among the capitals of columns: chickens and pigeons perch and nest in great (stone) lotus leaves... dogs run barking along the walls. So stirs a mini-life amid the debris of a life that was far grander...'
Gustave Flaubert in Egypt (April 1850)

▶▶▶ **Luxor Temple**   135D1

Open: winter 6–9pm, summer 6–10, 6–5 and 8–11 during Ramadan. Admission fee, half price at night.

In ancient times ordinary people were barred from entering temples, but now the Temple of Luxor lies in the heart of town. Verdi's opera *Aida* was staged here in 1987, with thousands of extras, and for several weeks no other music was heard in Luxor's coffee-houses. The Temple of Luxor is far more coherent than Karnak because it was mainly built by two kings. Amenophis III (18th Dynasty), who also built the Colossi of Memnon and the Third Pylon at Karnak, founded the temple on the site of an older sanctuary. Ramses II (19th Dynasty) added the impressive pylon with obelisks, colossi (giant figures) and a colonnaded court. Luxor Temple, dedicated to the Theban Triad of Amun-Min, Mut and Khonsu, was known as the 'Harem of the South' where Mut and her son Khonsu resided, while Amun-Min

When the mudbrick houses were cleared away from the temple, the Mosque of Luxor's patron saint Abu el-Haggag had to stay

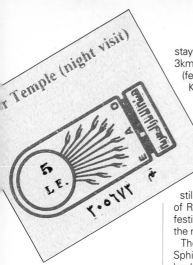

r Temple (night visit)

5 L.E.

r·orvr

Floodlit temple
The temple is well worth a second visit in the evening when it is dramatically lit and has less visitors. It seems more mysterious and imposing then, more like the temple might have felt in ancient times. The depth of the reliefs is intensified by the play of light and shadow.

The Luxor visitors' centre
A new visitors' centre for tourists has opened on the Corniche opposite the Mina Palace Hotel (open 5am–11pm).
It has telephone and fax facilities, shops, a small museum and a luxurious cinema where films are shown about the monuments. There is a scheme to computerise ticket sales for the West Bank monuments, to avoid overcrowding of these sites. Visitors will be given time-controlled tickets to spread visits more evenly throughout the day. Tourist ferries for the West Bank leave from the quay outside the centre.

stayed in Karnak. The two temples were connected by the 3km-long Avenue of Sphinxes and during the annual Opet (fertility festival), Amun's statue was escorted from Karnak by a grand procession of *barques* (holy barges) to be reunited with his wife Mut at Luxor.

The temple is well preserved, especially the pylon reliefs, as it was mostly covered by sand and, until the late 19th century, by the town itself. In 1885 when excavations began, the houses were slowly cleared away, but the people of Luxor refused to allow the mosque and tomb of their patron saint, Abu el-Haggag, to be destroyed. The mosque is still there, hanging above the northeast corner of the court of Ramses II. The *moulid* of Abu el-Haggag is the largest festival in Upper-Egypt. One or more boats are carried up to the mosque, a distant reminder of the Opet festivities.

The temple is best approached from the Avenue of Sphinxes, erected by Nectanebo I (30th Dynasty), which leads to the First Pylon. The pylon, built by Ramses II, was originally 24m high and 65m wide, with splendid reliefs exaggerating Ramses' victory in the Battle of Qaddesh. The right wall shows Ramses presiding over a war council in the Egyptian encampment, while on the left wall, seated in a chariot, he pursues his enemies in Qaddesh. Originally there were six statues of Ramses in front of the pylon, but only two seated colossi and a badly damaged standing one remain. An exquisite obelisk, supported by dog-headed baboons, stands in front of the pylon. Its twin, given to Louis-Philippe of France, now stands in the Place de la Concorde in Paris.

The entrance passage to the Court of Ramses II was decorated by 25th-Dynasty Nubian and Ethiopian kings. The court is surrounded by a double row of papyrus-bud columns which once formed a roofed arcade. Unlike other pharaonic courts, this one doesn't continue along the same axis as the Court of Amenophis III. The reason for this is that Ramses II was incorporating an earlier shrine of Hatshepsut and Tuthmosis III, built 100 years before Amenophis III's court. Above the northeastern corner sits the Mosque of Abu el-Haggag (see page 147), rebuilt in the 19th century but with an original 11th-century minaret. At the back of the court, on the wall to the right, is an unusual relief showing the temple with its colossi, obelisks and banners. On the right wall of the court is a funerary procession led by 17 of Ramses' more than 100 sons. In front of the Second Pylon, two black granite colossi of Ramses are seated on bases decorated with tied-up Nubians and Hittites.

The portal leads into the main part of the temple, starting with the impressive Colonnade of Amenophis III. On either side there are high columns with calyx capitals supporting heavy architraves. The work was unfinished when Amenophis died, and Tutankhamun had the walls decorated with scenes of the Opet festival. Starting at the portal to the right, the pharaoh is seen making sacrifices before the *barques* at Karnak, followed by the floating procession and the arrival at Luxor; on the opposite wall is the happy return to Karnak after a 24-day honeymoon.

The colonnade leads into the Court of Amenophis III, with double rows of elegant papyrus columns and then a small hypostyle hall. On the back wall are reliefs showing Amenophis' coronation by the gods. Next is a columned

portico whose reliefs were plastered over in the 3rd or 4th century AD by Roman legionaries using it as a chapel. The smaller second antechamber was an offering chapel and the reliefs show the pharaoh making offerings to Amun.

Beyond lies a third antechamber which was converted by Alexander the Great into the Sanctuary of the Sacred Barque of Amun. It once had acacia-wood doors inlaid with gold and the walls bear reliefs of Alexander making offerings to the Theban Triad. Around the sanctuary there are several rooms which were used for storage, their reliefs showing what they contained.

From the side room to the left of the sanctuary, a door leads to the Birth Room, where reliefs show Amenophis' divine birth. His pregnant mother Mutemuia gives birth, led by Isis and Khnum. Isis then gives the baby to Amun, who holds Amenophis in his arms. Khnum is moulding the baby and his *ka* (soul) on his potter's wheel. It was near this room, in 1989, that an important cache of statues was found, now in the Luxor Museum. Further south, a columned Transverse Hall leads to the private apartments of the gods, now unfortunately badly damaged.

Ramses II is wearing the double crown of Lower and Upper Egypt as a symbol for the united country

The missing obelisk
'The obelisk that is now in Paris... Perched on its pedestal, how bored it must be in the Place de la Concorde! How it must miss its Nile!'
Gustave Flaubert (1850)

■ **Visitors to Luxor in recent years were shocked to find Tutankhamun's tomb closed for restoration, but it is just one of many monuments that are in danger of collapse. Rising groundwater, urban and industrial growth, pollution and even tourists all pose a threat. There is disagreement as to what should be done to preserve Egypt's antiquities for future generations.....■**

How you can help
Help preserve what is left of the monuments by paying attention to signs asking you not to touch them, or carve names, or use photographic flash, and by discouraging others who are less thoughtful.

Two views of the problem
'These monuments... do not belong solely to the countries who hold them in trust. The whole world has the right to see them endure.'
Dr V Veronese, Director-General of UNESCO, speaking at the Abu Simbel appeal, 8 March 1960
'They [foreign Egyptologists] let us bear the burden of restoring and maintaining the monuments alone – the monuments they excavate themselves. They pick up this and that and write books about their work and they tell us that it is not their work to restore the monument.'
Dr Mohammed Ibrahim Bakr, ex-Chairman, EAO (1993)

A modern problem An 18th-century Jesuit missionary, Claude Sicard, sailed up the Nile reading a Greek account of ancient Egypt and was lucky enough to find much of it exactly as described two millennia earlier. Travellers in the 19th century were just as awe-struck as the Jesuit, but a new tone creeps into their descriptions. The monuments were wonderful,' no doubt about it, but damage was being done by the modern Egyptians. The remains of ancient Egypt, some of them suggested, must be saved for the world. The argument that 'if I don't take it away it'll be destroyed' was the justification for the removal of statues, the cutting out of sections of walls and the transportation of shiploads of objects which became the basis of European and American museum collections. The French archaeologist, Auguste Mariette, who established the Egyptian Antiquities Organisation (EAO) in the 1850s, tried to limit unlicensed excavation and to clear the temples and tombs. While he succeeded in containing one problem, he laid the ground for another.

The problem of preserving monuments Before the EAO cleared the temples, many Egyptians lived in and around them and while they undoubtedly caused some damage – you can see the effect of their fires on the top of many temple columns – it was nothing compared to the threats the monuments are facing now. There was great concern about damage to monuments when the second Aswan Dam was being built and a successful campaign was fought by UNESCO in the 1960s which resulted in Abu Simbel and some of Nubia's other monuments being moved above the waterline. But the dam also appears to have caused a rise in the level of groundwater north of the dam, which threatens to erode the stone monuments. The spread of industry and increases in traffic, air pollution and urban encroachment are threatening monuments throughout Egypt. The monuments are also suffering from their own popularity as much as from neglect. For instance, tourists visiting the Valley of the Kings have been depositing litres of sweat every day in the unprotected tombs, causing paint and plaster to peel from the walls.

Excavation or conservation? Many people know the name of Howard Carter and can retell the story of his discovery of Tutankhamun's tomb (see page 164), but few would recognise the names of the people involved in its restoration. Conservation is not as glamorous as excavation and that is part of its problem. Egypt's own specialists lack the funds and the manpower to preserve ancient sites, and their bureaucrats tend to make things worse, while the people who could help – the foreign Egyptologists – are driven by the demands of their own, increasingly cut-throat occupation. To further their careers, they need to dig, to find something important and to tell the world about it, or else get involved in documentation, publishing detailed records of images that are fading as they work. Although the technology does exist to preserve many of the monuments faced with destruction, the money isn't available to pay for it in Egypt while the will, or the interest, is lacking to pay for it in the international community.

What happens next? No one knows what will happen next, except that more tombs will be closed and more buildings will have to be propped up by scaffolding unless something is done. The threat exists not just in Luxor, or with ancient monuments – Islamic buildings are also collapsing around the country. The only certainty is that many things included in this book will no longer exist when our children come to use it.

The temple of the world
'Two thousand years ago, an Egyptian scribe saw it coming. And he protested. He said, "Do you not know that Egypt is a copy of the universe? The temple of the world? And that if it goes, the world will be full of graves and dead men?" I think what the ancient scribe was saying is that if we let all this slip through our fingers without caring, a bit of our humanity will die.'
John Romer, in *The Rape of Tutankhamun*, Channel 4 Television (1993)

The fallen head of yet another colossal statue of Ramses II, in the Ramesseum

153

West Bank

►►► Deir el-Bahri (Mortuary Temple of Hatshepsut)

134B4

This temple, dramatically set against the Theban Hills, often disappoints at first sight. The courts and terraces look stark and too modern, but as you go closer, imagine them filled with perfumed gardens, fountains and myrrh trees and you'll start to understand how grand this place must have been. Hatshepsut (18th Dynasty), one of the few female pharaohs in history, called her temple Djeser Djeseru (the Splendour of Splendours). In ancient times a promenade lined with sphinxes probably ran from the Nile to the Lower Terrace. The reliefs on the colonnades on either side of the ramp were badly damaged by Tuthmosis III and Akhenaton. The reliefs on the Northern Colonnade depict the country life, with a fine picture of waterbirds caught in a net.

The lower ramp leads to the Middle Terrace. On the walls of the Birth Colonnade, to the right, Hatshepsut is shown with divine parents. At the end is the Chapel of Anubis with bright wall paintings. The Punt Colonnade, left of the ramp, has fine reliefs of the expedition to Punt (probably the coast of Somalia). Five ships leave the Red Sea port and upon arrival they are met by the chief of Punt and his fat wife. The ships coming back are laden with exotic trees, myrrh, incense and animal skins. At this end is the Chapel of Hathor, with cow-eared Hathoric columns, and inside the Sanctuary of Hathor is one of the few intact images of Hatshepsut. The second ramp leads to the Upper Terrace, which may be closed for restoration. Hewn into the mountain is the Sanctuary of Amun. To the left is the Sanctuary of Hatshepsut with fine reliefs, and to the right, the Sanctuary of the Sun.

The magnificent setting of the Temple of Queen Hatshepsut against the Theban Hills

Cycle The West Bank

If you want to see the main sights on Luxor's West Bank in a day, you will need to take a taxi. But if you have more time, there is nothing finer than cycling slowly from one site to another, taking in the glorious countryside and meeting people on the way. See map on page 134.

Practicalities You can rent bikes on the East and West Banks. There are places to eat on the West Bank, but a picnic under the trees at the Ramesseum is hard to beat. All sites are open 6–4pm in winter and 6–5 in summer. Less popular tombs may close earlier but the keeper is usually around. Tickets for the sites must be purchased in advance, either from the new visitors' centres on the East and West Banks, or from the ticket office at the crossroads past the Memnon Colossi, on the way to the Valley of the Queens. You need to decide in advance what you want to see as there are separate tickets for every temple or group of tombs. To use a camera inside the tombs you have to buy a photo permit.

First day itinerary: Village of New Gurna (Qurna), on the right past the el-Fadiya Canal, designed by the Egyptian architect Hassan Fathy (30 minutes) – Colossi of Memnon (30 minutes, page 157) – Temple of Madinet Habu (1 hour, page 156) – lunch at Shahhat's café opposite the temple – Deir el-Bahri (1 hour, page 154) – walk over the hill or cycle to the Valley of the Kings (2–3 hours, pages 160–3).

Second day itinerary: Valley of the Queens (45 minutes, page 166) – Deir el-Madina (30 minutes, page 156) – Valley of the Nobles (2–3 hours, pages 165–6) – Ramesseum (lunch and 30 minutes, page 158) – Temple of Seti I (30–45 minutes, page 158) and cycle back along the canal.

Pharaonic motifs are a common sight on houses on the West Bank

155

A humble Ramses III making offerings to the gods, Madinet Habu

▶▶ **Deir el-Madina**   *134A3*

Deir el-Madina was the Workmen's Village, home to the craftsmen and artists who worked in the Valley of the Kings. They recorded their daily life on *ostraca* (pottery fragments) or papyrus, from which we know that they worked in shifts of eight hours a day for ten days, and then returned to their families. In their free time they worked on their own tombs, built beneath small pyramids, often taking inspiration from the scenery in the royal tombs.

The ruined village is closed to visitors, but a few tombs in the necropolis are open and are worth visiting. A pyramid marks the Tomb of Sennedjem (No 1), a well-preserved tomb with colourful murals of funerary rituals and the owner making sacrifices to various gods. The Tomb of Iphy (No 217) has scenes of everyday life. The Tomb of Ankherkha (No 359) has a fine scene of Ankherkha and his wife listening to a harpist. To the north is a Ptolemaic temple, dedicated to Maat and Hathor. Christians turned the temple and village into a monastery, Deir el-Madina (literally the Monastery of the Town).

▶▶ **Madinet Habu (Mortuary Temple of Ramses III)**   *134A2*

This 20th-Dynasty temple, often overlooked by tourists, is one of the best-preserved and easiest temples to understand, a clear example of a classical temple, with few additions. It was built on an older sacred site: according to legend, the first land that appeared above the waters of chaos. Ramses III modelled his extravagant temple – the last great pharaonic temple – on the Ramesseum of his ancestor, Ramses II. Centuries after Ramses III's death, the Coptic town of Jeme grew up within the temple's vast mud-brick enclosure walls.

The enclosure is entered through the unusual gatehouse, which is modelled on a Syrian fortress. Inside, dilapidated stairs lead to Ramses' private pleasure apartments. Inside the temple's grounds, to the right is an older small temple, built by Hatshepsut on the site of the primeval hill.

The First Pylon of Ramses' temple is almost as high as the one at the Luxor Temple (a staircase leads to the top, with fabulous views). Like the temple's design, some reliefs were probably also copied from the Ramesseum, showing battles Ramses III never fought. His own struggle against the Sea Peoples is recorded in detail on the northern wall of the temple. Ceremonies and festivities were held in the First Court; ruins of the Royal Palace can be seen through the windows of its south wall. The Second Court was later used as a Coptic church and Christian symbols can be seen on the pillars, but a few Osiris figures have also survived. The colours of the reliefs under the western colonnade are exceptional. Beyond are three hypostyle halls with sanctuaries and treasure rooms on the sides and, off the inner hall, three main sanctuaries dedicated (right to left) to Mut, Khonsu and Amun; they were once covered with electrum (an alloy of gold and silver) and had a golden doorway. On the outer south wall there are fine reliefs of Ramses hunting and fishing.

▶▶ Memnon Colossi   134B2

Two colossi of Amenophis III, 19.5m high, sit peacefully amid sugar cane fields. They once guarded the gates of the mortuary temple of Amenophis III (18th Dynasty), of which nothing else remains. The right one was hit by an earthquake in 27BC, after which it made a noise like singing at dawn, which the Greeks believed was Memnon singing for his mother Eos. Many visitors, including Roman emperors, came to see it. Septimus Severus restored it in AD199, after which it was silent.

The colossi are covered in Roman and other graffiti. On the sides are reliefs of Nile gods binding together the flowers of the Two Lands. Small statues of Queen Tiy and Amenophis' mother Mutemuia stand on either side of the colossi's legs.

The Colossi of Memnon are no longer singing for their visitors

For once Ramses II chose the wrong site for a building: his mortuary temple suffered badly from Nile floods

▶▶ Ramesseum   134B3

This is the mortuary temple of Ramses II, known as Ramses the Great. Although Ramses II took great care to ensure his immortality, this temple, home to his immortal spirit, was built on weak foundations and is ruined, though broken columns and fragments of pylons are now being reassembled by French archaeologists.

The temple is entered from the north, which leads to the First Pylon, with scenes of Ramses II's victory over the Hittites in the Battle of Qaddesh. At the far end of the ruined First Court, steps lead to the Second Court and as you go down, to the left, the famous statue of Ozymandias, the inspiration for Shelley's poem. This was one of the largest free-standing monuments in Egypt, 17.5m high and weighing over 900 tonnes. The fragments, scattered around, are still astonishing for their size and perfect finish. The Second Pylon is partly decorated with the Battle of Qaddesh and has a top register portraying the god Min. The Second Court is lined with an Osiris colonnade. Near the stairway leading to the West Portico lies another smaller granite colossus. The Great Hypostyle Hall, with 29 of its 48 columns still standing, is also decorated with military scenes. The vestibules lead to the sanctuary, which has been totally destroyed.

▶ Mortuary Temple of Seti I   134C3

The works of Seti's reign (19th Dynasty), particularly his temple in Abydos, are the finest of the New Kingdom. He built this temple for the worship of the god Amun and of Ramses I, his father. The first two pylons and courts have been destroyed and only the temple building remains. The columns in the hypostyle hall are decorated with fine reliefs of Seti and his son Ramses II making offerings to the gods. In the chapels and sanctuary beyond there are more superb reliefs of Seti. This temple is rarely visited, another good reason to see it.

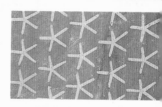

■ Earlier Egyptians had often been buried in tombs cut into rocks, but it wasn't until the 18th Dynasty that pharaohs and their families built tombs in the valleys of the Theban Hills. Their tombs, in the Valleys of the Kings and Queens, are among the most spectacular remains along the Nile.....■

Theban tombs Pharaohs were breaking with a 1,000-year tradition when they were buried in hidden tombs, far from their mortuary temples. They were hoping to secure their remains forever, but the promise of funerary treasure brought robbers to the desolate valleys. Accordingly, tombs became more complex and included pits to trap robbers, but New Kingdom pharaohs still seldom remained in their tombs for long. As the New Kingdom collapsed, so the guardian-priests abandoned the tombs and treasure altogether and reburied the mummies in unmarked pits elsewhere. Even Tutankhamun's tomb, the best preserved of all, was broken into and then resealed by the priests of the necropolis.

Decorations Entering royal tombs at Thebes is like following the pharaohs on their journey to the underworld. The walls are decorated with passages from the Book of the Dead and the Book of the Gates, anticipating what was lying in store for the dead soul: the unworthy were assaulted by snakes or crocodiles, while the worthy had their hearts weighed for purity in front of Osiris.

The tombs today European travellers in the 18th century found local villagers making use of opened tombs as houses. The prospect of finding gold has attracted locals as well as foreigners and there are many stories, mostly unsubstantiated, of villagers uncovering tombs and trying to sell the contents. The government has tried to clear villagers out of old Gurna (see page 165), but they are loath to leave which suggests there might be some truth in the rumours.

Top: in ancient as well as modern-day Egypt, professional mourning women beat their chests and threw sand in their faces in grief

Above: Old Kingdom rulers were buried in sarcophagi, which were symbolically equated with the body of the sky-goddess Nut, therefore affording the deceased the protection of the goddess

Walks in the Theban Hills

The hike from the Valley of the Kings to Deir el-Bahri can be done in about half an hour, but is worth doing slowly. Start at the trail near tomb No 16 and avoid the donkey boys if you can. Where the path forks, turn to the left and walk along the cliff for magnificent views of the temple and the abundant, green Nile Valley. Follow the path along the wire fence and where it forks turn to the left. Along the path young boys often sell fake antiquities which are occasionally mistaken for the real thing.

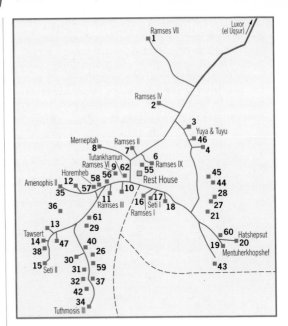

►►► **Biban el-Muluk (Valley of the Kings)** 134A4

From Tuthmosis I (18th Dynasty) onwards, all the New Kingdom pharaohs and occasionally a high official were buried in this secluded *wadi* (dry gully), the 'Place of Truth', as the ancient Egyptians called it, hidden in the barren Theban Hills. These secretiv/e tombs, hewn into the rock and decorated by the best craftsmen, were meant to preserve the royal mummies for eternity. Pharaohs usually started the work on their tombs as soon as they came to power, but many died before the decoration was finished. Although every precaution was taken to protect tombs from intruders, the treasures buried with the deceased were too attractive a proposition to resist. The powerful pharaohs of the 18th and 19th Dynasties kept the tombs under close supervision, but under the weaker rulers of the 20th Dynasty looting was rife, often by craftsmen

Wall paintings in the tomb of Ramses IV

who had worked on the tombs or officials who were supposed to be supervising. By the end of the New Kingdom the priests had to rebury the mummies and some of the objects in two secret caches, which weren't discovered until the end of the 19th century.

At the end of the 18th century, other intruders arrived on the scene to disturb the pharaohs' eternity: Egyptologists and early travellers. In 1922, Howard Carter discovered the Tomb of Tutankhamun, the last of the 62 tombs that have been uncovered to date. The fine and brightly coloured murals survived for thousands of years, but sadly, some have now been irreparably damaged, partly through the effects of mass tourism (see pages 152–3). A rotation system is now being introduced whereby only a small number of tombs will be open at any one time, and many of the decorations on tomb walls can now only be seen behind glass. The most radical of the plans under discussion involves closing all of the tombs and building a replica of the Valley of the Kings elsewhere.

Not all of the tombs have electric lighting, so only the ones that are lit will be described below.

Tomb of Ramses IV (No 2)►► (20th Dynasty) The bright lighting and delicate pastel colours of the murals make up for the poor quality of the carvings and an awful lot of Coptic graffiti. The ceiling of the sarcophagus chamber is adorned with a double image of Nut, while on the enormous pink granite sarcophagus, Isis and Nephthys were supposed to protect the mummy.

Tomb of Ramses IX (No 6)► Ramses IX was one of the last kings of the 20th Dynasty. The walls of his tomb are covered with extracts from the Book of Caverns and images of Ramses worshipping various gods. The ceiling of the burial chamber is unusual for its Book of Night in yellow on a dark blue background.

Tomb of Merneptah (No 8)► Merneptah (19th Dynasty) has been claimed as the pharaoh of the Exodus. Along the stepped corridors, descending at a sharp angle, are extracts of the Book of Gates and other texts. The lid of the outer sarcophagus was left in the antechamber by tomb robbers, while the lid of the inner sarcophagus, carved with a relief of Merneptah as Osiris, was found in the burial chamber.

All about mummies
Dead ancient Egyptian peasants were left to the goodwill of the dry climate, but the kings were mummified as an extra insurance for eternity. The brain was pulled out through the nostrils with a metal hook, while the viscera were removed via an incision in the abdomen, to be preserved in canopic jars. The heart was normally left in place, but a stone scarab would be placed over it in the mummy bandages. The body was then washed and pickled in natron (a sodium bicarbonate compound) for over a month, after which it was dried out. Once it was ready for the final stages, all orifices were plugged and the corpse was then swaddled in bandages.

The view over the Theban Hills towards the Valley of the Nobles, Deir el-Madina and the Valley of the Kings

The astronomical ceiling of the second pillared hall of Seti I's tomb (scenes from the Book of Amduat)

Decorative themes
Most of the decorations in the royal tombs are categorised as various books. The Book of the Dead encompasses the Old and Middle Kingdom pyramid texts. The Book of Amduat or the Underworld and the Book of Gates give instructions to the dead pharaoh, who sails in his solar barque through an underworld inhabited by demons and deities. The Book of Night and Day describes how every morning, after her nocturnal voyage, the goddess Nut gives birth to the sun. The Litany of Re contains texts or chants to announce to the solar god Re that his son is arriving.

Tomb of Ramses VI (No 9)▶▶▶ (20th Dynasty) This tomb, originally built for Ramses V, was already popular with tourists in ancient times, as the Greeks believed it was the tomb of Memnon. The first corridors are covered in graffiti, but in general the colours have been very well preserved. This tomb may well be closed for a long time, as it has suffered immensely from recent tourists. The walls are covered with the Book of Gates, the Book of Caverns and the Books of Day and Night. The pillared burial chamber has a magnificent ceiling decorated with Nut, the sky goddess, encircling the Book of Day on one side and the Book of Night on the other.

Tomb of Ramses III (No 11)▶▶ (20th Dynasty) This exceptionally large tomb, the only one in the valley with depictions of everyday life, is only partly lit as the second half is ruined. In side niches off the corridor are scenes of baking and butchery, and displays of hunting equipment, furnishings and agricultural scenes. It is called the Tomb of the Harpers because in one of these side chambers two harpists are shown playing for the gods. The corridor leads into a pillared hall decorated with texts from the Book of Gates and then descends into the ruinous burial chamber, now off limits to visitors.

Tomb of Ramses I (No 16)▶ (19th Dynasty) As Ramses I only ruled for a couple of years, his tomb was very modest. The decoration was not carved, but painted in bright colours against a grey background. On the left wall is a fine scene of 12 goddesses representing the hours of the night.

Tomb of Seti I (No 17)►►► (19th Dynasty) This is the most magnificent tomb in the valley, but because of damage caused by, among other things, the perspiration of visitors, it has been closed for several years. Restoration is underway but it is not certain when, if ever, it will be opened again. The exceptional carvings, painted in delicate colours, are only rivalled by the work in Seti's temple in Abydos. In the first descending corridors Seti is shown accompanied by various gods. Further down, the walls are decorated with various scenes from the Book of Gates. In the second pillared hall, the anteroom to the burial chamber, is an important astronomical ceiling with scenes from the Book of Amduat. The sarcophagus is now in the Sir John Soane Museum in London, while Seti's mummy is on display in the Egyptian Museum in Cairo.

Tomb of Tuthmosis III (No 34) (18th Dynasty)►► This is one of the oldest tombs, hidden high up in the valley and reached by a steep wooden staircase. The design of the tomb is most unusual with its circular burial chamber. The mummy of Tuthmosis is in Cairo, but his red granite sarcophagus remains here. A bridge crosses over a pit to reach the vestibule where 741 deities are represented as stick figures, painted in black and red only.

Tomb of Amenophis II (No 35) (18th Dynasty)► As this is one of the deepest tombs, with only decorations in the

163

Wall paintings in the tomb of Tuthmosis III

sarcophagus chamber, it is rarely visited by tourists. The walls in the burial chamber are decorated with the entire Book of Amduat on a yellow background, intended to imitate papyrus. Not only was Amenophis' mummy found in place in the sarcophagus, but in the side rooms 12 other mummies, perhaps hidden there by priests, were also discovered.

Tomb of Horemheb (No 57) (18th Dynasty)►► With an almost identical plan to Seti I's tomb, Horemheb's tomb is only sparsely decorated, but the images are finely executed. Work was never finished in the burial chamber so it is possible to see the progressive stages of decoration. (*Continued on page 165.*)

■   The tomb of Tutankhamun is not the most spectacular in Egypt and its contents were probably modest compared to the burial of a great pharaoh like Ramses II. But Tutankhamun's is the only pharaoh's tomb found intact and the amazing story of its discovery continues to attract visitors from around the world.....■

A vision for the world
'Outside this great sarcophagus stood huge golden shrines, and over there were the gods of Egypt, again in gold and lapis lazuli. And over there were the royal chariots, the armour, the chairs. All the paraphernalia of a royal household. It was a treasure which nobody had ever even imagined. When old Egyptologists who studied the profession all their lives first came into this tomb, they left weeping. It was a vision for the world, you might say.'
John Romer, *The Rape of Tutankhamun*, Channel 4 Television (1993)

Howard Carter removing the consecrating oils from the mummy of Tutankhamun

The lord and the archaeologist Lord Carnarvon was a wealthy, well-educated British aristocrat with an unusual hobby: excavating in Thebes. For six years he and his hired Egyptologist, Howard Carter, uncovered nothing spectacular. In 1914 they started digging in the Valley of the Kings, but it wasn't until 1922 that Carter uncovered steps cut into the rock and 'a magnificent tomb with seals intact'. It belonged to Tutankhamun. It took Carter almost ten years to empty the tomb, leaving the pharaoh's mummy in its inner sarcophagus.

The pharaoh's revenge Rumour that all who entered the tomb were cursed turned the discovery into one of this century's great media events: in three months of the 1926 season, 12,300 people went to visit the tomb. The first victim was Carnarvon himself. He was bitten by a mosquito in the Valley of the Kings, the bite became infected and a few weeks later the 57-year-old lord was dead. Many other Tut-related deaths were claimed over the next couple of years.

The price of success Tutankhamun's tomb is small and not particularly interesting, but it is the most famous. The price of success has been high: every day, litres of sweat have been left by fleeting visitors so that now the plaster is peeling from the wall and fungi attack the paintings. The tomb is often closed for repair, but restoration will only delay, not stop, the destruction.

BIBAN EL-MULUK (VALLEY OF THE KINGS) – VALLEY OF THE NOBLES

(*Continued from page 163.*) **Tomb of Tutankhamun (No 62)**▶▶▶ The tomb of the boy-king was intended for a high official because, however young the king was, he deserved more than this. The walls are mostly undecorated, another sign that the tomb was prepared in haste. But small as it is, this is the most important tomb to be discovered because its contents were more or less intact when Howard Carter found them. Steps lead into an ante-room with a storeroom, which was filled with grave goods, now on show in the Cairo museum. The walls in the burial chamber show the king's *barque* (royal barge) travelling through the underworld, Hathor with Isis and Anubis offering the *ankh* (looped cross) to the king, the funeral procession and Ay, the king's tutor, opening the mummy's mouth. The pink quartzite sarcophagus still contains the mummy, too badly decayed to be moved. (See also page 32.)

The death mask of Tutankhamun

▶▶▶ **Valley of the Nobles**   *134B4*

Government officials and high priests were buried in this valley near and underneath the old village of Gurna. These tombs may be less elaborate and less mysterious than the royal tombs, but instead of magical formulas and scenes from the Book of the Dead, they depict fascinating scenes of daily life in ancient Egypt.

Tomb of Rekhmire (No 100)▶▶▶ Rekhmire (18th dynasty) was a vizier (high official) under Tuthmosis III and Amenophis II. The entrance leads into a transverse chamber with, to the right, scenes of hunting, treading grapes and of Rekhmire inspecting workshops and agriculture and collecting taxes. The left wing of the chamber has an interesting register of Rekhmire receiving tributes from foreign lands like Crete, Syria, Punt and Nubia. In the corridor, on the left wall, Rekhmire makes the voyage to Abydos (see pages 128–9) while to the right, images of a funerary banquet and procession are mixed with gardens and lakes of the afterworld.

Tomb of Sennufer (No 96)▶▶▶ Known as the Tomb of the Vines, this is one of the most moving in this valley. Sennufer (18th Dynasty) was mayor of Thebes and overseer of Amun's gardens under Amenophis II. The themes in his tomb are similar to those of other tombs, but the difference is in the expression of love between Sennufer and his beautiful wife Meryt. There is a sense of beauty in every picture, the colouring is magnificent and here ancient Egypt feels very much alive.

Tomb of Menna (No 69)▶▶ Menna was an 18th-Dynasty inspector of estates, whose enemy had his eyes scratched out so he wouldn't enjoy the afterlife. The tomb decorations, of rural scenery, are finely painted and well preserved. In the entrance he and his wife and daughter are worshipping the sun. In the right wing of the first chamber the couple is seen in front of offering tables. In the second chamber, among scenes of mourning, are beautiful hunting and fishing scenes.

Old and New Gurna (Qurna)
Walking around Old Gurna you can see that some of the houses have been built over the tombs, and many a Gurnawi will claim to have found real antiquities under his kitchen floor. In the 1940s the government, aware of the grave-robbing, attempted to move villagers to a new town nearby, designed by the Egyptian architect Hassan Fathy. Fifty years later, the villagers still refuse to move and New Gurna, designed as a traditional mud-brick village, is now inhabited by people from outside Luxor.

Tomb of Nakht (No 52)►►► Nakht was a scribe and high priest of Amun during the 18th Dynasty. The only decorated part of his tomb, the transverse chamber, has well-preserved and very bright murals of country life. On the left, Nakht is supervising the harvest, while on the rear wall there is a banquet scene where beautiful dancers and a blind harpist entertain the guests of the deceased. On the right side is a traditional hunting scene and another of treading grapes. In the inner chamber is a copy of the funerary statue of Nakht; the original was lost when the ship transporting it to America sank.

Tomb of Ramose (No 55)►►► Ramose (18th Dynasty) was vizier and governor of Thebes under Amenophis III and Amenophis IV, who later became Akhenaton. His tomb is unusual in having some exquisite carvings in the classical style, especially the banquet scene left of the entrance, as well as reliefs from after the Amarna revolution in the typical Amarna style (see pages 124–5). On the rear wall, to the left, Amenophis IV is seen, under a canopy with Maat, while on the right he is seen worshipping Aton. A dark tunnel leads into the burial chamber.

Tomb of Userhat (No 56)►► The tomb of Userhat, 18th-Dynasty royal scribe, is unusual for its fine murals, mostly in pink tones. There are beautiful paintings of him hunting in the desert and fowling and fishing in the marshes.

Tomb of Khaemhat (No 57)►► Khaemhat was another 18th-Dynasty scribe and the carvings in his tomb are as fine as those in the Tomb of Ramose. In the chapel are various seated statues of Khaemhat and his family.

Tombs of Khonsu (No 31), Benia (No 343) and Userhat (No 51)► This group of tombs was only opened to the public in 1992. The scenes are traditional: hunting, the pilgrimage to Abydos, mourners, offerings and so on, but they have been well restored.

►► **Biban el-Harim (Valley of the Queens)** *134A3*

There are some 70 tombs belonging to queens, princesses and princes, mostly of the 18th, 19th and 20th Dynasties, in the valley. Queens were clearly far less important than pharaohs, as is suggested by the sober tomb decoration: sometimes the walls were painted, but often they were left unfinished. Several tombs have recently been closed to stop further damage.

The most remarkable tomb in the valley is the **Tomb of Nefertari (No 66)**►►►, but for the moment it can only be visited by special permission. It has some exquisite portraits of Nefertari, wife of Ramses II, in front of various deities. A smallpox epidemic killed several of the sons of Ramses III and they were all buried in the valley. In the **Tomb of Prince Set Her Khopshef (No 43)**► and the **Tomb of Prince Khaemwaset (No 44)**►►, Ramses is shown introducing his sons to the gods and making offerings. The sons are taken by the hand to the gates of the underworld, guarded by strange-headed figures. A third son buried in the **Tomb of Amun Her Khopshef (No 55)**►► is also led by his father, who is explaining about the afterlife. In the burial chamber to the right of the sarcophagus, a glass case contains a six-month-old foetus. It is believed that the mother miscarried when her other sons died so suddenly.

Death of a world
'How pleasant it is to find oneself in beautiful country once more, in this glorious plain, all surrounded by those violet-coloured hills, with rich fields bordering the blue Nile, and groves of palm trees and acacias, and tamarisks, overshadowing the ruins of a world. It is not the deathbed of a city which you come to visit here, it is the death of a world. And what a world!' Florence Nightingale, *Letters from Egypt* (1849–50)

VALLEY OF THE NOBLES – BIBAN EL-HARIM (VALLEY OF THE QUEENS)

For the moment, the **Tomb of Queen Tyti (No 52)▶** is the only queen's tomb that can be visited without special permission. The simple, cross-shaped tomb is lavishly decorated. In the central room are scenes of guardians of the underworld. In the chamber to the right is a strange scene: Queen Tyti with the cow goddess Hathor, coming out of a mountain in front of a sycamore tree, where a human Hathor pours rejuvenating water over the queen. The chamber to the left contained the sarcophagus.

The tomb of Nefertari after its extensive and successful restoration

UPPER EGYPT AND NUBIA

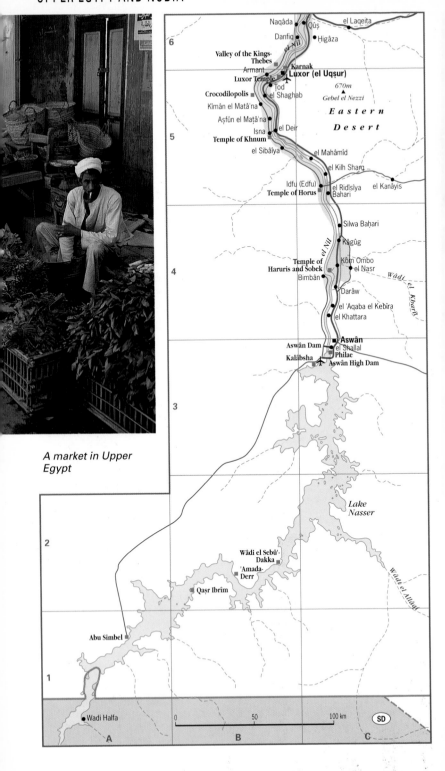

A market in Upper Egypt

el Laqeita
Naqâda
Qûş
Danfiq
Higâza
Valley of the Kings-
Thebes
Karnak
Armant
Luxor (el Uqşur)
Luxor Temple
Tod
670m
el Shaghab
Gebel el Nezzi
Crocodilopolis
Kîmân el Matâ'na
E a s t e r n
Aşfûn el Maţâ'na
D e s e r t
Isna
el Deir
Temple of Khnum
el Mahâmîd
el Sibâîya
el Kilh Sharq
Idfu (Edfu)
el Ridîsîya
el Kanâyis
Temple of Horus
Bahari
Silwa Baḥari
Kâgûg
Kôm Ombo
Temple of
el Nasr
Haruris and Sobek
Bimbân
Darâw
el 'Aqaba el Kebîra
el Khattara
Aswân
Aswân Dam
el Shallal
Philae
Kalâbsha
Aswân High Dam

el Nîl

Wâdi el Kharît

*Lake
Nasser*

Wâdi el Sebû'-
Dakka
'Amada-
Derr
Qaşr Ibrîm

Wâdi el Allâqi

Abu Simbel

Wadi Halfa

0   50   100 km

SD

6
5
4
3
2
1
A   B   C

Upper Egypt and Nubia It is rewarding to travel through the Upper Nile Valley, with its rich farmland, beautiful temples and traditional villages. It is easy to think of Aswan as the end of the line, now that the High Dam has cut the Nile's flow. But although most of the land of Nubia lies beneath Lake Nasser, its deeper rhythms and darker-skinned people, their culture as old as the pharaohs, are still to be found.

The thinning line The Nile becomes increasingly dramatic towards the south. The fat plains around Luxor, trimmed by limestone hills, begin to shrink, the riverbed changing from limestone to granite as you go upstream. Where the river fails to reach, the desert claims. The sands lie close around Aswan and beyond the dam, as they did through Nubia.

End of empire Divisions between people who cultivated the Nile Valley and others who lived off herding, fishing or trading along the river existed far back in antiquity.

UPPER EGYPT AND NUBIA

Beyond the cataracts
Tourism on Lake Nasser is getting a boost. In addition to specialist holidays offering fishing tours, a cruise service now operates between Aswan and Abu Simbel allowing visits to the out-of-the-way sites at Wadi el-Sebua (Sibu), Dakka, Derr, Amada and Qasr Ibrim.

Egyptians controlled Nubia and extracted its mineral wealth at various times in their history, while there were also Nubians who became pharaohs. But the two countries remained separate with Aswan acting as the border-post between them.

A great resort Aswan is often used as a place of transit to reach cruise boats, Philae, Abu Simbel or even Sudan, but it rewards closer inspection. It has been spared some of the worst excesses of mass tourism by its lack of an international airport, and it has a relaxed and unhurried feel to it. The valley is narrow, more intimate, forcing you down to the river, whose slender stream is divided by islands and rocks. In ancient times, dissident Romans were sent to Aswan as a punishment, but a few days spent in the town now are just a pleasure.

The last flood In antiquity offerings were made, prayers recited and a watch was kept each summer on the Nilometer (measuring station) on Elephantine Island to see how fast the river was rising. The news was then relayed to the north. Villagers on Elephantine Island still talk about a booming sound that was heard if you placed your ear to the rocks at the time of the flood. But the Nilometer is abandoned, the rocks are silent, and since the Aswan dams were built the Nile's flow has been regulated throughout the year.

The Nile at Aswan, caught between narrow banks

The job of camel-driver is taught from the cradle

Nubian architecture
Hassan Fathy reacted with enthusiasm to the Nubian houses he saw near Aswan, 'tall, easy, roofed cleanly with a brick vault, each house decorated individually and exquisitely around the doorway with claustrawork – mouldings and tracery in mud.' It was, he suggested somewhat prophetically, as if it had come 'from Atlantis'. Nubian architecture has been on the decline since Nubia was submerged, but Fathy took Nubian craftsmen to Luxor in the 1940s to work on his New Gurna (Qurna) village project (see page 165) and their influence can now be seen throughout the region.

The lost world Nubia was a harsh, arid place, but it was home to around 100,000 people, who were dependent on Egyptians to share the abundance of their harvests. The construction of the Aswan dams earlier this century caused the flooding of the entire Nubian homeland, and many Nubian men went looking for work in Egyptian towns and cities – Nubian clerks, cooks and watchmen are common throughout the country – but wherever they went, they maintained a separate identity based on their land.

The Egyptian architect Hassan Fathy understood that their sense of individuality was based on their architecture. 'There was nothing else like it in Egypt,' he wrote, 'a village from some dream country.' It was a dream Nubians have struggled to preserve, along with the distinctive character of their music, dance and cuisine. It is still possible to feel something of their character in the island villages around Aswan, but without their land the Nubians, dispersed between Sudan, Aswan and the Upper Nile Valley, are slowly losing their identity.

Modern Nubia The new museum in Aswan promises to be a good starting point to understanding Nubian culture, but the best place is with Nubians themselves. There are also remains of Nubian monuments along the shores of Lake Nasser. Some 23 temples were saved as the High Dam was being constructed. Some went to foreign museums in thanks for their help in the salvage operation, but others, most famously Abu Simbel and Philae, but also Wadi el-Sebua (Sibu), Bayt el-Wali and Kalabsha, were simply lifted above the waterline.

Painted column, the Temple of Kom Ombo

Upper Egypt

172

Twin-temples
The Temple of Hathor in Dandara was modelled on the Temple of Horus as they were closely connected, like the temples of Luxor and Karnak. In the annual procession Horus went to Dandara to visit his wife Hathor.

▶▶ **Isna (Esna), Temple of Khnum**   168B5

Open: winter 6am–5:30pm and summer 6am–6:30pm. Admission fee. The ticket office is on the quay.

Esna lies 54km south of Luxor and 155km north of Aswan. The temple is a short walk from the quay, through a narrow *souk* (market) street. Completely hidden beneath houses, it was partly excavated in 1860.

The temple, probably once as large as the Edfu temple, was rebuilt by Ptolemy VI (*c* 180BC) on an earlier structure. It was dedicated to the ram-headed god Khnum, god of creation, often depicted modelling man on his potter's wheel. Only the hypostyle hall, added by the Roman emperor Claudius (1st century AD) was totally excavated; it is now approached from a staircase descending 10m below the current street level. Its roof is supported by 24 colourful columns with various fine capitals, like an enclosed garden with different flowers. The fine astronomical ceiling has almost disappeared under a black residue of smoke from the fires of earlier Christian occupants. The carvings on the walls portray several Roman emperors in front of Egyptian deities. In front of the temple are several blocks from an early Christian church.

In the streets around the temple, some old houses have retained fine *mashrabiya* (carved wood) screens, but it is hard to imagine that it was in these houses that travellers like Flaubert tasted Egyptian pleasures of the flesh.

▶▶▶ **Idfu (Edfu), Temple of Horus**   168C5

Open: winter 7–4 daily and summer 6–6 daily. Admission fee.

Edfu lies 115km south of Luxor and 105km north of Aswan. The Temple of Horus is, after Karnak, the largest temple in Egypt. It is also the best-preserved as it was almost completely buried in the sand until the 1860s, when Mariette started excavating the main building. Dedicated to the falcon-headed god, Horus, it was built on a site inhabited since the Old Kingdom, believed to be the site of Horus' fight with his uncle Seth for control of the world. The temple was built 237–57BC, during the Ptolemaic period, but it faithfully maintains the traditions of pharaonic architecture and gives a clear idea of what all ancient temples must have looked like. It is also the temple we know most about as there are plenty of foundation and building texts inscribed on its walls.

The temple is now entered from the back of the court, but the visit should start at the massive pylon, built by Ptolemy IX. The reliefs on its outer walls show Neos Dionysos in front of Horus the Elder. The inside walls record the Festival of the Beautiful Meeting, when Horus joined Hathor in Dandara. In front of the First Hypostyle Hall stands one of a pair of majestic hawk-statues of Horus, its twin lying headless in the sand. The back wall of the hypostyle hall has some fine reliefs of the temple foundation rituals, in which the king is shown making mud bricks. The Second Hypostyle or Festival Hall is lined with

Different flower- and plant-shaped columns in the Temple of Esna are highly suggestive of a garden

The god Horus was often represented as a falcon or, as here at Edfu Temple, a hawk

side chambers. The walls of the first room to the left, the laboratory, are covered with fine reliefs of flowers and recipes. In the next hall, two staircases lead to the roof where Horus was revitalised by the sun. Beyond lies the strangely lit holy-of-holies, the Sanctuary, where the statue of Horus was believed to be inhabited by the living god. It once contained his sacred *barque* (royal barge), a copy of which is found in the middle room behind the sanctuary. The New Year Chapel, containing a beautiful depiction of the sky goddess, Nut, is to the left as you leave the Sanctuary. In the outer corridor around the temple is a relief of Horus' victory over Seth, depicting Seth as a hippopotamus. Outside the pylon is the Birth House.

Between Luxor and Aswan
All cruise boat and *felucca* (sailing boat) trips between Aswan and Luxor include a visit to the temples in Esna, Edfu and Kom Ombo (see pages 176–7). It is also possible to visit these three temples on the overland route if you hire a private taxi. Tell the driver you want to visit the temples and agree beforehand on a price. The route is beautiful through desert, villages and green farmland, often touching the Nile banks.

The impressive First Pylon of the Ptolemaic Temple of Horus in Edfu

Boats and Cruises

■ Some 200 years ago early travellers started to sail up the Nile for pleasure. Nile boats were adapted to their needs, bedrooms and salons were added, and visitors were able to admire the country from the comfort and safety of their own, well-ordered decks.....■

The standard tour

Cruise boat itineraries often look the same. They differ in the level of accommodation and service, the expertise of the Egyptologist and the length of stay. Some cruises include visits to Dandara and Abydos. Beyond Luxor, the temples of Esna, Edfu and Kom Ombo are visited before reaching Aswan. There are often delays at Esna due to the number of boats passing through the lock, forcing some companies to transfer passengers to a sister boat on the other side of the lock.

Feluccas

Note that the boatmen have to notify the river police before they take you out overnight on their feluccas. Stock up in the market on food and water before you leave. The trip from Luxor to Aswan is possible if the wind is blowing upriver, but from Aswan to Luxor, the river's current will carry you down if the wind fails.

Cruising on the Nile today is more popular and more affordable than it has ever been

Early cruises Early historians like Herodotus sailed up the Nile. Movement on the river is dictated by the seasons: in autumn a strong wind from the north propels sailing boats into Africa; coming back is easier, riding with the river's flow. This seasonal timetable suited the early tourists perfectly and Egypt quickly earned a reputation as a place to spend a warm winter, as travellers like Florence Nightingale and Gustave Flaubert knew. Lady Lucie Duff Gordon was one of the first Europeans to travel far afield for their health; initially sent to winter in Egypt, she remained by the Nile and died in 1869, her seventh year in Egypt.

The rapids, known here as cataracts, were a big obstacle to boats wishing to go south of Aswan into Nubia. No amount of sails could take boats over them, so they were pulled over by the men of the 'Sheikh of the Cataracts' who extracted a sizeable fee for the service.

The first Cook's tour By 1869, the year of the opening of the Suez Canal, tourism was already developed in Egypt. In 1863 Lucie Duff Gordon had marked the first regular steamer service up the Nile. Thomas Cook took it all one step further. Instead of tourists having to make their own arrangements with boatmen and interpreters, Cook promised to look after them and make sure that the linens were clean, the food familiar, the temples open – and all for a reasonable sum. It was a great success, especially among people who couldn't afford to pay their way on their own. It was Cook who brought the masses to the Nile and he was the first to set up agencies to ensure that everything was ready for them when they got there.

Cruising today There are a multitude of cruise boats on the Nile today offering a wide choice of accommodation, but the itineraries they follow are invariably the same. The differences, reflected in the cost, are mostly in the standard of service and accommodation and the number of

cabins – the newer luxury boats are getting smaller. Some boats carry a small library of books on ancient and modern Egypt and all cruises also provide the services of a guide to help make sense of the monuments along the river.

Sailing on the Nile The nearest thing to that old-fashioned feeling of sailing up the Nile is to be had on *feluccas*. These open-topped sailing boats can be hired by the hour or day in Luxor and Aswan, but the big thrills are to be had sailing between the two, drifting slowly past villages, seeing river life, eating with the boatmen and sleeping under the stars on the river's bank at night.

The new steamers
'The new passenger-steamers... will not now go till after the races – 6th or 7th of next month. Fancy the Cairo races! It is growing dreadfully Cockney here, I must go to Timbuctoo....
Lucie Duff Gordon, 1863)

A modern eye of Horus to keep the evil spirits away

The hypostyle hall of the Temple of Haruris in Kom Ombo

Something of Greece
'The temple... Its elevation, its seclusion, the combination of sun and water flowing past as though in slow but determined search for the Mediterranean, at last suggests something of Greece... there is something in its stones of that Hellenic response to light...'
Michael Haag, *Discovery Guide to Egypt* (1987)

A relief showing medical instruments

▶▶ Kom Ombo, Temple of Haruris and Sobek
168C4

Open: 6–6 daily. Admission fee.

Kom Ombo lies 170km south of Luxor and 45km north of Aswan. As the temple stands on a promontory beside the Nile, the most spectacular approach is from the river, by boat or *felucca*, in the late afternoon when the setting sun turns the sandstone a deep golden colour. The Nile has swept most of the pylon, forecourt and birth house away, and the temple was seriously damaged during the earthquake in 1992, but what is left is well worth seeing. The temple is unusual for being dedicated to two gods: the right side is dedicated to the crocodile god Sobek, the left side to Horus the Elder or Haruris. Ptolemy VI (c.180BC) started building the temple, but most of the work was done under Neos Dionysos (80–51BC). The Roman emperor, Augustus (30BC–AD14), added the pylon, court and outer enclosure wall.

The temple is approached passing the massive Gateway of Neos Dionysos and, to the right, the small Chapel of Hathor, its mummified crocodiles found in a cemetery nearby. Little remains of the **pylon** and the **court**, but at the back is the façade of the First Hypostyle Hall, with dual passageways leading to the twin sanctuaries. On the left wall of the façade Neos Dionysos is purified by Horus, while on the right he appears in front of Sobek. The hypostyle hall has lofty columns with floral capitals and a ceiling decorated with flying vultures. On the inner wall of the façade is a fine relief of Neos Dionysos' coronation by the gods. Inside the older Second Hypostyle Hall, reliefs show Ptolemy VII making offerings to the gods. Beyond are three vestibules, decorated by Ptolemy VI with reliefs of temple rituals, leading to the two, mostly ruined sanctuaries. Between the doors to the sanctuaries is a splendid relief of Ptolemy VI and his wife receiving a palm stalk with the Heb-Sed sign from Haruris (painted blue) and Sobek (green).

Behind the sanctuaries off the inner corridor are seven decorated chapels; the middle one has a stairway leading up for a good view of the temple complex. The most interesting of the Roman reliefs in the outer corridor are on the walls at the back of the seven chapels, especially the display of medical instruments, proof that Egyptian surgeons were already sophisticated almost 2,000 years ago. Also look out for the carvings of ears which heard pilgrims' prayers. The birth house in the northeast corner of the complex has almost entirely disappeared in the Nile.

Nubian and Upper-Egyptian camel drivers in Daraw market

►► Daraw   168C4

Daraw, 5km south of Kom Ombo and 40km from Aswan, can be reached by bus or taxi from either town.

Only one thing distinguishes Daraw from other concentrations of mud-brick compounds along the road from Kom Ombo to Aswan: it marks the end of the Forty Days Road and plays host to the main camel market (*suq el-Gimal*) between the Sudan and Cairo. The market is held every Tuesday of the year and sometimes, in winter, on Sundays as well, from 6:30am to 2pm, with most of the trading completed by 11am. The location varies, but from the crowds and trucks loaded with camels it soon becomes clear where it is.

The camels are brought from Darfur and Kordofan in the Sudan, through the Libyan Desert to Dongola, and from there they follow the Nile into Egypt. This desert trail, one of the last surviving desert trading routes, takes about a month of walking and is appropriately called the Darb el-Arba'een (the Forty Days Road). The Sudanese camel drovers mostly come from two nomadic tribes and are often dressed in their traditional gear, daggers included. The camels, cheaper here than in Cairo (see page 93), are sold to local peasants or traders from Cairo. The picturesque market attracts increasing numbers of tourists, but it remains a spectacular and exotic sight.

Horus the Elder or Haruris
Of all the Egyptian gods Horus is the most complex and most confusing, appearing in many different forms. One of his main forms is as the falcon-headed Horus the Elder or Haruris, known as the Good Doctor, and pilgrims came to his temple in Kom Ombo seeking healing. Another popular form was Horus the Younger, the son of Isis and Osiris, who fought against Seth, his father's brother and murderer.

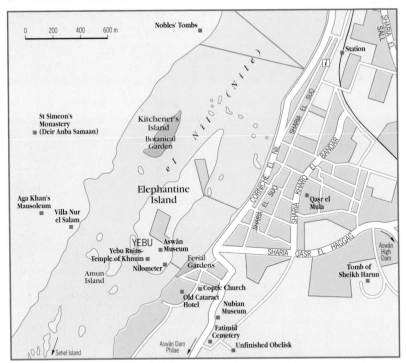

Map labels:
- 0 200 400 600 m
- Nobles' Tombs
- SHARIA EL SAIL
- Station
- St Simeon's Monastery (Deir Anba Samaan)
- Kitchener's Island
- Botanical Garden
- el Nil (Nile)
- SHARIA EL SUQ
- SHARIA KHARQ EL BANDAR
- CORNICHE EL NIL
- Aga Khan's Mausoleum
- Villa Nur el Salam
- Elephantine Island
- Qasr el Mula
- YEBU
- Yebu Ruins
- Temple of Khnum
- Aswân Museum
- Amun Island
- Nilometer
- Ferial Gardens
- SHARIA QASR EL HAGGAG
- Aswân High Dam
- Tomb of Sheikh Harun
- Coptic Church
- Old Cataract Hotel
- Nubian Museum
- Fatimid Cemetery
- Sehel Island
- Aswân Dam Philae
- Unfinished Obelisk

Nubian women

Tourist information

The tourist office (tel: 323297) is in a shopping arcade just off the Corniche, two blocks north of the Abu Simbel Hotel. It is open Saturday–Thursday 9–2 and 6–8, Friday 10–noon and 6–8. It has a list of the official prices for private taxis and feluccas (sailing boats). The tourist police also have an office here (tel: 324393) as well as near the railway station, both open 24 hours.

Shopping

Things to buy in Aswan's *souk*: Karkadeh (dried hibiscus flowers for infusions), spices, peanuts from Sudan, colourful silk and cotton hand-woven shawls, cotton tablecloths, bright Nubian baskets and strange charms.

▶▶▶ **Aswan** 168C3

Aswan, 886km from Cairo and 215km from Luxor, is Egypt's southernmost town, and it is totally different from the rest of the country. Here the green cultivated land disappears as the desert closes in on the river, which also changes from a flat and peaceful stream into a dramatic mass of water flowing between dark, dramatic granite rocks. Aswan feels more African and the majority of its inhabitants are Nubians, darker and taller than Upper

Egyptians, speaking a different language and having different customs.

Even in ancient times this was where Egypt ended and Nubia began. Yebu on Elephantine Island was the Old Kingdom border town and an important religious centre, as the Nile was believed to well up from under the nearby first cataract (rapids). Two thousand years later it marked the southernmost town of the Roman Empire, and in the 19th century it was the starting point for the conquest of the Sudan.

Aswan's position made it an important market for caravans passing with gold, slaves, incense and ivory and today it remains the best bazaar outside Cairo, bustling with Nubian and Egyptian traders selling more exotic goods than anywhere else in Egypt. Even if it has become more tourist-oriented recently, it is still a delight for the senses with strong smells of perfume, spice and incense, brightly coloured fabrics and everywhere the soft melodic tunes of Nubian and Sudanese musicians.

There may be less activity than in the past, apart from an occasional attack on the police force by Islamic militants, and there is little to see compared to Luxor and Cairo, but Aswan is a wonderful place to rest. You can stroll around, take sailing boats, spend afternoons on the terrace of the Old Cataract Pullman or wander around the bazaar without having the feeling of missing out on history. The town is so pleasant, its people so relaxed and friendly, that it is always hard to leave.

Aga Khan's Mausoleum▶▶ (*open: Tuesday–Sunday 9–4:30*) This mausoleum, beautiful in its simplicity, is where the Aga Khan III (1877–1957) chose to be buried. He was the spiritual leader of the Ismailis, a Shi'ite sect coming from India, and his grandson Karim succeeded

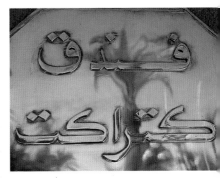

The brass plate of the Old Cataract Hotel

The Old Cataract Pullman
For nostalgia, romance and wonderful views stay in the Old Cataract Pullman (see page 275). Built in 1902, the hotel which appeared in Agatha Christie's *Death on the Nile* has recently been refurbished and is once again one of the nicest hotels in Egypt. If you don't stay, at least walk around, have a drink on the grand terrace, watch the sunset or have dinner in the splendid Moorish Room.

179

The busy boatyard near the Aswan Dam

The simple mausoleum of Aga Khan has wonderful views over the Nile and the town of Aswan

Nubian weddings
Nubian weddings are week-long celebrations at which foreign guests are considered auspicious. They are also fun. If you are invited to one, do offer some money for the musicians. Beware of invitations by touts selling this as an excursion.

him as the Aga Khan IV. His wealth was phenomenal and so was his weight: on his diamond jubilee, in 1945, his weight in diamonds was distributed among his followers. He fell in love with Aswan because of its beauty and perfect winter climate and he liked to spend the winter in the white villa he built on the west bank, as his wife, the Begum, still does. When she is there she lays a red rose on his tomb every morning.

Aswan Museum and Nilometer▶▶ (*open: 8:30–6 daily; admission fee includes the Ruins of Yebu*) This small museum on Elephantine Island is housed in the villa of Sir William Willcocks, the British engineer who designed the old Aswan Dam. On display are local finds from pre-dynastic to the Byzantine periods: statues, pottery, jewellery, a fine golden bust of Khnum, a mummified ram and several mummies. At the back of the house are pleasant and shady gardens where tea may be offered in return for a small *baksheesh* (tip). Beside the Nile is a Nilometer with scales in pharaonic, Greek, Roman and Arabic numerals. The height of the river dictated the level of taxes, so this was a very important instrument until the High Dam stopped the annual inundation.

Gezirat el-Nabatat (Kitchener's Island)▶▶ (*open: 8am–sunset daily; admission fee*) Behind Elephantine Island lies a small, lush island which was offered to Consul-General Kitchener for his military achievements in the Sudan. He developed a passion for exotic flora and imported trees and seeds from all over the world. In the late afternoon, the shady garden, full of bird songs and sweet fragrances, makes a perfect retreat.

Deir Anba Samaan (Monastery of St Simeon)▶▶ (*open: 9–4 daily; admission fee*) Start at the landing stage

below the Aga Khan's mausoleum and make the steep climb through soft sand (25 minutes) or hire a camel to the ridge. This is one of the most beautiful and romantic of Egyptian monasteries, built like a fortress in the 7th century and rebuilt in the 10th century. It was originally dedicated to Anba Hadra, a 4th-century local saint, and later to the little-known St Simeon. Salah ad-Din destroyed it in 1173 when Nubian Christians used it as a refuge. The roofless basilica has badly damaged paintings. In a nearby chamber, St Simeon is said to have stood reading the Bible for days on end, his beard tied up to the ceiling. The keep housed more than 300 monks. The setting is impressive: surrounded by desert, it is most spectacular around sunset.

Nobles' Tombs▶ (open 8–4 daily; admission fee) The tombs belonged to princes, priests and governors, mostly of the Old and Middle Kingdoms. They were hewn in the rock and have simple decorations. The two finest and best-preserved tombs belonged to Sirenput I (No 36) and Sirenput II (No 31), with colourful scenes of the governors and their family. On top of the hill, Qubbet el-Hawa (Dome of the Wind) is the tomb of a local sheikh, with a fantastic view over the Nile, the cataract and the desert.

Ruins of Yebu▶ (open: 8:30–6 daily) The southern end of Elephantine Island is covered with the ruins of ancient Yebu. Sites are still being excavated and include the temples of Khnum (30th Dynasty) and his wife, and a Temple of Jaweh, built in the 6th century BC by a Jewish colony.

An old Nubian man selling lemons from his garden, at the market in Aswan

Walk On Elephantine Island

Above: the elephant-like rocks

The island takes its name from the dark granite rocks at its southern end, which – especially after attending a Nubian wedding – may resemble a herd of elephants bathing in the river. Yebu was once an important frontier town, but for most people the ruins and the museum are merely a pretext to visit: the real interest lies in the tranquil Nubian villages and the sweet promise of Africa. See the map on page 178

Start from the Aswan Museum (see page 180) and wander towards the ugly tower of the Oberoi Hotel at the northern end of the island (ferries leave for the museum from the landing opposite the Egypt Air office and there is a private ferry back from the hotel). The first houses beyond the football pitch are modern concrete structures, as in many other Egyptian villages, but the further you go the more beautiful the houses become. These traditional houses, which so delighted the Egyptian architect Hassan Fathy, are built using the same mud bricks as the ancient Egyptians. They are often finely decorated with intricate patterns in mud. Every house is painted in different shades of ochre yellow or bright blue as a background, beautifully contrasting with the bright green of the surrounding gardens. If the owner of the house has made a *hajj* (pilgrimage) to Mecca, the façade will be decorated with drawings of the Holy Kaaba in Mecca and usually the means of transport he took to get there. Some doorways are carved with crocodiles and have a woman's hand as a door knocker. The people don't always enjoy their village being a showpiece, but if you walk through and offer a *salaam allaykum*, your greeting will be returned with a smile. After sunset, children push home-made boats out on the river and fill the air with melancholic songs.

Boat trip   *Felucca* trips

It takes an adventurous spirit to undertake a long *felucca* (sailing boat) journey from Aswan to Luxor, but in Aswan everyone can safely enjoy the tranquillity and beauty of the old River Nile. There is the traditional tour around the islands, the best way to see these sights, as well as a longer trip to Sehel Island. See the map on page 178.

Island tour (2–3 hours) *Felucca* trips are offered all along the Corniche, but decide where you want to go and for how long before you settle a price (check official prices with the tourist office). The traditional tour passes Elephantine Island; stops at Kitchener's Botanical Garden (see page 180), dropping you at one end of the island and picking you up from the other; visits the Aga Khan's Mausoleum (see page 179–80) and returns past the elephant-shaped rocks to the south of Elephantine Island and the Old Cataract Pullman. Longer tours include the Nobles' Tombs (see page 181) and even the Monastery of St Simeon (see page 180–1). At the end of a hot day, what could be more pleasurable than sitting back, catching the breeze from a *felucca*, and enjoying the sense of serenity that the Nile can inspire?

Sehel Island (3–5 hours) If by now you are hooked on *felucca* sailing, a trip to Sehel past the first cataract (rapid) is highly recommended. Try to avoid the west side, where commercialised tea-stops are offered in a Nubian house, and land on the east side. Walk towards the south of the island to see granite boulders with inscriptions from the Middle Kingdom to the Ptolemaic Period, recording Egyptian expeditions south of the first cataract. By far the most interesting is No 81, relating how King Zoser (3rd Dynasty) ended a seven-year famine by building a temple on Sehel dedicated to Khnum. From Sehel there is a magnificent view of the cataract, where the river turns into a rapid stream divided by granite rocks.

183

Villagers on Elephantine Island still earn their living from their boats

The Aswan Dam

■ If, as Herodotus wrote, Egypt is the gift of the Nile, it is a gift that constantly needs renewing. With only negligible rainfall, Egyptians are still dependent on the river for all their water needs. The Aswan Dam seemed to offer Egyptians control of the Nile and with it their destiny, but it was a controversial project from the start.....■

The first dam The British recognised the benefits that a dam would bring to Egypt and built the first Aswan Dam between 1899 and 1902. On completion it was the largest dam in the world and was hailed as a great engineering achievement – particularly by the British, whose engineers had carried out the project, using Egyptian and Italian labour. The dam was opened by the Duke of Connaught, brother of the British King Edward VII. Lord Cromer, the British agent in Egypt who was also present at the ceremony, later wrote that it was 'by far the most popular step we have ever taken.' The dam allowed an extra 10–15 per cent of land to be farmed between 1881 and 1911.

Driving in the cast-iron piles for the foundations of the dam, 1902

Early problems The original dam created a reservoir which stretched 225km back towards Sudan, partially submerging Nubian villages and monuments for up to eight months a year. The most famous monument to suffer was the Temple of Isis on Philae Island and photographs of the period show tourists being taken by boat, or swimming among the columns, beneath the stone roof. Another problem with the dam was that it wasn't high enough: originally just over 30m high, it was raised several times and by 1933 stood at 42m. But the biggest problem posed by the dam was its function. Although it

was desirable to control the flow of the river, it was less desirable to control the flow of silt. The Nile is fed by rain from the East African highlands and the water that flooded across the Nile Valley in Egypt deposited an important layer of silt when the waters receded. This silt fertilised the valley and without it, farmers had to use chemicals to replace the loss of their natural fertilisers.

Nasser and nationalism The Aswan High Dam project was swept forward by the surge of nationalism that followed the overthrow of the monarchy and the nationalisation of the Suez Canal, and President Nasser presented it as another step on the road to making his country strong and self-reliant. The dam was going to provide the country with sufficient water resources and would meet the country's electricity needs as well. When Nasser was refused aid for the project by western countries, he turned to the Soviet Union. Throughout its construction, the dam project was a source of national pride.

The price paid No progress without sacrifice: the benefits of the dam were considered great enough to allow the destruction of many important monuments. UNESCO and other national and international agencies became involved in saving the Nubian monuments, removing some to higher ground and others to foreign museums, but many disappeared beneath the man-made lake. The world community was less successful in saving the Nubian culture. With their villages and lands submerged, their contacts with nomadic tribes cut and their homes relocated further north, the Nubians lost the most obvious components of their cultural identity.

The price to pay There were also other, apparently unforeseen consequences of the dam whose effects will be felt far into the future. The vast surface area of Lake Nasser is posing a number of problems, changing rainfall patterns and raising the level of underground water far to the north. This, in turn, is now causing damage to monuments in places like Luxor whose stonework, preserved for millennia by the arid sand, is being eaten away by salty water.

In addition to flooding Nubian villages and ancient monuments, the large surface area of Lake Nasser appears to be influencing the climate

185

The Aswan High Dam Monument

The Temple of Isis at Philae

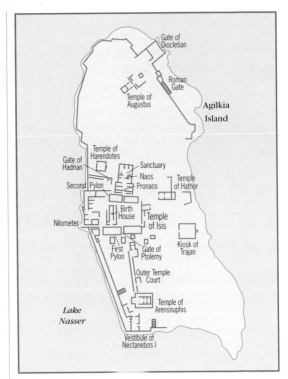

Old Nubia
'Between these two huge and barren expanses [of desert], Nubia writhes like a green sand-worm along the course of the river. Here and there it disappears all together, and the Nile runs between black and sun-cracked hills, with the orange drift-sand lying like glaciers in their valleys. Everywhere one sees traces of vanished races and sub-merged civilisations. Grotesque graves dot the hills or stand up against the skyline... everywhere graves. And occasionally... one sees a deserted city up above... with the sun shining through the empty window squares.'
Sir Arthur Conan Doyle (1897)

If finished, this obelisk would have been the largest work of stone in Egypt, but a flaw was discovered and it was left behind in the quarry

Nubia

▶▶ Nubian Museum   168C3

The first museum dedicated to Nubian culture and traditions is due to open on a hill behind the Cataract Pullman. The collection will be housed in a new building constructed in traditional Nubian style. Until now little attention has been paid to Nubian culture or history, which was dealt a great blow by the construction of the Aswan dams and the creation of Lake Nasser. As the lake's waters rose, Nubian families were forced to leave their villages and traditional land, many of them being resettled in Kom Ombo, Esna and other villages in the Upper Nile Valley. The common theme in modern Nubian art is the expression of a strong sense of loss of freedom, of the Nubian heritage and of their attachment to the land of their forefathers. There is a selection of antiquities found in Nubia on display in the Egyptian Museum in Cairo, but the Aswan museum is the first attempt to bring this heritage into the spotlight, as well as to illustrate living Nubian culture.

▶▶ Unfinished Obelisk   168C3

In an ancient granite quarry along the road to Philae lies a gigantic unfinished obelisk measuring 41.75m. The obelisk was probably intended to join the so-called Lateran Obelisk, now in Rome, in front of the temple of Tuthmosis III at Karnak, but it was abandoned after a flaw was discovered in the stone. Had the work been completed, this would have been the largest piece of worked stone in history, weighing about 1,200 tonnes. Its loss

must have been a disaster for the ancient masons, but for modern archaeologists it is an invaluable source of information on ancient quarrying techniques.

Near by in the **Fatimid Cemetery►** are some fine 10th-century, mud-brick tombs where local saints were buried including Sayyida Zaynab, the granddaughter of the prophet Muhammad. Most of the inscriptions were moved to Cairo in the late 19th century without any record being kept of which tomb they came from.

►►► Philae, Temple of Isis 168C3

Open: 7–4pm daily in winter, 7–5 daily in summer. Admission fee.

As Biga Island, identified with the burial place of Osiris, was only accessible to the priesthood, it was the neighbouring island of Philae that developed into a popular cult centre. The Temple of Isis was built over more than 700 years, mainly by Ptolemaic and Roman rulers who wanted to identify themselves with the Osiris and Isis cult. The temple shows a wonderful blend of Egyptian and Graeco-Roman architecture, in perfect harmony with its magnificent natural surroundings. In Roman times, this was the most important pilgrimage centre in Egypt. It was also the last functioning temple of ancient religion and only closed down in AD551.

When the first Aswan Dam was built, the Temple of Isis was partly submerged for most of the year. Travellers described their boat trip around the temple as one of the highlights of their Egyptian visit, but the annual rise of the waters soon started to erode the reliefs. With the construction of the High Dam, the temple was threatened with complete and permanent submersion. In a massive operation led by UNESCO and the Egyptian Antiquities Organisation, the island of Agilkia was reshaped into an exact replica of Philae and the Temple of Isis, the Temple of Hathor and Trajan's Kiosk were relocated to its drier ground. The relocated Philae was reopened in all its splendour, and with tide marks, in 1980.

The Temple of Isis at Philae, approached by boat

Boats to Agilkia Island
Taxis will drop you at Shallal dock, where tickets for the temple are sold and where you take a motor-boat to Agilkia Island. A notice-board near the ticket window gives the official prices for motor-boats, which are cheaper if you are travelling as part of a group as there is a minimum charge per boat.

Water marks stain the pylon from when the Temple of Isis was submerged

Temple of Isis▶▶▶ Stairs from the landing lead to the Vestibule of Nectanebo I (30th Dynasty), beyond which stretches the outer court flanked by colonnades. The windows in the well-preserved West Colonnade once overlooked Biga and the columns are decorated with reliefs of Tiberius making offerings to the gods. The First Pylon was decorated by Neos Dionysos (80–51BC). Its reliefs, showing the Ptolemy in traditional pharaonic scenes, were badly damaged by the Copts.

The gateway, built by Nectanebo I, leads into the Central Court. To the right lie the colonnaded quarters of the priests, with reliefs of the king performing rituals. To the left of the court is the Birth House of Ptolemy IV (221–205BC) with some fine reliefs depicting the myth of Horus rising from the marshes as a falcon. Behind the Second Pylon, the small court leads to the hypostyle hall, converted into a church in the 6th century AD. Beyond, three dark vestibules lead into the Sanctuary, dimly lit by two small windows, where a pedestal which once supported Isis' sacred *barque* (royal barge) is still in place. On the top of the right-hand wall Isis suckles her son Horus, while below she suckles a young pharaoh. On the left wall the pharaoh, here a Ptolemy, stands in front of Isis who protects Osiris with her wings.

A staircase in one of the vestibules leads to the Osirian shrine, where the Osiris myth is illustrated in beautiful reliefs – usually closed but sometimes the guard opens it for *baksheesh* (a tip). The western door of the first vestibule leads to Hadrian's Gate. An interesting relief on the right wall of its ruined vestibule depicts the source of the Nile as the Nile god Hapi, who pours water from two jars; the ancient Egyptians believed that the Nile sprung up at the first cataract, from where one branch flowed towards Africa and another towards the Mediterranean.

To the right of the Second Pylon, the small **Temple of Hathor▶▶** has a beautiful relief of musicians; Hathor was the patroness of music. Further south is the most eye-catching structure on Philae: the **Kiosk of Trajan▶▶▶**, with beautifully carved floral columns, which was intended as the formal entrance to the temple. From here there are splendid views over the lake, where the metal coffer dam used during the relocation marks the original Philae Island, now totally submerged.

Raised hieroglyphs at Isis' temple

▶▶ New Kalabsha 168C3

Open: 6am–5pm daily. Admission fee.

The Temple of Kalabsha now lies somewhat forgotten on a promontory beside Lake Nasser, in the shadow of the High Dam. The monuments were relocated here from other sites in Nubia in 1970 to save them from the rising waters of Lake Nasser. The temple is now in a military zone and became accessible only a few years ago.

The original site of Kalabsha – Talmis in ancient times – was 50km further up the Nile. The **Temple of Mandulis▶▶** was dedicated to the Nubian fertility god Marul, called Mandulis by the Greeks. It was built during the reign of Augustus (*c* 30BC) on the site of 18th-Dynasty and Ptolemaic structures. It later became a Christian church. The once imposing causeway leads to the unadorned Pylon, which lies slightly askew of the axis of the temple. Both the court and the hypostyle hall have columns with differing floral capitals, clearly suggesting the idea of a garden. The three chambers beyond, of which the last one is the sanctuary, are decorated with reliefs of Augustus in front of the entire Egyptian pantheon. A stairway in the first chamber leads to the roof, with splendid views over Lake Nasser.

The **Kiosk of Qertassi▶**, a Ptolemaic structure with two surviving Hathor-headed columns, came from further south. The **Temple of Bayt el-Wali▶▶** came from near the original site of Kalabsha and is known by its Arabic name, which means House of the Governor. It was hewn out of a rock by the Viceroy of Qush in commemoration of Ramses II's successful military expedition in Nubia. On the southern wall of the court, reliefs show Ramses II leading the campaign against the rebellious Nubians and receiving heaps of gold, ivory and exotic animals as a tribute after the victory. The reliefs have retained a remarkable amount of their original colour.

Sound and Light at Philae
There are two or three shows nightly, but check with the tourist office for the latest schedules. The temple looks spectacular when floodlit at night, but it must have been even more magnificent under a bright full moon, as the 19th-century travellers described it.

When Lake Nasser is high the Kalabsha temple can only be reached by boat

Staring at posterity: Ramses II's statues are positioned to catch the sun's first rays

Getting there
Most tourists fly the 280km to Abu Simbel, which is the easiest way to see the temples. Egypt Air sells an excursion, including return flights, bus transfers and a guided tour, which allows two hours on the site. This is usually sufficient. But be warned that if the outbound flight is delayed, you are still required to check in for the incoming flight at the published time, which can reduce time at the site to as little as 45 minutes. Travelling by air-conditioned bus (four hours each way, book the day before at the bus station) or shared taxi is less comfortable but allows more time on the site and is much cheaper.

▶▶▶ Abu Simbel, Temples of Ra-Harakhte and Hathor — 168A1

Open: 6am–5pm daily. Admission fee, which should include services of a guide.

Abu Simbel lies 280km south of Aswan and 40km from Wadi Halfa and the Sudanese border. Nineteenth-century travellers, having sailed 1,000km up the Nile from Cairo, were awe-struck by the sight of the newly uncovered colossi of Ramses II in front of the temple. Nowadays these giant figures are often first spotted from an aeroplane, dwarfed by the vastness of Lake Nasser, and the speed of organised visits leaves many visitors wondering what all the fuss is about. The two temples were built by Ramses II (19th dynasty), the larger one flanked by four colossi of the pharaoh, the smaller one with colossi of his wife Nefertari. Originally, the rock-cut temples overlooked a bend in the Nile and no doubt succeeded in their main purpose of impressing visitors from the south with Egypt's might and power and scaring off raiding Nubians.

In 1965, as the waters of Lake Nasser threatened to overwhelm them, a huge operation was undertaken by UNESCO to save the temples, which were hand-sawn into 1,050 blocks, to be rebuilt block by block on an artificial hill, 210m from and 61m higher than their original site. The reconstruction is nearly perfect, and every year on 22 February and 22 October (1 day later than originally planned) the dawn rays of the sun reach to the heart of the sanctuary to revive the cult statues, but somehow it feels almost too good to be true.

The Great Temple of Ra-Harakhte▶▶▶ The façade of the temple is dominated by two pairs of seated colossi of Ramses II, each 20m high, hewn into the cliff. Only the faces and torsos are finely carved, the rest of the bodies were crudely finished. The first head on the left is the most beautiful. The façade is crowned by a corvette cornice surmounted with baboons adoring the rising sun, and a niche holds a falcon-headed statue of the sun-god Ra-Harakhte, to whom the temple was dedicated, holding a sceptre and a figure of Maat. The sides of the thrones, near the temple entrance, are decorated with Nile gods symbolically uniting Egypt, and below them, on one side there is a row of African prisoners and on the other a row of Syrians.

Inside is the hypostyle hall with four columns on either side, flanked with 10m-high Osirid statues of Ramses. The walls are decorated with fine reliefs of Ramses' campaigns in Syria and Nubia, played up for propaganda purposes. Facing the back of the temple, to the right are reliefs of the Battle of Qaddesh in 1300BC (which Ramses failed to capture). On the opposite wall (left) he storms a Syrian fortress, while in the centre he kills a Libyan with his lance, returning from the victorious battle with black captives. The eight side-chambers probably stored tribute from Nubia. In the small hall with four pillars are reliefs of Ramses and Nefertari facing the gods. Beyond lies the sanctuary, its four mutilated cult statues once gloriously covered in gold. Outside, beside the temple entrance, a door leads to the innards of the futuristic structure which now supports the temple.

Temple of Hathor►►► Hathor was the wife of the sun god during his day's passage and mother of his rebirth at dawn. The façade here is flanked by six statues of Nefertari and Ramses, their children standing between them. The hypostyle hall contains Hathor-headed columns and reliefs of the beautiful Nefertari watching Ramses killing his enemies, and of the royal couple in front of the gods. The sanctuary contains a ruined cow statue of Hathor and is decorated with reliefs of Nefertari offering incense to Mut and Hathor, and of Ramses adoring himself and his wife.

Sunrise at Abu Simbel
'There was a morning of mornings when we lay opposite the rock-hewn Temple of Abu Simbel ... one felt rather than saw that there were four figures in the pit of gloom below it... The stronger light flooded them red from head to foot, and they became alive – as horridly and tensely yet blindly alive as pinioned men in the death-chair before the current is switched on. One felt that if by a miracle the dawn could be delayed a second longer, they would tear themselves free, and leap forth to heaven knows what sort of vengeance.'
Rudyard Kipling (1913)

Ramses II and his wife Nefertari at the Temple of Hathor, the only time in Egypt that a woman was portrayed at a temple entrance

OASES IN THE WESTERN DESERT

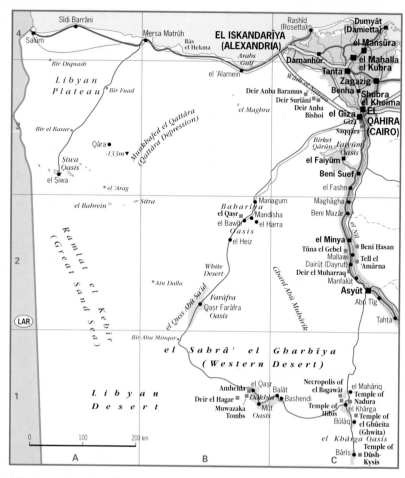

LAR

Life in the oases is still very traditional

A place apart The Western Desert has traditionally been a place apart for Egyptians, the antithesis of the generous Nile Valley. But more and more of them, as well as visitors to their country, are turning to the desert and being surprised by what they find.

The Western Desert Ancient Egyptians believed that Seth, the brother and murderer of Osiris, ruled the desert. Not surprisingly for a king-killer, he was associated with chaos and the desert was seen as a place to avoid. But they couldn't ignore it. It was too big for that – it is the eastern edge of the Sahara, the largest desert on earth. Stretching from the Nile to the Fezzan in Libya, from the Mediterranean coast to Kordofan in central Sudan, the Western Desert covers nearly 3 million sq km.

Islands of the Blest Herodotus, who visited several of the oases, called them the Islands of the Blest. But rather

OASES IN THE WESTERN DESERT

In spite of the town's rapid development, many houses in el-Kharga are still built of mud

Further reading
To get the most out of a desert trip, look out for the following books:
Ralph Bagnold, *Libyan Sands* (Bristol, 1935); Ahmed Fakhry, *The Oases of Egypt: Siwa Oasis* (Cairo, 1973) and *Bahriyah and Farafra Oases* (Cairo 1974); and Cassandra Vivian, *Islands of the Blest: a Guide to the Oases and Western Desert of Egypt* (Cairo, 1990) with excellent maps.

A landscape to get lost in: here, unlike the Eastern Desert, there is plenty of sand

than standing out like islands above the sea of sand, Egypt's oases are sunk below them in geological depressions. It is these depressions that have created the oases: being at or below sea level, they allow easy access to underground water. When, in prehistory, the climate became drier, people of the area congregated around these watering holes to survive and began to develop the first communities.

Early writers Apart from the fabled Siwan Manuscript, the inhabitants of the desert have left few records and most of what is known about the history of their communities comes from the accounts of travellers. Nothing is recorded of the visit of Hercules, but Herodotus in 450BC and the historians following Alexander in 331BC all left detailed accounts, and early Arab writers, following the pilgrims' routes, contributed essential information. Although Europeans had been to the more accessible oases, it wasn't until the 19th century that European explorers really began to penetrate the Western Desert. Exploration continues now, for the desert has yet to reveal the answers to the many questions it poses.

Romance of the Desert The desert has a great romantic appeal. It isn't just the image of the Bedouin shaped by Hollywood and Rudolph Valentino. The stories of lost oases, hidden treasure, impossible journeys, brave deeds and honourable behaviour, increasingly rare elsewhere, are still credible in the desert. The enormity of the place and its wilderness brings out an aura of romance, whether you are lying on your back watching the brilliant

night sky in the White Desert outside Farafra Oasis, or walking into the Great Sand Sea outside Siwa, with nothing but sand to be seen in all directions, the wind blowing away traces of your passage. It was partly because it was possible to get away from it all that religious hermits began the habit of monasticism in the desert; the remoteness of Wadi Natrun and the monasteries of the Eastern Desert seemed to bring supplicants closer to God.

The New Valley The New Valley is the largest governorate in Egypt and includes the oases of Kharga, Dakhla and Farafra. Some years ago the area was earmarked for considerable development in the belief that its many industries, from tourism to farming and phosphate mining, would support immigrant workers from the Nile Valley. This has been unsuccessful as a way of reducing the population of the Nile Valley, but it has led to improved communication and transport between Kharga and Asyut.

Hope for the future As their cities become overpopulated and the ban on building on agricultural land stops some development, Egyptians are looking to the desert for solutions to some of their problems. The Western Desert oases are seeing an increasing number of immigrants from the Nile Valley, but that is nothing compared to some of the other schemes that are being discussed by Egyptian planners. Among the most daring is the exploitation of subterranean water resources around Gebel Uwaynat to support a community in the heart of the desert where the Sudanese, Libyan and Egyptian borders meet.

Local customs
People in the oases are more conservative than in the rest of Egypt. Their lives and customs, strongly influenced by religion and their particular social code, have made the oases safe places, where crime is rare. Visitors are also expected to observe local custom and should wear decent, modest clothes. Women especially should try to keep most of their bodies covered. Locals consider it strange when a woman wanders off on her own in the gardens. One of the attractions of the oases is bathing in the hot springs, but while men can wear a bathing suit, women should bathe in a dress.

195

Making pots the traditional way

Drive The Great Desert Circuit

Above: volcanic stones give the desert its black tones

The Western Desert is still a place of mysteries and legends and the relatively new 1,000km road, connecting Cairo with Asyut via the four oases, offers one of the most exciting drives in Egypt. See the map on page 192.

A four-wheel drive is recommended, but if you stick to the main road a normal car will do. It is probably wise to start in Cairo and, if circumstances allow it (see page 126), to end in Asyut. The alternative is to fly back from Kharga, which is expensive, or return the same long way you came.

The drive starts behind the Pyramids of Giza and follows the rail-

way line used for transporting iron to Helwan. Once past the new 6th-of-October City, there is nothing but desert and a few rest-houses half-way. After 310km the road enters **Managum**, the checkpoint for Bahariya oasis, and continues on to Bahariya's capital, **el-Bawiti** (see page 197). Not long after el-Bawiti you enter the **Black Desert**, so-called because the desert is covered with black stones. After 47km you pass through **el-Hayyiz (el-Heiz)**, with several villages and a ruined Roman camp.

After 60km and a signpost for Ain Della, you enter the surreal landscape of the **White Desert▶▶▶**, and after another 20km, **Farafra** (see page 198) comes into sight. The 310km Farafra–Dakhla road, which was never finished, goes through flat sandy desert until **Abu Minqar**, a major checkpoint only 100km from the Libyan border, where the escarpment bordering the Dakhla oasis joins you to the right. Beyond **Dakhla** (see pages 198–9) the 197km road to **el-Kharga** (see page 199) is often threatened by moving sand dunes. The last 227km stretch to **Asyut** offers some of the most spectacular scenery in Egypt, with beautiful mountains and *wadis* (dry gullies), sand dunes and several Roman forts.

A wind-sculpture in the White Desert

Desert animals
Usually the only wild creatures encountered by visitors to the Western Desert are ants, beetles, mosquitoes, flies, fleas, scorpions and, if they are lucky, a herd of gazelle. But happily there are many more creatures adapted to the hard desert life and they include cheetahs, oryx, hyenas, Barbary sheep, cats and fennec foxes, as well as smaller animals like rats, hedgehogs, hares and weasels. There are several species or varieties of snakes which hide in the sand dunes. Kharga and Dakhla are a stopover for several migrating birds and throughout the desert are birds of prey like vultures and hawks.

▶▶▶ **Bahariya Oasis**   *192B2*

Beyond the checkpoint at Managum, as the road descends, there are spectacular views over the oasis, covering more than 2,000 sq km. Most of Bahariya's 24,000 inhabitants live in the capital **el-Bawiti▶**, which has merged with the old capital **el-Qasr▶▶**. El-Qasr, with picturesque houses and narrow streets, was built on the site of the ancient village of Qasr. Most of the monuments lie unexcavated under the houses. Of the excavated sites, several were looted or vandalised and may be closed for restoration. The most impressive building was the Roman Triumphal Arch until its stone was reused to build houses around it in the mid-19th century. Qarat Qasr Salim has two burial chambers with blackened murals and at Qarat el-Faragi (Hill of the Chicken Merchant) is a cemetery with mummies of ibises, falcons and armadillos.

A **Temple of Bes▶** from the Late Period was recently discovered in the middle of el-Qasr. The ancient Qasr extended 3km further north to Ain el-Muftillah, where in Gara, four unusual 26th-Dynasty chapels were found and re-covered with sand for preservation. From the dune beside the chapels there is a wonderful panorama over Bahariya, particularly at sunset.

The hot springs in towns like Ain Bishmu and Ain Bardir, surrounded by the gardens they irrigate, may look idyllic but visitors are warned against bathing here. Tour operators organise trips to the secluded springs of Bir Mattar, cool and refreshing, and Bir el-Ghaba. To the north of el-Bawiti on the road to el-Harra is the village of el-Agouz, founded by families who were banned from Siwa because of their women's loose morals. A little further, Mandisha, set in palm groves, is one of the oldest and most beautiful villages. About 5km further is Qaseir Muharib with impressive ruins of a Roman Christian village, where local women still come to seek the help of ancient gods in becoming pregnant.

Mr Kadafi, the barber of Bahariya, shows his skill

►► Farafra Oasis
192B2

Farafra, the most isolated and also the most beautiful of the oases, has only one inhabited village, Qasr Farafra. Many houses are decorated by a local artist, Badr, who has opened a small museum in a wonderful mud-brick house he built himself. Until the 1950s, every family had their own room to shelter in the fortress of Farafra and it is still partly inhabited. Farafra has no ancient monuments but a walk in its beautiful gardens and shady palm groves makes up for that. Local guides can lead you to Ain Dalla (Spring of Shade), 80km to the north of Farafra and the last water hole before the Great Sand Sea. Its refreshing clear water has saved many desert travellers from dying of thirst. However, the main attraction in the area is undoubtedly the magnificent **White Desert►►►**, with fantastic chalk sculptures eroded by the wind, which change with the light from white to gold to deep purple at sunset. Many visitors camp here to see the rock formations by night, when they seem surreal.

►►► Dakhla Oasis
192B1

Driving in from the desert, visitors see the oasis of Dakhla as a feast of colours, with vibrant green fields, red earth and a pink-coloured escarpment. During the New Kingdom, Mut was the capital of Dakhla, as it is again today. The most interesting sites are on the outskirts of the oasis, but Mut is a good base with simple accommodation. Its only sights are the **Museum of the Inheritance►** (*for visits call the tourist office, tel: 407 or the culture office, tel: 311; admission fee*), arranged as a traditional Islamic home, and the hot springs near the Gumhuriay Rest House, recommended for colds, rheumatism and skin diseases.

El-Qasr►►, about 30km west from Mut, is the medieval capital of Dakhla built over a Roman settlement.

Above and below: the mud-brick centre of el-Qasr, Dakhla's medieval capital

An Ayyubid mosque, a *madrasa* (theological school) and many four-storey houses have survived and it is a delight to walk around. The 1st- and 2nd-century AD **Muwazaka Tombs►►**, 5km away, are finely decorated. About 8km further, **Deir el-Hagar►**, a Roman temple dedicated to the Theban Triad, stands in the desert. **Amheida►►**, 3.5km from el-Qasr, has Dakhla's most important ruins, including a temple, cemeteries and interesting Roman wall paintings in the central building. Balat, 35km east of Mut, thrived on trade with Qush and **Bashendi►**, which has 1st-century BC tombs and good carpet-weaving.

Outposts of empire: a Roman fort at the el-Kharga Oasis

►► el-Kharga
192C1

After the peace and quiet of the desert and the other oases, the modern town of el-Kharga appears like a nightmare, its 35,000 inhabitants living in concrete blocks that sprawl into the desert. But the town makes a good base for exploring some fine pharaonic and Christian ruins, though it isn't a pleasant place to walk around. The opening of Kharga Museum has been delayed since its collection of pharaonic and Islamic antiquities was looted in 1989. The only old mud-brick houses, painted in blue and soft orange, are found in Darb el-Sandadiya, the area around the *souk* (marketplace).

North of the city are the ruined Ptolemaic Temple of Nadura and, further down the road at Hibis, surrounded by palm trees, the **Temple of Amun►**, one of the rare Persian monuments (6th century BC) to have survived in Egypt. It is always open and admission is free. Beyond, in the **Necropolis of el-Bagawat►** (*open 8–5 daily; admission fee*), Christians were buried in chapels with fine murals (3rd–7th centuries).

South of el-Kharga, the road to Baris follows the slave route which until 1884 crossed the desert from Darfur in the Sudan to Asyut; el-Kharga was the last stop en route. On the way is the 27th-Dynasty Temple of el-Ghwita and a ruined Temple of Amenebis. To the south of Baris, the second largest town, are the Roman Temple of Dush and the ruins of the ancient town of Kysis.

The Great Sand Sea
The Great Sand Sea is the biggest and most dangerous dune field in the world. It runs from the southwest of Siwa oasis to the west of Farafra and Dakhla oases, and goes 800km south to the Gilf Kebir, with dunes reaching heights of 150m. Nothing lives here, and it is one of the last unexplored areas in the world. The few expeditions to come this way have found big chunks of green glass, some weighing as much as seven kilos, all over the area; although the glass was worked by prehistoric man, it isn't manmade and is thought to have been produced by a natural chemical reaction.

OASES IN THE WESTERN DESERT

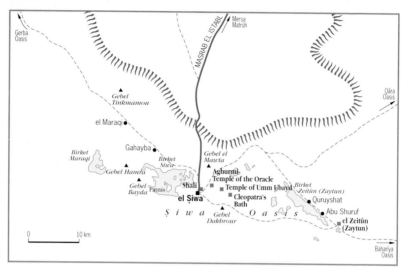

Being unable to live outside the walls of the Shali, Siwans built upwards as the community grew, until rains started to dissolve their mud-brick houses

A slip of the tongue
'Some say, Ammon's prophet being desirous to address him [Alexander] in an obliging manner in Greek, intended to say, 'O Paidion', which signifies 'My Son'. But in his barbarous pronunciation, he made the word end with an 's' instead of an 'n' and so said: 'O Pai Dios', which signifies 'O Son of Jupiter'. Alexander, they add, 'was delighted with the mistake and from that error was circulated a report that the god Jupiter himself had called him his son.'
Plutarch, quoted in Ahmed Fakhry's *Siwa Oasis* (Cairo, 1973)

▶▶▶ Siwa Oasis
192A3

The road from Mersa Matruh (see page 222) to Siwa follows the ancient caravan route; its name, Masrab el-Istabl, translates as 'the Course of the Stable'. Alexander the Great took eight days to cover the 300km in 331BC with a handful of companions. The Egyptian King Abbas II, with 300 camels, herds of other animals and supplies of water, took seven days in 1907. But after King Fuad

visited Siwa in 1928, a road was laid and the journey can now be done in under four hours.

Dominated by the ruins of its past, Siwa Town is undergoing rapid change. A few years ago the main streets were covered in sand, cars were rare, and most people lived in traditional Siwan houses. When Egyptian TV arrived in the 1980s, as many as 1,000 television sets were immediately ordered and in cafés, television rather than conversation is becoming the main attraction at night. The new town, where concrete houses are replacing mud-brick houses, is still a quiet and sleepy place where some old traditions are obviously being maintained: women are most commonly seen hidden beneath their *milayah* (wrap) in the back of a donkey cart.

Founded, according to the Siwan Manuscript, in AD1203, Shali►► was originally surrounded by high walls to counter Bedouin attacks. Siwans, forbidden to build outside these walls, were obliged to build extra floors on their houses to accommodate a growing population. The shortage of space was further exacerbated by the need to bring the animals in each night. In 1820 Siwa was conquered by Egyptian troops who made the area safe enough for the town council to permit building outside the walls. As at Aghurmi, Siwans built using the local *karshif* (mud), strong enough to support eight storeys, but with a high salt content that dissolved in the occasional, heavy rains, which accounts for the Shali's present, melted appearance. The mosque is the best-maintained building; the *muezzin* (prayer caller) here sometimes calls the faithful to prayer using his own, unamplified voice.

Although the centre of the Shali has been abandoned, some houses on the edge of the old town are still habitable

Siwan culture
Siwans are unlike the people of the other oases. Descended from Berbers, intermarried with Arabs and Negroes, they speak their own dialect of Berber although they are obliged to speak Arabic for official matters. They had interesting traditions regarding sex: young workers, known as *zaggalah*, were forbidden to marry and also forbidden to live inside the town, to keep them away from women; homosexuality became accepted among them. To further safeguard their women, who continue to be completely covered when they leave their houses, Siwan men ensured that animals of different sexes were also segregated.

Siwan manuscript
The history of Siwa is recorded in the Siwan Manuscript, a document based on oral traditions that date back to the mid-7th century AD. Listing blood lines, customs, history and songs, the manuscript is a complete record of Siwan culture up to 1960, when the record was discontinued.

The bright spot.
'It is no longer the romantic medieval fortress which still existed up to the beginning of this century. The place is also very different from the town of Siwa which I had known 20 years ago. But in spite of all the changes which have taken place, it is still one of the most romantic and interesting of places – not only in our deserts, but in all of Egypt. It will always be a bright spot in the memory of the visitor.'
Ahmed Fakhry, *Siwa Oasis* (Cairo, 1973/1982)

Shali precautions
Take care when walking in the Shali. Although many surfaces are safe, great damage was caused by a two-day storm in 1982 and occasionally a floor or path will sound hollow underfoot – it will be, and may be about to fall.

Gebel el-Mawta► Just outside the town is the Hill of the Dead, its harsh outline sculpted by the wind and riddled with tombs from the 26th Dynasty to the Graeco-Roman period. Ptolemaic corpses were prepared in the same way as mummies in the Nile Valley which, as author Ahmed Fakhry has pointed out, suggests the oasis was completely Egyptianised at that time. Four tombs are open, the Tomb of Si-Amun being the most important. Its decoration, particularly images of the owner and his family, and of the goddess Nut in front of a sycamore tree, shows Greek influences. Some 20m away, the north-facing Tomb of Mesu-Isis shows signs of having been reused in the Roman period. The Ptolemaic Tomb of the Crocodile, with one decorated chamber, takes its name from a painting of a crocodile, further proof that Siwans were in touch with el-Faiyum, where the crocodile god Sobek had his centre, from an early date. These three tombs were discovered in 1940, when Siwans hid on the hill to escape Italian bombers. The Tomb of Niperpathot, which was already uncovered, is largely ruined.

About 4km (a 20-minute walk) from Siwa Town lies the fortified settlement of **Aghurmi►►**, surrounded by palm trees. The door to the main gate is off its hinges. A path leads to the inner court, still inhabited in the early 20th century. The restored mosque has excellent views from its minaret. Below, in the court, several holes serve as reminders of the legend that there is treasure buried beneath the town. The houses are even more ruined than those in the Shali. At the back of the town, raised on the rock of Aghurmi, lies the Temple of the Oracle.

It isn't often that you can locate the exact spot on which an event took place more than 2,000 years ago, but you can at the **Temple of the Oracle►►►** at Aghurmi. The building dates from the reign of King Amasis (26th Dynasty) who is mentioned in the sanctuary. The temple, dedicated to Amun-Ra, is well preserved, although the rock on which it is built is cracking. Only the sanctuary has decorations. It was here in 331BC that Alexander the Great, hidden from the eyes of the priests and his companions, approached one of the ancient world's most revered oracles. Alexander never repeated what he heard. He had promised to tell his mother the answers he received from the oracle when he returned to Macedonia, but he died before he saw her. Whatever was said, from then on Alexander claimed descent from Amun.

Also known as the Spring of the Sun, **Cleopatra's Bath►►** is the most famous of Siwa's many springs. Cleopatra's visit is a matter of legend, but Herodotus was there, fascinated by its apparent bubbling at night, which he took to be due to a warming of the water after dark. Presumably, Alexander the Great also refreshed himself here after his desert journey. It is still a popular place for men of the oasis and visitors to swim, but the nearby road has made it too public a place for women to feel at ease.

Six kilometres from Siwa Town, the road runs through palm groves until it opens on to salt flats and **Birkat Siwa (Siwa Lake)**. Foreigners started coming in large numbers to swim more privately in the spring on Fatnis Island, a hop away from the shore, but this has recently become just as popular with local males. The lake itself, backed by vast eroded rocks on the far side, is worth the journey.

Through the palm groves

Siwan dates; famous all over Egypt

This walk (3–4 hours) from Siwa Town through the beautiful groves and gardens of the oasis visits Siwa's original settlement and famous temples. See the map on page 200.

As you leave Siwa Town past the marketplace, houses quickly give way to gardens. The oasis is famous for its fruit trees, some 25,000 olive trees and an estimated quarter of a million palms. Siwan custom allows anyone to eat dates from the trees, but it is an offence to carry them away.

A couple of miles on, the road forks. The right-hand path, through eucalyptus trees, leads to **Gebel el-Dakhrour**▶▶, known in Siwan as Daran Breek. There are three hills close together, believed to be the site of lapis and emerald mines, referred to by Arab writers. A large festival is held here on the full moon of October. The hill allows excellent views of the oasis.

Returning to the fork, take the other path to follow the loop around the oasis, following a sign (occasionally obscured) to **Cleopatra's Bath** (see page 202). Continue along the road to the Temple of Amun, also known as the **Temple of Umm Ubayd**▶. It was standing in the early 19th century, but an earthquake in 1811 and, more disastrously, a governor in need of building material in 1896 have left it a sad ruin. It still deserves a visit before you reach the **Temple of the Oracle**▶▶▶, to which it was said to be connected by an underground passage.

Continue along the road to the new village of **Aghurmi**. At the crossroads, the right-hand turn leads to the abandoned village of Zaytun (Zeitan) and to the Darb Siwa, the road to Bahariya and Cairo. The left-hand road leads back to Siwa Town, passing **Ain Tamousi**▶▶, where Siwan brides used to bathe on the eve of their wedding, and a garden where the German general Rommel is said to have stopped for tea.

OASES IN THE WESTERN DESERT

▶▶▶   **Wadi el-Natrun**   192C3

The valley of Wadi el-Natrun, lying off the desert road from Cairo to Alexandria, takes its name from the deposits of natron salts, used in Pharaonic times for embalming mummies and still mined today. Monasticism began in the Eastern Desert (see pages 236 and 238–9), but the rules were developed in Wadi el-Natrun and it is from here that Coptic popes have been chosen for the last 1,500 years. The current Pope Shenuda III, enthroned in 1971, was a monk at Deir el-Suryani and lived for several years as a hermit in desert caves. He has done much to revive monasticism and encourage a greater involvement of the monks in the Coptic community. Nineteenth-century visitors described the monks as dirty, anti-intellectual, even ignorant, but today many monks are highly educated and speak several languages.

The four monasteries in Wadi el-Natrun follow a similar plan. Surrounded by heavy walls, originally without an entrance as visitors and provisions were winched up over them, they have a keep where monks hid during the frequent Bedouin attacks in the Middle Ages. There are several churches, traditionally divided into three sections: the *haikal* (sanctuary) with the altar hidden behind a screen, the choir and the nave. The monasteries are now easily accessible and admission is free. Visitors are welcomed with a chat and a cup of tea, for which the monks never accept money, although a donation in the offering box is much appreciated.

Deir Anba Bishoi▶▶ (*open: daily 8–5, 6 in summer*) This monastery with 150 monks and 22 hermits receives the most Coptic pilgrims, and it is still expanding. St Bishoi (320–407AD) was one of the first monks in Wadi el-Natrun, arriving at the age of 20. As an old man Bishoi had a vision of Christ, whose feet he washed and who permitted him to drink the hallowed water. He was buried in the Church of Anba Bishoi (9th century AD) together with his friend Paul of Tamweh, who was canonised after attempting suicide seven times. Apparently Bishoi's body is as well preserved as on the day he died and from time to time he stretches out his arm to the believers. Pope Shenuda lived in the domed building away from the entrance during his exile (1981–5), which was ordered by President Sadat. He still returns here on retreat.

Deir el-Suryani▶▶ (*open: daily 9–3, 5 in summer*) The monastery was founded (6th century AD) by disgruntled monks from Deir Anba Bishoi. After the monks were persuaded to return to Deir Anba Bishoi, their new monastery was taken over by Syrian monks. The 10th-century Church of el-Adhra (the Virgin) has a magnificent inlaid Door of Prophecies and striking frescoes in the semi-domes of the choir. St Bishoi used to pray for days in his cave, which is now part of the church, his hair attached to the ceiling to keep himself upright. In 1837 Lord Curzon discovered several ancient manuscripts in the keep, which are now in the British Museum.

A new icon in 6th-century Deir el-Suryani

Monks, Deir el-Suryani

Deir Anba Baramus▶▶ (*open: daily 9–5, 6 in summer*) is the most remote and oldest monastery in Wadi el-Natrun. Baramus is Coptic for 'two Romans', as the monastery is ascribed to two young sons of the emperor Valentine, buried here after they died from excessive fasting. Recent restorations in the 9th-century Church of el-Adhra have revealed medieval frescoes. About 2km out in the desert is the Cave of Pope Kyrillos VI, Shenuda's predecessor, which has become a shrine.

Deir Abu Maqar is closed to visitors, unless you have a letter of introduction from the Coptic patriarchate in Cairo. It was founded by St Makarius, who died in 390 after he had spent 60 years as a hermit in the desert. In 1978 the monks claimed to have the head of John the Baptist, an assertion also made by Aleppo, Damascus and Venice.

About the monasteries
The monasteries are open daily, except during the many fasting periods. Visiting hours vary. To find out if and when the monasteries are open, contact the Coptic patriarchate, next to the Cathedral of St Mark, 222 Sharia Ramses, Abbaseya, Cairo, tel: (02) 828513 or 825806. Women visitors are now welcome.

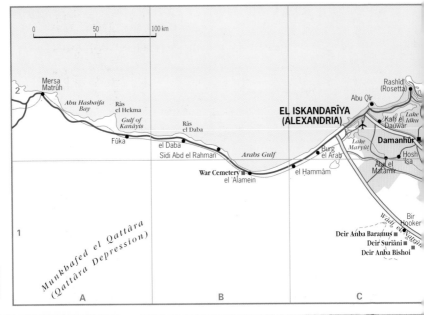

Above: the Alexandria Museum of Antiquities contains many precious exhibits
Right: the corniche at Alexandria

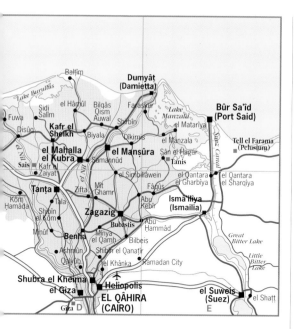

ALEXANDRIA AND THE DELTA

A natural barrier After running as a single thread of water from Khartoum to Cairo, the Nile fans out into several branches and creates the luscious Delta, separating Cairo and the Nile Valley from the north coast. The Delta lacks the archaeological splendours of the Nile Valley, but visitors who do no more than pass through on their way to the north coast are missing some beautiful and fascinating country.

The north coast Egypt's Mediterranean coastline stretches 1,181km from the Israeli to the Libyan borders, a sparkling line of sand, Nile silt and sea. Although much of the coast east of Alexandria (el-Iskandariya) is either poorly served by roads and facilities, or overlooked by industry, the old ports of Rosetta and Damietta, with their distinctive Ottoman architecture, are worth travelling to see. Some of Egypt's finest beaches lie to the west of Alexandria, but as the coastline becomes filled with low-cost holiday resorts for middle-class Egyptians, most visitors heading north of Cairo are on their way to Alexandria or, like Alexander the Great, heading west to the oasis of Siwa.

Legendary Alexandria Few cities in the world lean so heavily upon legend as Alexandria. At first sight Egypt's second-largest city, with a population of over 4 million, appears to offer nothing but illusion and disillusion. Where is Alexander's city? Where is the city of the Pharos and Library, as famous for its loving as for its learning in the ancient world? Where is the more recent city conjured out of words by four great writers in the 20th century? The pictures are all distorted and your first sight, whether you approach from the sea or across the marshes to the south, is likely to be of industrial chimneys and too much concrete. It is easy to leave thinking that the magical city lives on only in the work of Cavafy, Forster, Durrell and

The grand sweep of Alexandria's corniche

Mahfouz. But stay awhile and slowly those other cities will reveal themselves, and you might hear what Cavafy called 'the exquisite music of that strange procession', because there *are* remains from almost all of the city's many epochs. To get the most out of the city, follow Ibn Duqmaq's advice and make that pilgrimage: walk around it and piece the pictures back together.

A great start When Alexander the Great conquered Egypt in 332BC, he needed a capital to serve as a bridge between the Mediterranean and the Nile. Rhakotis, a fishing village with a natural double bay, offered the ideal solution: according to legend, Alexander himself marked the city's boundaries before leaving for Siwa. Alexander never saw the city, but after his death in 325BC, his body was sent to Alexandria by the priests of Memphis with the warning: 'Do not settle him here, but at the city he built at Rhakotis. For wherever his body must lie, that city will be uneasy, disturbed by wars and battles.' But the warning was not heeded and one of those disturbances, in the 4th century AD, supposedly destroyed Alexander's

The intricate dome of the Abu el-Abbas Mosque

Getting around
Guided tours can be arranged from Cairo or at the reception of most Alexandrian hotels. Otherwise, one of the most pleasant ways of getting around the city is by calèche, an old horse-drawn carriage. Used by tourists in the centre of town, they are also an essential means of transport for people all over Egypt who need a cheap local taxi. Drivers and horses come in various states of fitness. Be prepared to haggle hard for the price, making it clear what you want to see and how long you intend to spend.

tomb and the rest of his city. Legends of that 'lost city' within the city have left Alexandria with a haunting sense of loss. While it may no longer deserve the epithet 'the pearl of the Mediterranean', it is still glistening.

The modern city When the American Civil War in the 1860s created a worldwide cotton shortage, Alexandria's traders monopolised the market and the city rose to prominence among the Levantine ports. The opening of new ports along the Suez Canal after 1869 took some of that business away, but Alexandria maintained its wealth and, as the summer capital for Egypt's rulers, also its social importance. The current president still prefers to spend his summers by the sea, but the city has changed. Most of the Italians, British and Greeks have gone and Alexandria's traders are now mostly Egyptian. But in its museum, its ruined temple to the Mediterranean god Serapis, the remains of the Pharos – wonder of the ancient world – and most recently in its Levantine cafés, it is still possible to trace the development of the inspiration that came from across the water in Europe.

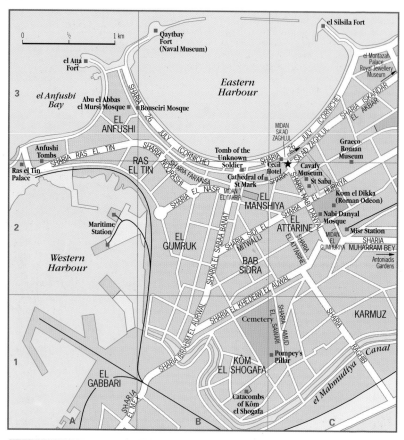

Map legend and labels:

Scale: 0 — ½ — 1 km

Qaytbay Fort (Naval Museum)
el Silsila Fort
el Atta Fort
el Montazah Palace Royal Jewellery Museum
el Anfushi Bay
Eastern Harbour
Abu el Abbas el Mursi Mosque
Bouseiri Mosque
EL ANFUSHI
SHARIA 26 JULY (CORNICHE)
SHARIA ISKANDAR EL AKBAR
SHARIA 26 JULY (CORNICHE)
Anfushi Tombs
SHARIA RAS EL TIN
RAS EL TIN
SHARIA MOGRESBI
SHARIA FARANSA
Tomb of the Unknown Soldier
MIDAN SA'AD ZAGHLUL
SA'AD ZAGHLUL
Gracco-Roman Museum
Ras el Tin Palace
Cecil Hotel
Cavafy Museum
St Saba
Cathedral of St Mark
SHARIA EL NASR
MIDAN EL TAHRIR
EL MANSHIYA
Kom el Dikka (Roman Odeon)
SHARIA NABI DANYAL
SHARIA HURRIYA
Maritime Station
EL GUMRUK
SHARIA EL SABAA BANAT
SHARIA SIDI EL MITWALLI
EL ATTARINE
Nabi Danyal Mosque
Misr Station
MIDAN EL GUMHURIYA
SHARIA MUHARRAM BEY
Western Harbour
BAB SIDRA
EL ATTARINE
Antoniadis Gardens
210
KARMUZ
SHARIA EL KHEDEIWI EL AWWAL
Cemetery
SHARIA AMUD EL SAWARI
SHARIA RAGHIB
EL GABBARI
SHARIA IBRAHIM EL AURYAL
KÔM EL SHOGAFA
Pompey's Pillar
el Mahmudiya Canal
SHARIA EL MEX
Catacombs of Kôm el Shogafa
A   B   C

► **el-Anfushi**   210A3

El-Anfushi is a fascinating old quarter at the centre of the city. Originally part of the island of Pharos, it was connected to the mainland by the Heptastadion dike. Over the centuries the dike broadened into a neck of land, which later housed the Turkish town, an interesting place to walk.

Five tombs, their occupants unknown, comprise the **Anfushi Tombs►** (*Sharia Ras el-Tin; admission fee*). The walls are painted to imitate marble and alabaster, and date from the 3rd century BC. Tomb No 2 has paintings of deities, a Greek inscription and two sketches of boats very much like the present-day *felucca* (sailing boat). Rising groundwater is threatening the tombs.

Just beyond the tombs, the 19th-century Ras el-Tin Palace was originally Muhammad Ali's summer residence. It was from here that King Farouk left Egypt after abdicating (26 July 1956). The palace is now used to house visiting dignitaries and is closed to visitors.

► **Antoniadis Gardens**   210C2

Near Nuzha Gardens. Open: daily 8–4. Admission fee.
Peaceful formal gardens surround the 19th-century villa of the Greek philanthropist, Sir John Antoniadis. The villa, now another government guest residence, is officially

closed to the public, but the man selling Coke outside will sometimes get you in after 2pm. The gardens are understandably popular for an afternoon stroll, away from the noise of the city. Across the neighbouring Nuzha Gardens is the zoo, less interesting than the one in Cairo.

►► Cavafy Museum   192C2

4 Sharia Sharm el-Sheikh. Open: Tuesday–Sunday, 10–3. Constantine Cavafy's furniture and books, formerly housed in the Greek Consulate, have been returned to the apartment where he lived for 25 years until his death in 1933. Until recently it was a run-down pension; now sketches and photographs of Cavafy stare from the walls of the bedroom, salon and three well-stocked reading rooms. If there is any of his spirit in the apartment, it is in the pictures, the books and the view over the city where he lived and the hospital where he died of cancer (see Walk in Literary Alexandria, pages 216–17).

Fishy business
In spite of wildlife preservation agreements, baskets of turtles are sometimes on sale in el-Anfushi's fish market – the meat is sold to eat, shells for ashtrays and turtle blood as an aphrodisiac.

The older parts of Alexandria, like Anfushi, are full of character and crumbling buildings

211

Mummification survived the advent of Christianity (Graeco-Roman Museum)

Museum guide
'...the visitor who "goes through" it will find afterwards that it has gone through him... He should not visit the collection until he has learned or imagined something about the ancient city, and he should visit certain definite objects, and then come away – He may then find that a scrap of the past has come alive.'
E M Forster, *Alexandria: a History and a Guide* (1922)

Masonry displayed in the museum's garden

Sharia el-Mathaf, off Sharia el-Hurriya. Admission fee.

If there is time to see just one thing in Alexandria, head for this museum, which covers an intriguing period too often overlooked in Egypt's long history. Most of its exhibits have come from Alexandria, the Delta and from al-Fayoum. On-going reorganisation might result in room numbers being changed, but at the moment, most exhibits are displayed chronologically, starting, to the left off the entrance hall, with Room 6. It contains two magnificent Roman busts – one in marble, the other in sycamore – of Serapis, the god of Alexandria who was a hybrid of Dionysos and Osiris, intended to unite the Greek and Egyptian cults. Along with the gigantic 2nd-century AD sculpture of the Apis bull, they came from the Serapeum, destroyed in 4th-century riots.

The Ptolemies maintained the cult of the Pharaonic crocodile god Sobek. Room 9 contains the remains of a Sobek chapel from el-Faiyum, including the extraordinary mummified crocodile on a bier.

Rooms 12–17, mostly devoted to sculpture, include an imposing bust of Marcus Aurelius; marble heads of Alexander (Room 12) and of Roman emperors including Julius Caesar, Augustus and Hadrian (Rooms 13–14); some fine Greek torsos (Room 16a); and the largest known statue from a single block of porphyry, which some believe to be Diocletian (Room 17).

The museum's most pleasing collections are the encaustic paintings – lifelike portraits painted on to mummy cases (Rooms 7 and 10) – and terracotta *Tanagra* figurines (Room 18a), 4th–2nd century BC. Found in the tombs of children and young women, these figurines were intended as a celebration of youth and beauty and give a fascinating insight into fashion and hairstyles of the period – strangely sad to see in all their realism.

Christian antiquities (Rooms 1–5) include an unusual mummy with a black cross in his neck (Room 1) and some beautiful textiles (Room 4), for which the Copts were renowned. When you need some air, stroll around the stone sarcophagi and architectural fragments in the garden.

Ancient Alexandria

■ **The Egyptian government has started building another Alexandrian Library, but you don't have to wait until it is finished to rediscover Alexander's city. If you know what to look for, you'll see fascinating traces all around you.....■**

The ground plan Alexander's city was bisected by two principal streets: Canopic Street and the Street of the Soma. With their long vistas and cooling breezes, they survive in the modern city as Sharia el-Hurriya and Sharia Nabi Danyal. The entrance to the sparkling western harbour is also as it was, although the 15th-century sultan, Qaytbay, built his fairy-tale fort over the ruins of the ancient lighthouse and the Egyptian navy occupies the site of the Temple of Isis near the eastern point.

The palace area Stop in front of the Cecil Hotel, facing out to sea, and you are standing near the ancient palace area. Ptolemy, Caesar and Cleopatra were here before you. The Caesareum – Cleopatra's gift of a temple for Mark Antony – was directly beneath you. Until the 19th century, two obelisks brought from Heliopolis marked the site of the temple; they now grace New York's Central Park and London's Victoria Embankment.

Alexandria's glory Alexandria's harbour bridged the gap between Egypt and Greece, but the Mouseion was an

Eratosthenes
Eratosthenes was born in Cyrene in 276BC. He believed that the earth was round, and measured its circumference by measuring the sun's shadow at midday on midsummer's day in Alexandria. Knowing that in Aswan, on the same longitude, the midsummer sun cast no shadow at all, he calculated that the distance between the two was 1/50th of a complete circle. Estimating Alexandria to Aswan as 500 miles, he calculated the world's circumference as 25,000 miles and its diameter 7,850 miles, only 50 miles out.

213

essential link between the knowledge of the ancient and medieval worlds. The Mouseion stood at the centre of the city, probably near the crossing of those two main streets; the ancient pillars adorning the Abd el-Razzaq Mosque, across from the Nabi Danyal Mosque, may have originally stood in the Mouseion. Within its complex of libraries, parks and halls dedicated to the development of all knowledge, Homer was edited, Eratosthenes measured the earth's circumference, our 'Julian' calendar was devised, sciences from mathematics to medicine were developed and the city's reputation was assured.

Street stalls on Sharia Nabi Danyal, with pillars decorating the Abd el-Razzaq Mosque that came from the ancient Mouseion

ALEXANDRIA AND THE DELTA

Forgotten grandeur
The Kom el-Dikka odeon is
Egypt's only surviving
Graeco-Roman theatre, but
according to the Arab general Amr Ibn al-'As, there
used to be more. In AD642,
he wrote to the caliph,
Omar: 'I have taken a city
of which I can only say
that it contains 4,000
palaces, 4,000 baths, 400
theatres, 1,200 greengro-
cers and 40,000 Jews.

▶▶▶ Kom el-Dikka (Roman Odeon)   210C2

*Sharia Abd el-Muneim, Misr Station. Open: 9–4, closed
Fridays 11:30–1:30. Admission fee.*

When you walk down into the odeon at Kom el-Dikka you
are walking through layers of the city's history. Polish
archaeologists in the 1960s removed the ruins of a late
18th-century fort, several centuries of Muslim graves and
later Roman remains to uncover what you see now. The
small theatre, dating from the 2nd century AD, underwent
several alterations in antiquity to become this elegant,
covered auditorium for musical performances. The well-
preserved monochrome mosaic flooring in the vestibule
originally covered the entire area. A Graeco-Roman street
runs past the odeon and disappears beneath the hill.

▶▶▶ Kom el-Shogafa Catacombs   210B1

*Off Sharia Amud el-Sawari. Open 9–4, closed Fridays
11:30–1:30. Admission fee.*

Originally a series of 2nd-century AD private tombs, the
complex was later enlarged for the community, creating
the largest Roman funerary complex known in Egypt. The
tomb decorations show a surprising blend of Egyptian and
classical styles, so typical of Alexandria.

A spiral staircase winds around the shaft where bodies
were lowered and leads to a vestibule on the first level.
Beyond the vestibule is the Rotunda and the Banquet
Hall, where families came to feast in memory of the dead.
Through a fissure in the rock to the right of the rotunda is
the Hall of Caracalla, where four painted tombs contained

*The eerie depths of
the catacombs of
Kom el-Shogafa, a
typically Alexandrian
mix of Egyptian and
Roman influences*

the remains of young men and their horses, reputedly massacred for insulting the emperor.

The strangest part of the complex is the second-level Central Tomb, reached via the staircase in the rotunda. Limestone statues on either side of the vestibule probably represent the deceased and his wife. The entrance is guarded by two bearded serpents wearing the double crowns of Upper and Lower Egypt and, above them, a Medusa in a disk. The confusion of styles and religions becomes even more notable inside the tomb where the three sarcophagi are decorated in classical style. Niches above the sarcophagi show bas-reliefs with Egyptian motifs: a mummy on a lion-shaped bed being administered to by Anubis, Thoth and Horus, and a prince offering a collar to the Apis bull. On the way out, note the hybrid figures on either side of the door: the Egyptian gods Anubis and Sobek dressed as Roman legionnaires.

The third level is flooded and therefore inaccessible. Rising groundwater has left even the Central Tomb vulnerable to serious damage from occasional floods. Check at the ticket office whether there is electricity, although if your nerves are strong, frequent power cuts add to the eeriness of the place. If the prospect doesn't excite you, be on the safe side and take a torch.

▶▶ el-Montazah Palace and Gardens   *210C3*

El-Montazah. Gardens open 24 hours. Admission fee.
Khedive Abbas II's turn-of-the-century, Turko-Florentine folly is now the presidential summer residence, but its 350 acres of well-tended pleasure gardens are open to the public. In summer, join Alexandrians making the 15km trip from downtown for a picnic. Fast-food restaurants are sprouting among the greenery, but it's still a good place for a stroll and a swim (see page 221).

▶ Nabi Danyal Mosque   *210C2*

Sharia Nabi Danyal.
This unprepossessing mosque is tucked behind a girls' school off a busy downtown street. Some claim that in the crypt below the prayer hall (entirely rebuilt in the 19th century), beyond the two visible tombs ascribed to Sheikh Danyal el-Maridi and Lukman the Wise, lies the tomb of Alexander the Great. Archaeologists dispute this, but until the foundations are excavated, or the tomb found elsewhere, the mystery will remain. For a small bribe the guardian might let you look for yourself.

President Mubarak lives in this extravagantly decorated palace when Cairo gets too hot

The allure of Alexandria
'If a man make a pilgrimage around Alexandria in the morning, God will make for him a golden crown, set with pearls, perfumed with musk and camphor, and shining from the East to the West.'
Ibn Duqmaq

Mind the gap
Rumours easily become legends in Alexandria as the ancient city, mostly unexplored beneath the modern one, constantly reminds Alexandrians of their heritage. Excavations had been going on around the Kom el-Shogafa for eight years when, in 1892, the ground gave way beneath a donkey to reveal the complex of catacombs. An even more bizarre occurrence took place within living memory when a bride, in her wedding procession, fell down a hole in the road. Searches proved of no use and the bride was never seen again – one more treasure lost beneath the modern city.

Walk **Literary Alexandria**

Above: the Cecil Hotel

E M Forster, in the preface to his 1922 guide, wrote, 'The "sights" of Alexandria are in themselves not interesting, but they fascinate when we approach them through the past.' In a house on Sharia el-Mamun, near the Mahmudiyh canal beyond the Kom el-Shogafa catacombs, Lawrence Durrell lived, in his own words, 'two and one half years of great, extravagant and colourful life in wartime Alexandria'. The modern city also comes alive on a walk (1½–2 hours) around places associated with Alexandria's literary figures, when its buildings resonate with the words of Constantine Cavafy (*Collected Poems*), Durrell (*The Alexandria Quartet*) and Forster himself (*Alexandria, a History and Guide*). See the map on page 210.

In the **Cecil Hotel** (Midan Saad Zaghlul), Durrell's Darley first saw Justine, '...among the dusty palms, dressed in a sheath of silver drops... Nessim has stopped at the door of the ballroom which is flooded with light and music...' Across the square,

The entrance to Qaytbay Fort

the **Trianon** patisserie used to contain a discreet bar frequented by the writers and above it, in what is now the Metropole Hotel, was the office where Cavafy worked.

Turn your back to the sea and walk along Sharia Safiya Zaghlul where Cavafy used to pick up his boys. Cross the junction with Sharia el-Sultan Husayn, past Cinema Rialto, and turn right into Sharia el-Hurriya to

leads into Sharia Sharm el-Sheikh, formerly Rue Lepsius. Here, more than anywhere else, fact and fiction mingle. At No 4 (previously No 10) where Cavafy lived, his second-floor apartment is now the Cavafy Museum (see page 211). In the basement of the building was a brothel, now a carpentry workshop. Balthazar, one of Durrell's characters, also lived on this street in a 'worm-eaten room with the old cane chair which creaked all night...' Cavafy is reported to have said, 'Where could I live better? Below, the brothel caters for the flesh. And there is the church which forgives sin. And there is the hospital where we die.' It is a reminder of how geographically circumscribed was the Alexandria of the writers.

Left off Sharia Istanbul, by the Panda clothes shop, is Sharia Nabi Danyal. Durrell's Darley and Pombal shared a 'little dank flat' here. At the

The terrace of Pastroudis

find **Pastroudis**, café-patisserie and a haunt of Cavafy and of characters in *The Alexandria Quartet*, many of whom lived nearby (Justine and Nessim in a house set back from Sharia el-Hurriya). Opposite the entrance to Pastroudis, beside a crumbling 19th-century building, Sharia Zangalola leads to the Greek Orthodox Church of St Saba, where Cavafy was mourned on his death.

Sharia St Saba, where Durrell's Clea had her studio, runs into Sharia el-Sultan Hasayn (also known as Sharia Istanbul). On this street, behind a high wrought-iron gate and advertising signs, is what is left of the Greek hospital. A left turn after the hospital

junction with Sharia el-Hurriya, near the café-patisserie **Venous** (its name written only in Arabic, green letters on a lime-green background), Durrell's Armenian barber Mnemjian had his shop. 'We were lifted simultaneously and swung smoothly down into the ground wrapped like dead Pharaohs, only to reappear at the same instant on the ceiling, spread out like specimens. White cloths had been spread over us by a small black boy while in a great Victorian moustache-cup the barber thwacked up his dense and sweet-smelling lather...'. A similar experience can be had in several of Alexandria's barber shops: the barber in the Cecil Hotel, like Mnemjian, also serves as 'the Memory man, the archives of the city'.

Making an impression
Midan el-Tahrir (Liberation Square), formerly Place Muhammad Ali, suffered badly in the 1882 nationalist uprising. After the British fleet bombarded the city, killing as many as 2,000 people, rioters destroyed almost all the buildings in the square except the Anglican church and the statue of Muhammad Ali. The square was later rebuilt along even grander, neo-classical lines and many of those buildings, suffering from neglect and alteration, are still standing.

Pompey's Pillar, cut from a single block of stone, fascinated early travellers in Egypt

▶▶ **Midan el-Tahrir (Liberation Square)**   *210B2*

This was once the centre of European Alexandria, known as Frank Square, and though it has lost most of its importance, it still carries reminders of its former grandeur. The equestrian statue of Muhammad Ali, who was responsible for Alexandria's 19th-century reconstruction, is now rather marooned in the middle of the square. The Bourse, Alexandria's Cotton Exchange, stood on the site of the car park opposite the Banque du Caire until it was burned down in the food riots of 1977. The Anglican Church of St Mark, with its memorials to the British regiments who fought in Egypt in 1882, looks abandoned in its quiet garden. The crowded bus stop on Midan Orabi was once the pleasant French Gardens. For a sense of how grand these late 19th-century buildings must have been, beyond Midan Orabi look for the Okelle Monferrato department store. A passageway cuts through the building into an arcade with one of the city's most atmospheric cafés, where men play dominoes and enjoy excellent waterpipes. Across the square are the Law Courts, and just to the south is the Passage Menasce. Beyond it lies Alexandria's largest food market.

▶▶ **Pompey's Pillar**   *210C1*

Sharia Amud el-Sawari. Admission fee.

Alexandria's most prominent antiquity, Pompey's Pillar, was named in error by the Crusaders: it was raised in honour of Diocletian in the 4th century AD and probably supported a statue of the emperor. The column, of pink Aswan granite topped with a Corinthian capital, is 27m high and 9m thick. Near by are two Ptolemaic granite sphinxes found in the vicinity; in front of these are the scant remains of the Serapeum, the temple of Serapis, one of ancient Alexandria's most important buildings. The Serapeum and the library Cleopatra established alongside it were destroyed so completely by 4th-century Christians that there is little now to interest the casual visitor. But

Taking the sea air
For an early evening stroll, follow the Corniche past Midan Orabi and the Tomb of the Unknown Soldier towards Qaytbay Fort. Near the Tikka Grill restaurant, you come to a square which is brightly lit and often lively in the evening. Across the square, facing the harbour, is the Bouseiri Mosque, where Egypt's sultans used to pray on Fridays. Behind it are the taller minarets and dome of the Abu el-Abbas Mursi Mosque, a 1940s replacement of a mosque built by Algerians in 1767 over the tomb of a 13th-century saint.

climb up to the pillar for the view beyond the crumbling tenements of the living city.

▶▶▶ **Qaytbay Fort**   *210B2*

End of eastern harbour. Open: 9–3:30. Admission fee.
In the morning, as the sun rises over the Mediterranean, this extraordinary 15th-century fort looks as if it is made out of butter. Sultan Qaytbay built the fort with the remains of the legendary Pharos lighthouse, which once stood on the site. The lighthouse, built in 279BC by Sostratus under Ptolemy II, was reputed to be over 125m high, with more than 300 rooms for the mechanics and attendants; it remains a mystery how the lantern worked. In the 14th century earthquakes brought the 1,500-year-old lighthouse to the ground. But the Pharos still serves as a symbol of ancient Alexandria's desire to combine aesthetic beauty and scientific knowledge. Excavations are underway to find whatever parts of it fell into the sea, and there is even talk of a new Pharos being built, with a hotel and restaurant complex. Nowadays the fort houses the Naval Museum. There are magnificent views over the Corniche and the sea from the ramparts.

▶ **Royal Jewellery Museum**   *210C3*

21 Sharia Ahmad Yahia, Zizinia. Admission fee.
Princess Fatma el-Zahraa's imposing palace contains a sparkling collection of jewellery, covering a period from the rise of Muhammad Ali to the abdication of King Farouk. The Egyptian royal family was noted for its extravagant tastes and it is not surprising to see rare jewellery – including a platinum crown inset with 2,159 diamonds – as well as gold and silver chessboards, ashtrays, *kohl* (eye make-up) pots and water-pipes encrusted with diamonds and precious stones. The displays here must be a mere fraction of what was confiscated after the revolution. Apart from all that glitter, the museum is worth visiting for its nymphs, cherubs and other kitsch interior decoration.

Part of the glittering display in the Royal Jewellery Museum

■ **Alexandria is famous for its food and for its eating places and, although they may have lost some of their old atmosphere, the many café-patisseries around the city are still good places to join the Alexandrians at play and watch the city reveal something of its character.....■**

Café fare
You can taste some of the influences that have shaped Alexandria in the fare on offer in its cafés, which resemble English tea-rooms more than anything else: English cream cakes, Swiss-style chocolates, French patisserie, Italianesque ice cream and, of course, delicious oriental sweets.

220

Alexandrian spirit Alexandrians, more liberal than other Egyptians, are known for their fondness for good living and while elsewhere in Egypt cafés are often exclusively for men, in Alexandria's café-patisseries you'll often be served by female waitresses. Around you will be elderly Levantine gentlemen reading the news from Greece or a well-thumbed volume of poetry, a well-dressed lady and her friends sipping *cappuccinos*, and couples making romantic plans for an impossible future from behind the cream topping of a black forest gâteau. Although many places have 'gone modern' and replaced wood and old mirrors with plastic and aluminium, beneath the glittering chandeliers in Athineos, or surrounded by the surviving art nouveau panelling in Trianon, you can still catch a hint of their former glory.

Different moods There are different places for different times of day. Watch Alexandrians rush to work while enjoying the set breakfast at Trianon, near Ramla station. The terrace of Pastroudis, the favourite hangout of Lawrence Durrell's characters, is particularly enjoyable on a sunny morning. Further down Sharia el-Hurriya, Confiserie Venous sits at the crossroads of ancient Alexandria near the reputed site of Alexander the Great's tomb – an excellent place for afternoon tea entombed by pyramids of sweets. Athineos, another old Greek café, has lost much of its charm, but at the end of a busy day it is welcomingly empty for a tea or an ouzo. Later, on a hot summer's evening, sit in Baudrot's garden and watch young couples hold hands under the trellis of vines.

Pastroudis is still famous for its European-style patisserie

■ **Every summer several million Egyptians escape the dazzling heat of the Nile Valley and descend on Alexandria to catch the sea breeze. Alexandria has sun and the azure Mediterranean, but to enjoy them to the full you will need to choose your beach with care.....■**

Crowds and pollution From May to September it is hard to find an empty patch of sand on Alexandria's beaches, a problem that gets worse at weekends with the arrival of additional thousands of Cairene and Alexandrian families. The most popular beaches are along the Corniche between the Cecil Hotel and el-Montazah. Easy to reach by public transport, they are also within 40m of some of the 47 pipes draining untreated sewage into the sea. Once alerted to this fact, many visitors to Alexandria prefer to look at the Mediterranean from a safe distance.

Peach of a beach The beach experience in Alexandria is unlike anything you can experience in the West. Egyptians prefer to picnic under canvas shades rather than expose their bodies to the sun and on most beaches, women remain fully dressed, some even veiled. Stray sunbathing foreigners often receive the same treatment as veiled women on the other side of the Med – they are a welcome source of entertainment. Foreign women in bathing suits, however, may be harassed or thrown off the beach.

In spite of alluring names, public beaches like Chatby, Cleopatra, Stanley, Glym, Sidi Bishr and Miyami are best avoided unless you want to make a sociological study of crowd behaviour. Swimming is more pleasant and umbrellas are available on the cleaner, fee-paying beaches of el-Montazah and, beyond it, Ma'mura. Agami, the most fashionable resort on the north coast and the choice of wealthy Cairenes, has some of the best and cleanest beaches within striking distance of the city and although most of them are private, they will often admit foreigners for a fee.

Abbas's bridge decorates one of the city's best beaches, at Montazah

The unthinkable
Be very careful on empty beaches along the Mediterranean coast: mines and unexploded shells from World War II, and from more recent confrontations with Libya, are still lying along the shoreline and in the desert. Shifting sands uncover them occasionally, resulting in loss of life.

Lest we forget: hard-ware left over from World War II

A turning point
Winston Churchill wrote of the battle at el-Alamein, 'Before Alamein we never had a victory. After Alamein we never had a defeat.'

West of Alexandria

▶▶ el-Alamein 206B1

El-Alamein, 106km west of Alexandria, was the site of a series of famous battles during World War II. On 1 July 1942, the German commander Erwin Rommel and his Afrika Korps arrived in the area, forcing a British withdrawal through the Suez Canal. In October the same year, the new British general, Montgomery, launched a counter-offensive that drove the German army westwards out of Egypt. Around 11,000 soldiers were killed and some are buried in the British, Italian and German war cemeteries. These are open to visitors, as is the Military Museum in the centre of el-Alamein town, which displays artefacts from the battle.

West of el-Alamein, the coast is infinitely beautiful and the empty desert dunes roll gracefully into the clear, azure waters of the Mediterranean.

▶ Mersa Matruh 206A2

Mersa Matruh, 290km west of Alexandria, is an increasingly popular beach resort. Until recently it was a quiet fishing village and trading post, but with the reopening of the border with Libya it is turning into a boom town. The town itself is of little interest unless you are en route for Siwa oasis and Libya, or you want to stretch out on a magnificent beach.

The beaches in town, as in Alexandria, are not really recommended for foreign women unless they are prepared to follow the local custom of swimming fully clothed, the exception being the private beach of the Beau Site Hotel, which welcomes non-residents for a fee. Of the public beaches, those around the bay tend to be covered with litter, so head for Rommel's Beach, where the Desert Fox is said to have taken a swim. A nearby cave has been turned into the small Rommel Museum with his maps and other objects of war. Further west is Cleopatra's Bath, where another unfounded legend has it that the famous queen enjoyed herself with Mark Antony. The best beaches lie even further west, out of town: Ubbayad Beach and Ajjiba Cove are among the most isolated and desirable, with magnificent turquoise water (but see panel, page 221).

Wild at heart
Sir Ronald Storrs, civil servant, Alexandria, 1905: '... I went for long walks alone by the canals or along the eastern shores without meeting a soul; sometimes bathing, sometimes riding, once combining both in an experimental gallop naked to see what it was like, and proving it to be better adapted for bronze or marble than for human contours.' (Orientations)

Drive Rosetta

This drive eastwards through country-side and along an increasingly industrial coastline to the town of Rosetta (Rashid) is 140km round-trip. Rosetta, renowned for the inscribed stone which led to the deciphering of hieroglyphics, is remarkable for its well-preserved Ottoman buildings. See the map on pages 206–7.

The Rosetta road follows Alexandria's corniche past el-Montazah ▶ ▶ (see page 215) and Ma'mura, through groves of date palms, orange and guava trees, then past some of the Middle East's largest factories – paper mills and fertiliser plants. For much of the journey, the road follows a canal and railway line (infrequent trains from Alexandria to Rosetta are only for people with time to waste).

Among the reeds on lakes Abu Qir and Idku ▶, you might see people fishing from rowing boats, using the same techniques shown on ancient Egyptian tomb paintings. Beyond the lakes, Tabia, el-Ma'diya and Man-shiyet el-Aman are concrete towns busy with donkey carts and vintage cars. Relief is on hand when you reach the sign 'Welcome to Rashied'.

The road into Rosetta ▶ ▶ leads along the Nile, and past warehouses from the 18th century, when this was Egypt's principal port. Leave the car by the two cannon in the main square to explore on foot (see page 224).

The Abu Mandar Mosque

The Rosetta Stone

From the square, follow the Nile 5km further north to reach Sultan Qaytbay's 15th-century Citadel ▶ ▶. Note the way ancient stones, some with cartouches and hieroglyphs, were reused. In 1799, Captain Bour-chard, serving with Napoleon's army, discovered the Rosetta Stone near here (see page 224). A copy of the stone is inside the fort, beside the modern mosque. Climb the ramparts for a view towards the Abu Mandar Mosque ▶ and, 5,440km from its source at Lake Victoria, the gaping mouth of the Nile.

Retracing the route to Alexandria, stop at Abu Qir, 24km before the city, and eat at the Zephirion restaurant, looking out over the water where Nelson sank Napoleon's fleet in 1798.

The Delta

The Delta Unlike the well-preserved temples and tombs in the Nile Valley, the Delta's monuments have all but vanished due to the changing course of the Nile, heavy Mediterranean rainfall and dense cultivation of the land. What remains is of most interest to scholars and specialists and few tourists do more than catch a glimpse of the Delta from the window of a train between Cairo and Alexandria. Even then, some of its attractions are obvious: the immense, flat landscape of carefully divided fields of cotton and rice, the ponderous buffaloes turning water-wheels, and *feluccas* (sailing boats) cutting through the green.

The Delta has other attractions and is particularly famous for its *moulids* (see pages 146–7). Much more than merely Islamic festivals, *moulids* echo pharaonic celebrations and have outlived the ancient Egyptian towns in which they were first celebrated. The Moulid of Sayyid el-Badawi in Tanta is especially popular, attended by up to 2 million people from all over the country. In winter, the northern lakes and marshes are a popular refuge for water birds, herons and storks, and also for people hunting them.

The Delta contains some of the most lush farmland in the world

Saintly behaviour
Among the Crusaders who attacked Damietta in 1218 was St Francis of Assisi, who valiantly crossed the battlefield to inform Salah al-Din's nephew, the Sultan el-Kamil, that he had come to convert them all to Christianity. El-Kamil replied by introducing him to the Christians in his entourage, offering him the usual hospitality and sending him back to his side of the lines.

Carved in stone
In the 2nd century BC, a declaration from the priests of Memphis was inscribed on a basalt slab in the three scripts current in northern Egypt – hieroglyphics, Egyptian demotic and Greek. The stone was recovered by a French officer at a time when scholars were trying to decipher hieroglyphs. The Rosetta Stone was handed over to the British after the defeat of Napoleon's expedition and the original was dispatched to the British Museum, but a copy was also sent to France, where, in 1822, Jean-Francois Champollion used it to read hieroglyphs for the first time since antiquity.

▶ **Dumyat (Damietta)** 207E2

Damietta, at the end of the eastern branch of the Nile, is a busy port and industrial zone. In the Middle Ages Damietta was a prosperous trading town, but it was vulnerable to seaborne attack and was twice sacked by the Crusaders. The Ottomans brought life back to the town and built Delta-style mansions, but like Rosetta, Damietta declined in importance when Muhammad Ali restored the fortunes of Alexandria. The main tourist attraction is now the excellent bird-watching on Lake Manzala.

▶ ▶ **Rashid (Rosetta)** 206C2

Rosetta is a sleepy town at the end of the western branch of the Nile (see page 223). Apart from its fine Delta-style mansions, some of which can still be visited, its real claim to fame is the Rosetta Stone, which is now in the British Museum in London. The Arab Killy House ▶ ▶ (*Sharia el-Gheish; open: 9–4 daily*) is remarkable for its black and red brickwork, typical of Delta architecture. This 18th-century house, once the town governor's residence, is now Rosetta's museum. The Mosque of Zaghlul ▶, at the end of Sharia el-Suq, is the most famous of Rosetta's 128 mosques. Built in the 17th century, its roof has fallen in but pillars still support the lintels and a forest of columns stand reflected in a pool of stagnant water. The Bayt el-Amasyali ▶ ▶ ▶ (*Sharia el-Gheish; open: 8–2 daily*) is one of the finest early 19th-century townhouses in Egypt, with beautiful painted ceilings and exceptional inlay work; it gives a fascinating glimpse into the life of the leading members of the town.

► Tanta
207D1

Tanta, in the centre of the Delta, is Egypt's fifth-largest city. The Ottoman-style mosque and tomb of Sayyid el-Badawi, founder of the Ahmadiya Sufi order, is visited by pilgrims from all over the Arab world.

Sais, northwest of Tanta, was Egypt's capital during the 26th Dynasty, but unlike Luxor, it is now only a few muddy holes.

►► Zagazig
207D1

Zagazig itself is an agreeable and bustling regional centre, but the main reason to visit is to get to the nearby ancient sites. Bubastis ►, 3km south of Zagazig, was one of the most ancient cities in Egypt, dedicated to the cat goddess Bastet. Her temple is in ruins, so we must trust Herodotus' claim that of all the temples in Egypt, this was the most pleasant to look at. Many fine bronze statues of Bastet were found in a nearby cat cemetery.

Tanis ►, northeast of Zagazig, is by far the most interesting archaeological site in the Delta. Tanis was long thought to be Pi-Ramses, birthplace of the Ramessid Dynasty and of Ramses II; it is mentioned in the Bible as having been built by Moses and the Israelites and as the departure point for the Exodus from Egypt. Recent excavations, however, are suggesting that Pi-Ramses might be near Qantara in Sinai. The Great Temple of Amun ► is in ruins but there remain many fragments of colossal statuary. The most significant finds – at the time as important as Tutankhamun's tomb – were the six, almost intact royal tombs from the 11th and 22nd Dynasties, discovered in 1939. The splendid collection of funerary equipment and jewellery is often overlooked in the Egyptian Museum in Cairo.

Egypt's most popular festival
More people attend the Tanta moulid (see pages 146–7) of Sheikh Sayyid Ahmad el-Badawi than any other festival in Egypt. El-Badawi, a 12th-century Moroccan Sufi, established his own *tariqa* (brotherhood), the Ahmadiya, in Tanta. The feast lasts for a week, at the end of which the sheikh of the brotherhood leads a chanting, flag-waving procession through the town.

Cat lovers
Lord Kitchener, the British general most famous for the capture of Khartoum in 1898, is reported to have said, 'I can't think much of a people who drew cats the same for 4,000 years.' But ancient Egyptians were clearly happy with cats – after all, the cat deity Bastet was a goddess of joy.

225

Fishermen fixing their nets at Rosetta

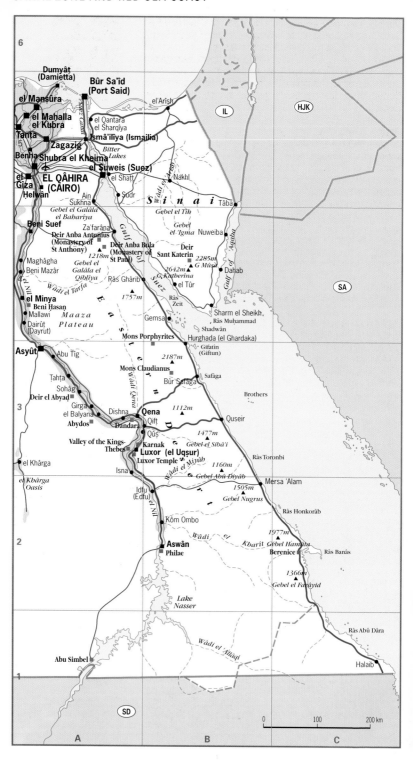

Canal Zone and Red Sea Coast The Suez Canal and Red Sea coast are different in character to the rest of Egypt. There are no great archaeological sites to visit and most traces of previous habitation have disappeared beneath water or sand. But along the canal, beneath the surface of the Red Sea and among the mountains of the Eastern Desert there are surprising and beautiful things to be found.

A lifeline Since its grand opening in 1869, the Suez Canal has been a lifeline in global transport. Cutting through the isthmus of Suez, linking the Mediterranean and Red Seas, it has been fought over several times this century. It was nationalised in 1956, and remains one of Egypt's largest earners of foreign currency. It also remains an object of inspiration and although the days of P&O passengers throwing their topees (hats) overboard at Suez have long passed, the canal still represents the divide between east and west.

Canal towns Suez, at the northern end of the Red Sea, was a thriving port before the canal was opened, an important stage along the overland route from Europe to the East via Alexandria and Cairo. Isma'iliya and Port Said

Left: the Suez Canal

CANAL ZONE AND RED SEA COAST

A tale of two towns
William Russell, the Times correspondent travelling in Egypt in the 1860s, wrote of Isma'iliya: 'You would be tempted, as you hear the click of billiard-balls and the rattle of the dominoes, and look in through the gauze blinds and see the smoking crowds, to imagine that you were in some country quarter of La Belle France.'

A less flattering view of Port Said was written by Major C S Jarvis in *Oriental Spotlight* (London, 1937): 'In 1860 it did not exist, but by 1890 it had achieved the distinction of being called the wickedest town in the East, and vice and evil were rampant on its streets.'

– both created by the canal – immediately eclipsed Suez, which has only recently regained some of its importance. Isma'iliya quickly developed an air of cosmopolitan gentility which somehow it has held onto, while Port Said, the main trading port and base of the Suez Canal Authority, earned a different sort of reputation as 'the wickedest town in the East'. It now has tax-free status in an attempt to lure cruise ships and freighters to its port, while Isma'iliya, with a large slice of world trade sailing past its doors, has become an alternative weekend resort for people wanting to escape Egypt's cities.

The Red Sea Early travellers expected to find a sea whose water was red, but instead they found the blue, black or turquoise waters; the sea seems more likely to have earned its name from the colour of the mountains behind it which glow red beneath a lowered sun. Gustave Flaubert described swimming in the sea as one of the most voluptuous pleasures of his life – like 'lying on a thousand liquid breasts that were caressing my entire body' – and its waters continue to exert a powerful attraction over visitors to the region. But throughout history it has been the Red Sea's importance as a trading route that has brought people to its shores.

A shoal of blackspotted grunt. The teeming waters of the Red Sea provide some of the best diving sites in the world

Natural resources Egypt has 1,250km of coastline between Suez and the Sudanese border. In antiquity the coastal plain was undeveloped, but several ports made trading contacts possible between the Nile Valley, Somalia and the Yemen. Some of those ports, such as Quseir and Safaga, are once again important trading posts for Egypt. Oil and gas reserves found offshore in the Red Sea have also led to development of some of the coastline. But the largest changes to Egypt's Red Sea coast have been to its tourism facilities. Ten years ago, these were scarce and unsophisticated, but Hurghada has developed quickly and is now an important resort with regular international flights and a growing range of hotels. As Hurghada grows, the search for new areas to develop has turned southwards and facilities in both Safaga and Quseir are being improved.

Eastern Desert Unusually, in this region you have to look to the desert to find signs of previous lives and of contemporary ones as well. The Bedouin moving their camels or goats in search of pastures, the miners digging for gold or valued stone, trading caravans passing through the wadis (dry gullies), hermits seeking religious enlightenment in solitude – now, as thousands of years ago, the traces of their lives are scant. Surrounding them are the beautiful, barren mountains of the Eastern Desert, with the highest peaks in Egypt outside Sinai and many of the last survivors of the country's wild animals.

Essentials
Isma'iliya, Monastery of St Anthony, Hurghada, Wadi Hammamat and the road to the Nile Valley.

St Paul's Monastery on the edge of the Red Sea Mountains

229

Qantara

Before the Suez Canal existed, pilgrims, armies and caravans used to cross the Isthmus of Suez at Qantara (meaning 'bridge' in Arabic), between Isma'iliya and Suez. The pontoon bridges have long gone but there are still ferries going from the west bank of the canal to the east bank on Sinai.

Darius's Canal

The canal dug by Darius in 500BC connected the Red Sea with the Nile at Zagazig. It was later improved by the Ptolemies and the Romans. The Arab conqueror of Egypt, Amr, had it restored to export corn to Arabia. But 100 years later it was abandoned, and many invaders had thoughts about restoring it until Napoleon proposed a canal from the Red Sea to the Mediterranean.

The distinctive dome of the Suez Canal Building, Port Said

►► Isma'iliya 226A5

Isma'iliya, by far the most pleasant of the canal cities, lies 128km from Cairo and can be reached by train (3–5 hours) or by bus (3 hours) from the Koulali bus station. It is cut in two by a railway line. The European-style garden city, south of the track, with its tree-lined boulevards and restored colonial villas, looks very much as it must have done in the 1930s. The other side of the track is less idyllic, with run-down apartment buildings built between slums, but this is where the majority of Ismailians live.

Near the intersection of Muhammad Ali Quay with Sharia Orabi, the House of De Lesseps ► (see page 232), containing his books and his belongings, is sometimes open for visitors (check with the tourist office). The small museum ► (open: daily 9–4, Friday 9–11 and 2–4), built like a Ptolemaic temple, houses a collection of Graeco-Roman and pharaonic objects and an exhibit about the building of Darius's Canal between the Nile and the Red Sea. Beside the museum is the Garden of Steles and opposite is the shady Fountain Park. The city lies on the shore of Lake Timsah (Crocodile Lake), whose fine beaches are mostly owned by beach clubs. It is possible to use the beach of the PLM Azur Hotel (the admission fee usually includes lunch); from here you can watch freighters slowly passing. Outside town, the suburb of Nimrah Sitta offers beautiful colonial villas and excellent views over the canal.

► Bur Sa'id (Port Said) 226A5

Port Said lies 80km north of Isma'iliya. It can be reached by bus or service taxi from Isma'iliya and Suez, by train (5 hours) from Cairo or by Superjet bus from the Abdel Muneem Riyadh Terminal; there are also buses from Alexandria (6 hours).

Port Said is now a duty-free port and is trying hard to forget its old reputation as a city of smugglers and prostitutes. The original wooden buildings on Sharia Gumhuriya vaguely suggest the colonial past, but the city is looking towards the future by attracting Egyptian holiday-makers to its new resorts and modern shopping centres.

The port's most famous landmark is the Suez Canal Building on Sharia Filastin with its three shiny green domes. The Military Museum on Sharia 23rd of July (open: daily 9–3; admission fee) has paintings and dioramas of the Egypt-Israel wars. The pleasant Port Said National Museum ► on Sharia Filastin (open: daily 9–4, closed Friday for prayers; admission fee) has a small but interesting collection of pharaonic objects, Coptic textiles and Islamic art, as well as objects from the 1869 canal opening, including the khedive's (viceroy's) carriage. A ferry leaves from the quay (opposite the tourist office on Sharia Filastin) to Port Fuad (15 minutes), which officially lies in Asia. This suburb, founded in 1927, has some interesting 1930s villas surrounded by lush, well-kept gardens, and makes for a pleasant afternoon stroll.

► el-Suweis (Suez) 226A5

Suez is 134km from Cairo and can be reached by express train (3 hours) or by bus from Koulali Terminal. Buses and service taxis come and go to Alexandria, Luxor, Hurghada (6 hours) and Sinai.

A typical building in old Port Said

Suez, at the southern end of the canal, suffered more than other canal cities in the 1967 and 1973 wars with Israel, and three-quarters of the city was totally destroyed. It has been rebuilt, with money from the Gulf states, as an important industrial centre for fertilisers, cement and petrochemicals. In the Middle Ages this was the port of Qulzum, a walled city important in the spice trade and as a stopover point on the pilgrimage to Mecca. For all its interesting history, there is little to attract the visitor beyond its seafront atmosphere and a few crumbling colonial houses, overwhelmed by neighbouring modern blocks. Sharia el-Gheish runs to the customs and docks at Bur Tawfiq (Port Tawfiq). The Ahmad Hamdi tunnel, 12km to the north of Suez, runs under the Suez Canal to Sinai.

On your bike
It is delightful to walk or ride a bike around the old town of Isma'iliya. Bikes can be hired from the PLM Azur or in the alleys off Muhammad Ali Quay, and information is available at the tourist office on Muhammad Ali Quay (closed Friday 8–2).

Building the canal

■ **It is hard today to imagine the fuss that was made over the idea of building the Suez Canal, but at the time of its construction it was considered the greatest engineering feat and proof of the progress possible in the Industrial Revolution.....■**

Some canal statistics

An estimated 20,000 Egyptians worked on the construction (thousands of them died in the process). 97 million cubic yards of earth were removed along the 167km-long canal. Work started on 25 April 1859 and the canal was officially opened on 17 November 1869. The distance between London and Bombay using the old route, via South Africa, is 11,000 miles; via the Suez Canal it is 5,800 miles.

232

Antecedents A waterway connecting the Mediterranean and Red Sea was completed in the reign of Darius (*c* 500BC). It was a series of canals: one from the Red Sea to the Great Bitter Lake, and one from there to the Nile. Extended under the Ptolemies and Romans, it was still in use in the 8th century, when the Arabs closed it.

The impossible project The merits of a canal had been discussed for hundreds of years, but in the 1790s Napoleon's engineers reported that the project was impossible: the two seas were at different levels. Only they weren't, and in the 1840s, when the French consul and engineer Ferdinand de Lesseps discovered the mistake, there was a boom in trade and transit between the two seas as European powers consolidated their eastern empires. The canal was a project of its time.

Pros and cons The canal project was caught up in Anglo-French rivalry. Britain, needing to guarantee fast passage to its colonies, had backed a British-built railway from Alexandria to Suez. After great difficulties, it wasn't the French government but the Egyptians and the independent Suez Canal Company, founded by de Lesseps, that financed construction.

Posterity De Lesseps assured Said, the Egyptian ruler, that his name would be 'blessed from century to century', but that has not been the case. Said died before work was completed and is remembered in the name of the port. Ismail, who opened the canal, had Isma'iliya named after him. And de Lesseps' commemorative statue, which stood beside the canal in Port Said, was blown up in 1952.

A dredger at work on the canal, 1869

Red Sea Coast

The road to Hurghada

▶ **el-Ghardaka (Hurghada)** 226B3

El-Ghardaka, 410km south of Suez, can be reached by air, bus (6–8 hours) from the Arbaeen terminal in Suez or by service taxi. The journey from Cairo takes 8–12 hours by bus (Ahmad Hilmi Terminal) or service taxi and 1 hour by ZAS or Egypt Air flight.

The small fishing village of el-Ghardaka has developed, in less than ten years, into one of Egypt's most popular resort towns. The town itself has little more to offer than guaranteed sunshine most of the year, good diving facilities and a wide range of accommodation. The modern town is ugly and completely dependent on tourism. Tourists fly in directly from Europe to sunbathe and dive, and most of them stay by the pool and forget about ancient Egypt. The majority of the hotels are resorts with restaurants, bars and shopping centres within the grounds, so there is no cause for adventure.

There is a public beach, but as it is usually covered in litter, most tourists opt for one of the private hotel beaches. Unlike in Sinai where the coral reefs are near the shore, it is necessary to take a boat to explore the coral islands, which are truly magnificent. In most hotels it is possible to book a day-excursion to Gifatin Island (Giftun Island), with fish for lunch and plenty of time to snorkel. More experienced divers can explore Gubal Island, the Careless Reef, Shadwan Island – popular with reef sharks – and, further away, the spectacular Brother Islands. For the less adventurous there are excursions on glass-bottomed boats – from Shedwan, Three Corners Hotel and some other hotels – to see the marine life around the smaller reefs. In town, the New Aquarium ▶ on Sharia el-Bahr (*open: 9am–10pm; admission fee*) has a small selection of fishes in its dark aquariums. The Oceanographic Museum, 10km north of town, has a quirky collection of dusty, stuffed fishes in very unnatural colours.

Ferry to Sinai
To avoid a long bus journey, it is usually possible to take a ferry from Hurghada to Sharm el-Sheikh. It leaves around 9:30 in the morning and takes 5–6 hours. Bookings should be made in advance through your hotel or directly from Spring Tours on Tariq el-Nasr. Take food, plenty of water and a good protective sun cream.

Hurghada's facilities, diving opportunities and clear water have helped it to develop into a major resort

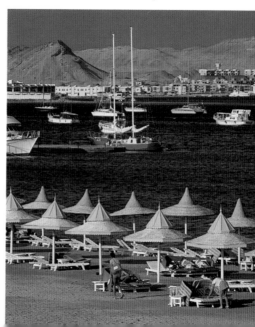

The Red Sea Mountains

■ Unlike the Western Desert, the desert to the east, between the Nile and the Red Sea, is a mountainous region which stretches to the Sudanese border. Rich in minerals, the beautiful but harsh Red Sea Mountains are still home to hermits, miners and tribes of Bedouin.....■

234

Old miners
The 1st century AD Jewish historian, Josephus, recorded that after the Romans sacked Jerusalem, Jewish captives over the age of 17 were sent to the Egyptian mines. Regimes before and after them adopted the same policy to provide labour for the mines. The earlier Greek writer Agatharchides explained that while the strongest men worked deep in the gold mines, 'the old men and children carried the ore to the crushers, where it was broken up by men and then further ground by women. It was then washed on sloping tables, the quartz being all washed away and the gold remaining behind.'

Composed mainly of granite, porphyry and breccia, the Red Sea Mountains rise to a maximum height of 2,187m

Ancient remains Long before St Anthony came looking for solitude (see pages 236–7), people searched for gold, copper and precious stone. There is little to see from the ancient Egyptians, but at Mons Porphyrites there are the remains of Rome's largest porphyry mine. The broken huts and ruined temple are from Hadrian's reign. Further to the south, at Mons Claudianus, there are the remains of a walled miners' camp, with the temple on its highest ground. From these mines, stone was carried 150km and more to the Nile, and from there throughout the Roman empire, where it was used in the great imperial buildings.

Bedouin tribes The mountains are divided between two main Bedouin tribes. The Ma'aza, to the north of the Qift-Quseir road, are descended from Arab nomads. The Ababda, to the south, used to graze their herds far into Sudanese territory and are of African descent. Like Bedouin elsewhere in Egypt, these tribes are being settled by the government in Cairo.

Last of the wildlife When the Red Sea Mountains were covered in forests, they were also home to a great variety of wildlife. As their cover and food supply disappeared, the animals became vulnerable. Earlier this century, great numbers of gazelle, ibex and Barbary sheep were hunted, many shot en masse with machine guns. Some of King Farouk's 'trophies' are now lining the walls of Cairo's Manyal Palace museum.

Modern miners Mining companies have been prospecting in the mountains, hoping to use modern techniques to further exploit the ancient mines, but so far Egyptian bureaucracy has proved more impenetrable than the rock.

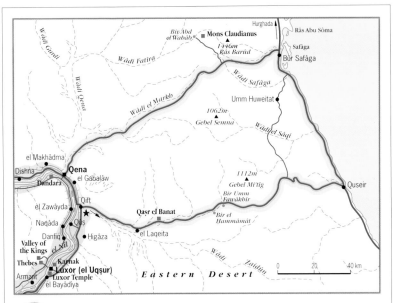

Drive In the Red Sea Mountains

The drive from Qift to Quseir can be done as a day-trip from Hurghada or Luxor, returning along the faster Qena-Port Safaga Road. Take enough water and food for the day'. The only way-station is the little hamlet of el-Laqeita, about 16km from Qift.

The well-paved road from Qift to Quseir (216km) crosses the Eastern Desert through the Red Sea Mountains. After a series of wells were dug in the reign of Ramses IV (1164—1157BC), trade flowed along the route between the Nile and the Red Sea. It has been in almost continuous use since then. The romance of caravans is gone, but there are some fascinating and rarely visited sights and beautiful mountain scenery along the way.

Qift was known as the place where Isis heard of her husband Osiris' murder. The road leaves to the east, away from the Nile, following the ancient route suggested by Greek and Coptic inscriptions at Qasr el-Banat (the Maidens' Palace), some 8km past el-Laqeita. The road winds upwards and after 75km enters the Wadi Hammamat, a beautiful route through the mountains. The Wadi was prized for its breccia stone and gold. At several places its walls contain ancient inscriptions and its hilltops preserve the remains of ancient and Arab watchtowers.

Bir Umm Fawakhir, 124 km from Qift, is an ancient well with hieroglyphic inscriptions. Further east, a long wire fence encloses el-Sid, a British gold mine abandoned after the Suez crisis of 1956, its equipment still untouched. The guardian may be persuaded to let you in. The remainder of the road to Quseir is lined with old gold and newer phosphate mines.

Road to the monasteries

There is no public transport to the monasteries, so it is advisable to book an organised tour with Misr Travel or hire a taxi for the day from Hurghada or Suez (about 160 km). It is possible to ask any bus driver, from Cairo or Suez to Hurghada, to drop you at the turn-off for St Paul's, 26km south of Za'farana. It is a 13km walk to the monastery, though you may get a lift. For St Anthony's, service taxis from Beni Suef to Za'farana can stop at the turn-off for this monastery, 33km south of Za'farana; you can then walk 15km uphill, or pray for a lift.

► ► **Deir Anba Antunius (Monastery of St Anthony)** 226A4

Open: daily 9–5. Closed: during Christmas and Lent.

The monastery was founded by followers of St Anthony shortly after his death in 356, and it is often mentioned as the oldest monastery in the world. It is set dramatically in the Wadi Araba, beneath a barren ridge of cliffs. The compound, surrounded by 12m-high walls, contains houses, gardens, churches and palm trees and looks very much like an Egyptian village. Until the beginning of the 20th century it took three or four days to get here by camel, so it is hardly surprising that visitors were rare. But nowadays there is a road, and busloads of Copts and tourists arrive here on a tour or a pilgrimage. Some monks do a small tour of the monastery in several languages.

The oldest structure is the **Church of St Anthony**► ► with paintings and murals from the 13th to 16th centuries. To the northwest of the church is the much more recent Church of the Holy Virgin. On top of a four-storey keep is the 16th-century Church of St Michael, and other churches include the Church of the Apostles and the Church of St Mark, both 18th-century. Near the south wall is the Spring of St Anthony, believed to be the place where Moses' sister took a bath during the Exodus; until recently it was the only water source in the compound. A path from the west side of the monastery makes the steep climb to St Anthony's Cave (see page 238), with magnificent views over the Red Sea.

► ► **Deir Anba Bula (Monastery of St Paul)** 226A4

Open: daily 9–5. Closed: during Christmas and Lent.

The Monastery of St Paul the Hermit (or Ascetic) has long been in the shadow of the Monastery of St Anthony; it is smaller, more dilapidated and very remote, not even on a caravan route. This St Paul (AD228–348) was the earliest

Walk across the mountains

It is possible to get a lift between the two monasteries (over 80km by road), but experienced walkers may prefer to do the three-day hike across the mountains, like St Anthony did when he visited St Paul. A map of the region is available at St Anthony's monastery, but take plenty of advice before you start as it can be dangerous. Beware of getting lost or running out of water.

Coptic monks at the Monastery of St Anthony. Recent years have seen an increase in the number of new monks entering the monasteries

The twin towers of St Anthony's Monastery, built at the foot of the hill where the saint went into retreat

hermit, but when, at the age of 113, he was visited in his cave by St Anthony (then aged 90), he acknowledged that St Anthony was spiritually his superior. Because of the monastery's remoteness, there are less visitors here and the monks are friendlier. Saint Paul's Cave, where St Anthony found him, is in the Church of St Paul; the sarcophagus near by is said to contain his remains. On top of the four-storey keep, where the monks hid from invading Bedouins, is the Church of the Virgin, adjacent to the Church of St Mercurius. In the 17th-century Church of St Michael there is an icon of the Virgin, believed to have been painted by St Luke in AD40.

► **Marsa 'Alam** 226B2

This small fishing village, 132km south from Quseir, has beautiful offshore coral reefs and is far less polluted than Hurghada. This is as far south as you are allowed to go on the coastal road without military permission. Further south is the ancient trading port of Berenice, founded by Ptolemy II and rediscovered by Belzoni in 1818.

► **Bur Safaga (Port Safaga)** 226B3

Port Safaga, 58km south of Hurghada on the junction of the road to Qena, is nowadays a commercial port which exports phosphates and imports grain from the USA. It has a few new resort hotels with diving centres.

► **Quseir** 226B3

Until the 10th century Quseir, 150km south of Hurghada, was the largest trading port on the Red Sea. In ancient times boats left from here on expeditions to the Land of Punt (either Yemen or Somalia) and until the 19th century it was the most popular port for pilgrims going to Mecca. Quseir lost its importance with the opening of the Suez Canal, but the small fort of Sultan Selim still dominates the town.

Muslim and Christian motifs mix on this decorative panel in the Monastery of St Paul

■ **Monasticism is one of Egypt's many gifts to civilisation. The idea of seeking understanding and coming closer to God by retreating from the world was a natural one to the inheritors of pharaonic Egypt.....■**

238

St Anthony
St Anthony (AD251–356) became a hermit at 18 when he heard Matthew's gospel: 'If thou wilt be perfect, go and sell that thou hast, and give to the poor, and thou shalt have treasure in heaven'. He started off in his own garden, then joined a caravan into the Eastern Desert and found his isolated cave in Mount Qalah, where he lived until the age of 105. He life was the inspiration for monasticism, which quickly spread to England, Ireland and Northern Europe where it soon had many followers.

St Anthony, one of the founders of Christian monasticism

Beginnings of monasticism The beginnings of monasticism are bound up with the beginnings of Christianity in Egypt. Tradition says that the Holy Family hid from Herod in Egypt, but of more importance to the growth of the church was the arrival of St Mark, who founded the Patriarchate of Alexandria in AD61. The translation of the scriptures into Coptic in the 3rd century AD gave the new religion a popular touch at the same time as Roman emperors were persecuting Christians with increasing severity, culminating in the outrages committed under Diocletian. During the persecutions of his predecessor Decius, two of the Coptic church's most revered saints left their very different homes and sought refuge in the Red Sea Mountains. Both St Paul and St Anthony renounced the pleasures of the world and retreated to caves in the hope of drawing closer to their God.

Martyrs or monks While tens of thousands of Christians were being slaughtered, 'so many,' according to a contemporary writer, 'that the exhausted executioners had to be periodically relieved,' huge numbers of others were also seeking sanctuary away from the Nile Valley. For Egyptians, to whom the river and its rhythms were life itself, leaving the valley for the desert was indeed like giving up life. Strangely, after Diocletian's rage had been replaced by Constantine's vision and Christianity was declared the favoured religion of the Roman empire, even greater numbers of Egyptians abandoned the valley in favour of a life of religious seclusion.

Monastic orders St Anthony is said to have forbidden his many followers to stay near the cave into which he had retreated, so they camped at the foot of the hill, forming a community which became a permanent settlement and the basis of today's Monastery of St Anthony. The next step in monasticism was taken back in the Nile Valley when, around 320, the soldier-convert St Pachom decided that these communities should be run along military lines. His ideas, which included the taking of vows, the wearing of habits and the regulating of every hour of the monks' days, were observed by the

dozen communities he founded. They also formed the basis of monasticism throughout the Christian church, and 19th-century Europeans, rediscovering his beliefs, nodded in admiration as they read, for instance, of his insistence that a healthy body leads to a healthy mind.

Hermits Visit a monastery in Egypt these days and the chances are that one of the monks will have recently ended a period of complete retreat, sometimes for a matter of days, sometimes for 20 or more years. For monks, the status of being a hermit is one that they must work towards, first spending up to ten years in a monastery, then securing the permission of monastic superiors and even the Pope. A new hermit must then find a suitable place to hide, usually a cave, where other monks can bring the weekly supply of food. But even out in the wilderness, the hermit's life is governed by rules which dictate how many hours a day he may spend in prayer, rest or physical activity.

Monastic revival Nineteenth-century travellers mourned the decline of Egyptian monasteries, but since Shenuda III was made Pope in 1971, the Coptic church has had a leader who himself spent many years in retreat. Neglected, understaffed, and underfunded for so long, the monasteries are again attracting the interest of the Coptic community, who are restoring the old buildings and paying attention to the farmland that provides food to support the community and thus reversing monastic fortunes. This in turn has led to an increase in new monks and in visitors to their monasteries.

St Paul the ascetic and the lions with which he is associated

Ostrich eggs
Some people insist that the ostrich eggs in the Coptic church, like other eggs popular at Easter, are a symbol of the resurrection. Others, less poetic, point out that they were often placed above oil lamps hanging from the chapel ceilings to discourage rats from climbing down.

Coptic monks with embroidered cowls

239

SINAI

Bûr Sa'îd
(Port Said)

Tell el Farama
(Pelusium)

Români

el Qantara
el Sharqîya

Ismâ'ilîya
(Ismailia)

Great
Bitter
Lake

Little
Bitter
Lake

Khatmía
Pass

Giddi
Pass

Mitla
Pass

el Suweis
(Suez)

el Shatt

Qalat el Jundi

Sudr

Ain Sukhna

Gebel
el Galâla
el Bahariya

1274m

Râs
Matarma

Râs
Abu
Darag

el Gharandal

Za'farâna

Deir Anba Antûnius
(Monastery of St Anthony)

Deir Anba Bula
(Monastery of St Paul)

1218m

Gebel el Galâla
el Qiblîya

Wâdi Hawashiya

Wâdi Araba

Râs Ghârib

Râs
Sharatib

Râs
Abu Bakr

Abu
Durba

Râs
Ghârib

1757m
Gebel Ghârib

el Tûr

Râs Dib

Zeitúna

Râs Zeit

Gemsa

E a s t e r n
D e s e r t

Mons Porphyrites

Hurghada

Gebel Shâyîb
el Banât
2187m

Tawîla

Shadwân

Gifâtin
(Giftun)

Sadot

el 'Arîsh

Abu
Aweigîla

el Quseima

Gebel
el Maghâra

Bir Hasana

1094m
Gebel Yi'allaq

Bir el Thamâda

Nakhl

el Thamad

Wâdi el 'Arîsh

Wâdi el Aqaba

Wâdi Abu el Gain

Wâdi el Ghaduyâl

G e b e l   e l   T î h

S i n a i

Gebel el 'Igma

1626m

Coloured
Canyon

Ain Umm
Ahmad

Râs el Gineina

Sarabît
el Khâdim

Abu Zenima

Abu Rudeis

Wâdi Seih

Ain Hudra

Nuweiba

Wâdi
Feirân

Wâdi el Sheikh

Deir
Sant Katerin
(Mon of St Catherine)

2285m
Gebel Mûsa

2642m
Gebel Katherina

Sharira Pass

2438m
Gebel el Thabt

2266m
Gebel Sabbâgh

Dahab

Nabq

Nursâni

Na'ama
Bay
Sharm el Sheikh

Râs Muhammad

Strait of Gûbâl

Gulf of Suez

Gulf of Aqaba

Strait of Tiran

Tâba

Pharaoh's
Island

IL

HJK

SA

0   50   100 km

Sinai Sinai is unlike the rest of Egypt. A varied and beautiful desert, a land of miracles and holy places, its importance in connecting Africa and Asia has often made it the scene of bitter fighting. Since its return to Egypt in 1982 under the Camp David agreement, the peninsula's tourist potential has been realised, first as a beach and diving centre and now for its cultural attractions.

The Land of Sin Sinai's first settlers were nomads from the east, who predated the Nile civilisation and worshipped a moon goddess called Sin. Five thousand years ago, as the Egyptian empire expanded, expeditions from the Nile came to the area looking for copper. They found it around Mafkah, east of modern-day Abu Rudeis. For nearly two millennia Egyptians extracted copper, manganese and turquoise from Sinai, and the ruins of their temples and settlements tell the tale of their hard lives on the peninsula.

West and East Sinai's position, standing firmly between two continents, rather than its mineral wealth has dominated its history and also the course of its main routes. The northern route, following the Mediterranean coast, was known as the Horus Road of War and its name suggests its function. Egyptians, Syrians, Canaanites and Israelites marched across it to fight for land and power. The Romans, who conquered them all, improved the route to allow easy access between their Syrian and Egyptian provinces and called it the Via Maris, reflecting a more peaceful period, although the Holy Family would have fled along it to escape the vengeance of King Herod. Muslims going to Mecca defined a more southern passage, the Darb el-Hajj (Pilgrims' Road), from Suez to Eilat, its route lined with the ruins of Arab and Crusader castles. These are still the peninsula's two main roads and, not for the first time, there is already an increase in traffic now that political stability is coming to the region.

Desert hideouts Sinai's climate is harsh, discouraging settlement, but the mountains at its heart provided Jews and then Christians with a sanctuary in which to hide. Particularly in the south, there was an abundance of wildlife and, if you knew where to look for it, of water as well. The Israelites settled around palm-filled *wadis* (dry gullies) such as Wadi Feiran – Moses received the Ten Commandments on a nearby mountain – and Christians escaping Roman persecution established settlements there. By the 5th century AD, the community was important enough to be made a bishopric, though continuous

attacks from nomadic tribes made it necessary to enclose the settlement, creating the Monastery of St Catherine.

Natural beauty Bird-watchers gather along Sinai's coasts to observe the migration of flocks between the continents in spring and autumn. The underwater wonders off Sinai's coasts are famed throughout the world and its coral reefs, particularly along the eastern coast from Ras Muhammad, are often described in superlatives by experienced divers. Its central mountain ranges, their jagged peaks rising over 2,500m, look like forbidding places but, as persecuted Israelites and Christians found, among the rocks there are beautiful *wadis* and canyons, abundant with water and vegetation. Here the more traditional of the desert's Bedouin live surrounded by wildlife, from lizards and scorpions to the last of Egypt's endangered wild animals.

A place of traditions Bedouin tribes used to control the peninsula and only the strongest of rulers in Cairo, Jerusalem or Damascus were able to claim sovereignty over them. But Israeli and now Egyptian control, and the reduction in Bedouin numbers, has led to the majority of Sinai's Bedouin being found around el-Arish on the northern coast, with the 1,000-strong southern group in the Wadi el-Aradi. While their tribes are a shadow of the hordes who fought alongside Lawrence of Arabia, and those that remain are increasingly subjected to outside influences, Sinai's Bedouin are still the guardians of ancient traditions.

Sinai's mountains look forbiddingly barren but they contain large reserves of water and sustain the Bedouin communities

Religious tourism
Nineteenth-century travellers scoured Sinai in the hope of finding evidence to support the Bible. By proving that Moses did exist and really did wander in the desert, they hoped to add credence to the Bible's other stories, especially its account of the creation, which had been called into question by Charles Darwin and his theory of evolution. Recent discoveries in northern Sinai are likely to revive religious tourism in the region.

Sinai style: going 'Bedouin' at Shark Bay

Camel treks
Bedouin in Nuweiba organise three- or four-day treks to the interior of Sinai and wherever you choose to go the scenery is wild and wonderful. The cost of the trip includes a Bedouin guide, who will also cook for you (Hatim Abed at Waha Tourist Village is recommended). Gazelles can be seen in the dunes of Wadi Ghazala, the scenery in the Coloured Canyon is magnificent, tradition claims the oasis of Ain Khudra as the site where Miriam caught leprosy and the steam in Ain Umm Ahmad offers welcome refreshment in the summer.

► **el-Arish** *240B5*

El-Arish, in northern Sinai, may be the peninsula's largest town, but its magnificent beaches are only disturbed by the rolling of the Mediterranean. The Romans called it Rhinocolorum because prisoners exiled here had their noses cut off. Until recently just a Bedouin settlement under the palm groves, el-Arish has become a resort, especially popular with middle-class Egyptian families. For all the changes, el-Arish is still more conservative than the resorts in southern Sinai, which means there are alcohol restrictions and few women in bathing suits on the beach. Bedouins sell rugs, jewellery and traditional dresses in the Thursday market.

►► **Dahab** *240C2*

Dahab means 'gold' in Arabic, the colour of its superb beaches. The town divides into three areas: upmarket el-Mashraba, around the Pullman holiday village; el-Masbat, the 1km-long beach where backpackers and old hippies relive the Woodstock years; and el-Asla, a friendly Bedouin settlement. Dahab can be a difficult place to leave, as some foreign women have found who have married locally and stayed on to run a bar or restaurant in el-Masbat or just to hang out. In Dahab, it seems the 1960s were only yesterday and yet, in spite of the relaxed atmosphere, topless or naked sunbathing is illegal and the police are known to be difficult about drugs. The best snorkelling and diving sites are just outside town. The most famous and most dangerous is the Blue Hole, a 67m-deep shaft, which is further north. The Lagoon and Napoleon Reef are near the holiday village.

► **Nuweiba** *240C3*

This sleepy town close to the Israeli border is the least developed of the resorts along the Gulf of Aqaba. As in Dahab there are two main tourist areas: Nuweiba itself is popular with well-off Egyptians and tourists on package holidays, while Tarabeen, the Bedouin village, attracts a younger public. Both places are a good starting point for camel treks into the interior. Two ferries a day leave Nuweiba for Aqaba in Jordan.

■ As much as anyone else in Egypt, the Bedouin provide a direct line back to another age, before the spread of nationalism and the arrival of the combustion engine. Although they are increasingly settled and their culture is being quickly eroded, they still value many of their nomadic traditions.....■

Mixed ancestry Bedouin in Sinai and elsewhere in Egypt claim descent from the Arab tribes of the Hejaz; others, particularly in the Western Desert and the mountains of the Eastern Desert, were living there long before Arabs arrived.

Romance of the nomad As nomads living in a harsh environment, Bedouins were constantly searching for pasture until tribes established feeding grounds to which they would return each year. Not having settlements, they placed strong emphasis on family and tribal structures. Their nomadic life forced them to reject anything that could not be carried, a habit that continues to be admired by people whose lives are ruled by their possessions.

Desert life Because they spent part of each year in the desert, Bedouin were forced to master their environment to support and protect themselves. Skills such as finding water, tracking animals and navigating by stars became second nature. While the Bedouin of Sinai have been able to use their skills and earn a living by guiding tourists, the future seems less comfortable for Bedouin elsewhere.

Settling the nomads Nomads who lived in places which other people (particularly those of the Nile Valley) found hostile, were difficult to control. But the helicopter and the four-wheel-drive car have tamed their wilderness, and the development of nationalism has forced them to conform to the will of central authority. Increasingly, Bedouin are being settled, often in unsuitable camps or villages where there is little prospect of work. Under these circumstances, Bedouin culture is bound to die out, even among the few groups who continue to be semi-nomadic.

The coming of cars
Bedouin girls, singing of their love, refer now to young men driving cars rather than riding horses or camels, as in:
'Welcome driver of the jeep I'll make you tea with milk if not shameful'
and
'Toyotas when they first appeared brought life's light then disappeared.'
Lila Abu-Lughod, *Veiled Sentiments: Honor and Poetry in a Bedouin Society*

245

Sinai's Bedouins have been settled but they still raise goats and camels as they did when they were semi-nomadic

St Catherine's Monastery, at the foot of the holy mountain

This Transfiguration is one of the Eastern Church's earliest mosaics

▶▶▶ **Deir Sant Katerin (Monastery of St Catherine)**   240B2

Open: Monday–Thursday and Saturday 9–12:30. Closed: Friday, Sunday and Orthodox holidays. Dress modestly.

The Greek Orthodox Monastery of St Catherine is set dramatically in the Wadi Deir, in the shadow of two mountains: Gebel Musa (Mt Sinai), where tradition says Moses received the Ten Commandments, and Gebel el-Deir. St Catherine's, a place of pilgrimage since long before the 4th century, is considered to be the oldest continuously inhabited monastery in the world.

In 337 the Byzantine empress, Helena, ordered the building of a chapel on the site of the Burning Bush, to which the 6th-century emperor, Justinian, added a fortress monastery to protect the monks and pilgrims from raiders. The monastery was only later dedicated to St Catherine, a beautiful 4th-century Alexandrian who converted to Christianity and was martyred for accusing the Roman emperor, Maximus, of idolatry. According to tradition, five centuries later priests found her previously-lost body glowing on top of Gebel Katerina (Mt St Catherine), apparently transported there by angels.

The lush gardens of olive and apricot trees surrounding the fortified walls contain a cemetery and Charnel House, where bones of the dead monks are stored. The present entrance and the south and west walls are original (6th-century), but the north and east walls were rebuilt after an earthquake in the 14th century.

The **Church of the Transfiguration**▶▶▶ (now called the Church of St Catherine) dominates the enclosure. Built in 542 by Justinian in memory of his wife, it is, along with the Chapel of the Burning Bush, the oldest structure on the site. The entrance is through the narthex (vestibule), added in the 10th or 11th century, where some of the world's rarest icons are displayed. From here, exquisite 6th-century cedar-wood doors lead to a high nave. The original 12 granite pillars represent months of the year, each bearing an icon of the saints to be worshipped that month. The wooden bracing beams of the 18th-century ceiling are original (6th-century) and finely carved with animals and cherubs. Between the nave and choir, a gilded iconostasis has 17th-century icons of Mary, Jesus, John the Baptist and St Catherine. Behind it, under the marble canopy, is what are believed to be the relics of St Catherine: her left hand and her skull.

In the sanctuary is one of the masterpieces of Byzantine art, the 6th-century mosaic of the Transfiguration of Christ, portraying Christ in the middle, with Elias and St John to his left, St Peter at his feet and to his right Moses and St James. Above the arch are medallions of the Virgin and John the Baptist, and beside the windows are biblical

scenes of Moses receiving the Holy Commandments (right) and Moses taking off his sandals in front of the Burning Bush (left).

Visitors with special permission can visit the Chapel of The Burning Bush, but must remove their shoes before visiting the earliest level of the monastery. Strangely enough, the altar was built over the roots of the bush, while the thorny bush itself was transplanted at the back of the church where everyone can see it flourishing. The monastery has more treasures, but a letter of introduction from the Coptic patriarchate in Cairo is needed to gain admittance. There is a priceless collection of around 2,000 icons and nearly 100 are exhibited in the Icon Gallery. They are all worth seeing, but the oldest 12 icons (6th and 7th centuries), made in the melted wax technique on wood, are particularly striking. The Library has the most important collection of religious manuscripts after the Vatican, with some 5,000 books and 3,000 manuscripts. To the left of the Church of St Catherine is Moses' Well, where Moses met his wife Zipporah. Opposite is a mosque that was originally a 6th-century hospice for pilgrims.

Icon of St Catherine. The monastery holds one of the most important collections of icons in the world

Codex Sinaiticus
Even with a letter of introduction the monks are hesitant to show their valuable manuscripts. This is not surprising since a 19th-century German scholar borrowed one of their rarest manuscripts, the 4th-century Codex Sinaiticus, and never returned it. It came into the possession of the Czar of Russia and the Communist regime later sold it to the British Museum.

Walk **Up Gebel Musa (Mount of Moses)**

Christians, Jews and Muslims believe that Gebel Musa – Mt Sinai of the Bible – is where Moses received the Ten Commandments. The climb takes about two hours and is best done early in the morning, to see the sun light up this wild and rugged landscape.

Gebel Musa is an important pilgrimage spot, so you will not be alone. To enjoy the best views, it is recommended to climb up before sundown, spend an extraordinary night on top of the mountain and be woken up by psalms sung by pilgrims greeting the sunrise. Luggage can be left in the monastery, but take warm clothes, a sleeping bag (you can rent blankets at the monastery, but nights can be very cold) and some food and drink, as the Bedouin who makes tea on top of the mountain sometimes takes a day off. A more comfortable alternative is to stay at the monastery and join the pilgrims in the early morning.

The monastery is built at an altitude of 1,500m, which makes walking up the 2,285m mountain less of a climb. There are two ways to the top. The Sikket Sayyidna Musa (Path of our Lord Moses), a 3,750-step 'stairway to Heaven', starts south of the monastery. It is the shortest but steepest route, best saved for the descent. The easier route, a camel path built in the last century, starts behind the monastery and winds slowly around the mountain, allowing plenty of photo opportunities. Along the way, Bedouins with camels wait for the feeble to collapse. The two routes meet just before the top for the last few hundred steps. In the simple chapel on the summit, near the cave where Moses stayed for 40 days, masses are held at dawn. Once there, you'll be overwhelmed by the sheer beauty and the spectacle of light and colours over these barren and dark mountain peaks.

Many pilgrims and visitors climb Gebel Musa to watch the sun rise over the spectacular range

▶▶ Sharm el-Sheikh 240C1

Sharm el-Sheikh, and especially Na'ama Bay, is rapidly becoming one of Egypt's most popular resorts. The town was developed by the Israelis when they occupied Sinai in the 1967 war, at first merely for strategic reasons and later as a tourist resort. When it was returned in the 1980s, Egyptians set up some camps and diving centres. Sharm itself still looks pretty much as it did under the Israelis, but since the opening of the airport and the first five-star hotel – the Fayrouz Hilton – Na'ama Bay has changed dramatically. Four- and five-star hotels are opening on the bay, which is becoming a popular package-tour destination, as well as a place for wealthy Cairenes. Backpackers now head straight for Dahab (see pages 244). There are no alcohol restrictions here and nightlife is pretty active.

Sharm's only 'sight' is Ras Kennedy, a rock formation resembling the face of John F Kennedy, the former US president. In Na'ama Bay, most waterfront hotels and restaurants lie along the promenade. The beach is all right, but the best reefs for snorkelling lie to the north of Na'ama Bay. Half an hour's walk beyond the pontoon pier are the amazing Near Gardens, full of brightly coloured fishes and strangely shaped corals. Another 30 minutes along the coast brings you to the Far Gardens, just as spectacular and often deserted.

▶ Taba 240C3

Taba is a tiny beach resort, with a small hotel, a Hilton and a police station. It was returned to Egypt in 1989 after ten years of negotiations. The Crusader castle on **Geziret el-Faraun (Pharaoh's Island)** ▶, outside town, was built around 1115 by King Baldwin I of Jerusalem to protect pilgrims on their way to St Catherine's monastery. A museum is planned to commemorate the 20th anniversary of the October War. Taba is one of the border crossings into Israel and from there it is now possible to cross to Aqaba in Jordan.

There are other things to do in Sharm el-Sheikh apart from diving

Camel treks
The manager of the Pigeon Hotel (Na'ama Bay) organises a week-long camel trip to St Catherine's, crossing some spectacular and wildly beautiful scenery. The guide is, of course, a Bedouin, who cooks and tells stories about desert life.

■ **Sinai and the Red Sea coast share the honours with Australia's Great Barrier Reef for having the best scuba diving in the world. As 'scuba-tourism' rapidly develops, the challenge for Egypt is to ensure that its underwater wonders are still there for the next generation to enjoy.....■**

Corridor of marvels
'The Red Sea is a corridor of marvels... The happiest hours of my diving experience have been there.'
Jacques Cousteau

Dive sites are often reached after treks across rough ground

The underwater landscape The Red Sea is warm enough and in some places shallow enough to encourage the growth of corals. Corals are minute polyps, anemone-like creatures, which group together in colonies and feed off other small organisms that live in their environment. When corals die, the next generation grows up on top of them. Over a long period of time, they accumulate into a myriad extraordinarily beautiful formations. Lagoon or fringe reefs are the most common formations, running along the coast, just under the surface, with a steep shelf or cliff on their sea side. Patch or pillar corals grow up directly off the seabed in a tower or spike, often reaching to just below the surface of the sea.

Creatures of the deep Corals and the organisms they feed off are part of a mini-ecosystem supporting more than 100 species of brilliant, warm-water fish. The most common inhabitants are yellow anemone fish and damsel fish and a host of other animal-named fish, like goat-, parrot-, turkey-, scorpion- and butterfly-fish. The big fish, usually found at greater depths, include various types of shark, barracuda, sting rays and whales.

Coral care
Significant damage has already been inflicted on the coral and underwater environment by diving boats dropping anchor on the reefs, divers taking trophies, rubbish and building rubble being thrown into the water and other acts of environmental vandalism. Egypt has no shortage of regulatory bodies, including the Environmental Affairs Agency and Coastal Protection Research Institute, but they have been ineffective. You can help by not touching the corals or leaving litter of any sort.

How to see them Especially around Sharm el-Sheikh, some coral reefs are accessible to the energetic snorkeller, but the real thrills are to be had further from the shore. For the safety of the diver *and* the coral, most scuba centres will want to see a diving proficiency certificate from a recognised association before renting equipment. If you aren't already trained, or want to improve your skills, there are excellent courses at diving centres all along the Sinai and Red Sea coasts. Many are attached to hotels, and sometimes their fees are included as part of a package with rooms and flights. Instructors should belong to an internationally recognised body, the largest of which is the Professional Association of Diving Instructors (PADI). A doctor's certificate, confirming fitness to dive, is usually required to enrol on a five-day course leading to the basic PADI certificate.

Dive options It is expensive to hire diving equipment and a boat on your own, but joining a club and diving as part of a group brings the price down considerably. At Sharm el-Sheikh it is possible to visit some fine reefs without hiring a boat, but the best reefs and most exciting dives will involve some transport. A boat is also a must for divers on the Red Sea Coast around Hurghada in Sinai. Diving clubs offer day-trips to popular reefs, but their accessibility means there can be crowds underwater as well as above it. Further afield, some of the dives within easy reach of Sinai's eastern coast present a formidable challenge: the Blue Hole is the most notorious, a 67m shaft which has

Trophy hunting
Photographs are the best souvenirs of your dive, and if you don't have an underwater camera you can rent one from the diving clubs or photographic shops in the resorts.

claimed the lives of several experienced divers. The ultimate dive experiences are probably to be had on 'liveaboard' boats – effectively Red Sea dive-cruises which spend several days or a week around the further-flung, less-visited reefs.

Diving clubs There is a choice of diving clubs in Sharm el-Sheikh, neighbouring Na'ama Bay, Dahab, Nuweiba and Taba. Their rates, group sizes and departure times in the morning (some leave very early) will be a deciding factor. The Sinai Divers, Camel Dive and Aquamarine clubs in Sharm are the longest-established.

The diving year Like the world above, the underwater world has its seasons. Among the highlights are: manta rays in the northern Red Sea (March–May), spawning season around Ras Muhammad (July–August) and the appearance of Napoleon wrasse (September).

Conspicuous against its background, a clown fish nestles among the protective forest of anemone tentacles

■ Most people visit Sinai for its beaches and world-class watersports, but the interior of the peninsula has much to offer. St Catherine's monastery has attracted pilgrims and tourists for centuries, but new discoveries are also drawing attention. As a change from Egypt's man-made treasures, the desert is also a place of remarkable natural beauty.....■

Newly discovered antiquities Egyptologists are still debating the implications of the latest archaeological discoveries in Sinai. A large fort, recently uncovered some 25km east of the Suez Canal, marks the starting point of the Horus Road of War, along which Egyptian armies marched into Palestine. Some claim the fort was built by Seti I, others that it is the city of Pi-Ramses. If it is the latter, then it may be the Old Testament city built by the children of Israel, from which Moses led the Exodus to the promised land. On the road to el-Arish, the mounds at Tell el-Faramah contain the remains of ancient Pelusium, where the Persians surrendered to Alexander the Great in 332BC.

Medieval ruins Many Arab ruins await rediscovery in Sinai, particularly along the pilgrims' route south to Sharm el-Sheikh or due east from Suez to Taba. The latest discoveries include buildings near el-Tur, an important medieval port, and the Mamluk citadel and two circular towers east of Taba, thought to date to the reign of el-Ghuri, the last sultan before the Turkish invasion.

Eternal treasures Although they are hard to visit without Bedouin guides, and are sometimes hard to visit with them, the wadis (dry gullies) of southern Sinai are worth seeking out. Treks of several days, preferably by foot or camel, will take you through desert mountains to brilliantly coloured valleys and cool, clear pools.

In Bedouin society the camel is still perceived as a measure of wealth

252

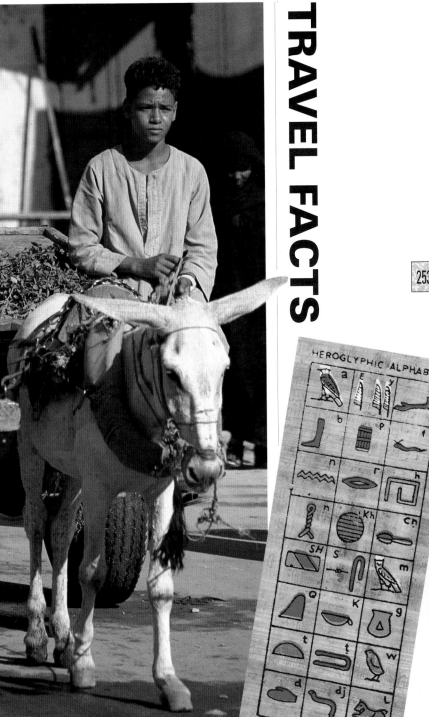

All visitors to Egypt must hold a passport valid for at least six months after the day of arrival and most will need an entry visa (see page 255). It is recommended that you carry your passport with you at all times. It is useful to make a photocopy of it, in case you lose it.

By air There are direct scheduled flights from all European capitals to Cairo and much cheaper charter flights to Luxor, Sharm el-Sheikh and Hurghada. Egypt Air flights arrive in Cairo's Terminal 1 (the old airport), while most European airlines arrive in the more efficient Terminal 2 (the new international airport). The easiest way to get into town is to take a limousine with a fixed price or to haggle with a taxi driver for a cheaper ride. Buses No 949 (24 hours a day from Terminal 2) and No 400 and minibus No 27 (from Terminal 1) leave regularly for Midan el-Tahrir, the main square in central Cairo.

By bus There are regular buses from Tel Aviv, Jerusalem and Eilat in Israel to Sinai and Cairo, crossing the border at Rafah or Taba, where Israeli departure tax and an Egyptian entry fee have to be paid. Frequent buses connect Cairo with Tripoli and Benghazi (Libya), but these days few tourists venture that way.

By car Most people avoid entering by car as the bureaucracy can be painful. You should be allowed to bring a car into Egypt for three months if you can show an *international triptyque* or a *carnet de passage de douane* issued by the automobile club in the country where the car is registered. An extension of three months can be given by the Automobile Club of Egypt, 10 Sharia Qasr en-Nil, Cairo (tel: 02/743355).

Signposting in Cairo has improved over the past few years

By sea Adriatica Lines runs regular ferries from Venice and from Piraeus in Greece to Alexandria and cheaper but more erratic ferries operate from Istanbul to Alexandria via Piraeus, but tickets can only be purchased in Istanbul, Athens or Piraeus. Daily ferries run between Aqaba (Jordan) and Nuweiba (Sinai).

Customs regulations
Visitors are allowed to bring in 200 cigarettes and 1 litre of alcohol. In Luxor and Cairo airports there are duty-free shops after customs where you can buy another

2 litres, and within a month of your arrival you can buy three more bottles and cigarettes from the Egypt Free Store at the end of Sharia Gama'a el-Duwal el-Arabiya in Mohandisseen. There is another shop in the Cairo Sheraton in Dokki and in the centre of Luxor (take your passport). Video cameras, computers and other electronic equipment should be declared on a D-form upon arrival. In case of theft always get a police report, otherwise the equipment will be considered sold and a duty of 100 per cent will have to be paid.

Departing
Always reconfirm your return flight with the airline, and during rush hours be sure to allow at least an hour to get from downtown Cairo to the airport. There is no departure tax.

Registration
Every foreigner must register with the authorities within seven days of arrival. Most hotels will arrange this for you, but do check for the triangular stamp in your passport, as there is a fine for not registering. If you have to do it yourself, the main passport offices are the Mugamma on Cairo's Midan el-Tahrir; on Sharia Khaled Ibn el-Walid near the Isis Hotel in Luxor; 28 Sharia Talaat Harb in Alexandria and in the port of Sharm al-Sheikh.

Visas
Most visitors to Egypt have to obtain a tourist visa. Egyptian consulates abroad issue visas, but it is cheaper and easier to buy one upon arrival at Cairo, Luxor and Hurghada airports or the Alexandria port. However, you **cannot** get a general visa at the land crossings. Visas issued at Rafah or Taba are valid for one week in Sinai only. No extension is possible. Both the single-visit and multiple-entry tourist visas are valid for one month and visa extensions can be applied for at the offices mentioned under 'Registration'. Take your passport, two photographs, money and bank receipts proving that you exchanged US$180 worth of foreign currency for every additional month you wish to stay. Overstaying your visa for a few days is usually okay, but after two weeks a fine has to be paid.

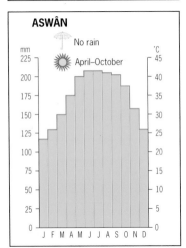

EL QÂHIRA

January & February

April–September

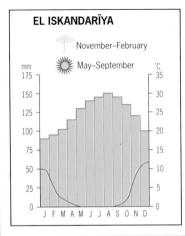

ASWÂN

No rain

April–October

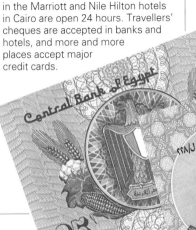

EL ISKANDARÎYA

November–February

May–September

Climate

Temperatures in Egypt differ greatly between night and day. The climate is less extreme on the Mediterranean coast, where it is always cooler than in the rest of the country. March and April can bring the *khamaseen*, a strong, hot wind which carries dust and sand from the Sahara. Cairo is extremely hot from June to September, but at night it becomes more bearable. It can be quite cold in the winter months, often with rain around Christmas. The air becomes drier and hotter towards the south, but although Upper Egypt is hot even in winter, the nights can be surprisingly cold. Aswan has a perfect climate in winter with daytime temperatures around 25 degrees Celsius.

When to go The tourist season in Egypt is traditionally from the end of November to February, but Cairo and even Luxor are quite chilly then, and hotels tend to be overbooked. The best time is either in May, when the heat is still bearable or, even better, October–November, when the long, hot summer comes to an end.

Money matters

The Egyptian pound (LE, *Guineh* in Arabic) is divided in 100 piastres (PT, *Irsh* in Arabic). There are notes for 25 and 50 piastres and 1, 5, 10, 20 and 100 pounds. It is now possible to buy Egyptian currency abroad.

Banks are generally open from Monday to Thursday and Saturday 8:30–1 and sometimes on Sunday 10–12noon. Banks in the airport and in the Marriott and Nile Hilton hotels in Cairo are open 24 hours. Travellers' cheques are accepted in banks and hotels, and more and more places accept major credit cards.

Independent exchange offices are quicker than banks and often offer a better rate. Always keep the bank receipts as you need them to apply for a visa extension, to buy an airline ticket or to pay the bill in a five-star hotel in Egyptian pounds.

National Holidays
Banks, offices and often shops close for public holidays as well as for religious holidays. These include:
1 January (New Year's Day)
25 April (Liberation Day)
1 May (Labour Day)
23 July (Revolution Day)
6 October (Armed Forces Day)
23 October (Suez Day)
23 December (Victory Day)

The Islamic calendar is lunar-based, and compared to the Western calendar the Islamic holidays come about 11 days earlier each year. There are 12 Islamic months and *Ras as-Sanna* (Muslim New Year) on the first day of *Muharram* is a holiday. The *Moulid el-Nabi* (Prophet Muhammad's birthday) is celebrated all over the country, while every neighbourhood, town and city celebrates the *moulid* (feast day) of its local saint (see pages 146–7). The most important Islamic holiday is the holy month of Ramadan when Muslims don't eat, drink or smoke from sunrise until sunset, and abstain from sex for the entire month. Non-Muslims don't have to observe the fast but should show some respect and refrain from eating, drinking and especially smoking in public. Many restaurants and cafés will be closed until the evening and it may be difficult for visitors to travel during this month. Everything slows

The concept of time is not necessarily a Western one

down in a big way, or at least closes much earlier in the afternoon, but the joy and the air of festivity at the end of a long day has some kind of magic, which compensates for the frustration. Shops and offices close for the few days of the *Aid el-Fitr* marking the end of Ramadan, and the *Aid el-Adha (Bayram)* when sheep are slaughtered in memory of Abraham's sacrifice. The main Coptic holidays are *Sham el-Nasseem* (the coming of spring) and Coptic Christmas on 7 January.

Friday is the Muslim Sabbath.

Time differences
Egypt is two hours ahead of GMT. Sydney is seven hours ahead of Egypt, and New York and Montreal are seven hours behind. But there is another time difference called the IBM of Egypt: *'Insha'allah, Bokra, Ma'alesh'. Insha'allah* (God willing) suggests that it may happen, but then again it may not; *Bokra* means tomorrow, or in two weeks, and sometimes never; *Ma'alesh* is what you will hear all the time, meaning 'never mind, don't worry, it wasn't that important anyway'.

Public transport

Buses Inter-city buses are inexpensive and often more comfortable and faster than the train, especially for short distances. For longer distances it may often be preferable to take a night bus. There are three main bus operators. The Upper Egypt Bus Company operates buses to the Nile Valley, el-Faiyum, Western Desert Oases and Red Sea coast. The East Delta Bus Company runs buses to the beach resorts in Sinai, St Catherine and the canal towns. Alexandria, Mersa Matruh and the Delta are served by the West Delta Company. The Arab Union Transport Company runs more expensive but brand-new Superjet buses, with air-conditioning, food, video, toilets and hostesses on board. They run between Cairo, Alexandria, Luxor, Aswan and Hurghada. Tickets should be bought in advance at the appropriate terminals (see pages 110–11). Air-conditioned buses are newer, more comfortable and somewhat more expensive than the old non-air-conditioned buses, but the air-conditioning doesn't always work.

Egypt has an excellent network of internal flights

Domestic flights The national airline, Egypt Air, operates frequent daily flights between Cairo, Luxor, Hurghada and Aswan. Less often there are flights to Alexandria and Kharga Oasis. There are several flights a day between Aswan and Abu Simbel; the return ticket is usually sold as an excursion (see pages 190–1). Air Sinai operates daily flights between Cairo, Luxor, Hurghada, Sharm el-Sheikh and the monastery of St Catherine, and the independent airline ZAS serves Cairo, Aswan, Luxor, St Catherine and Hurghada. The fairly average domestic air fares are calculated in US dollars. It is possible to pay in Egyptian pounds if you provide an exchange receipt. Always book as far as possible in advance as flights get quickly overbooked, especially in winter. All domestic flights leave Cairo from Terminal 1, the old airport. Domestic flights are often delayed and there is no entertainment in the airports, so always bring something to read. Needless to say, the aerial views over the thin Nile Valley strip and the rugged peaks of Sinai are magnificent.

Ferries The ferry between Hurghada and Sharm el-Sheikh makes for a pleasant alternative to the overland trip via Suez. Lately the service has been running frequently and almost daily, but check locally as the schedules change often.

Trains For short journeys trains are often unreliable and much slower than buses, but there are some comfortable trains between the major cities. Wagons-Lits runs three fast turbo-trains per day between Cairo and Alexandria (2 hours), and overnight sleepers to Luxor (11 hours) and Aswan (15 hours). Tickets should be booked in advance at the offices of the Compagnie Internationale des Wagons-Lits in Ramses station or Shepheard's Hotel (tel: 355.3900) on the Corniche in Cairo, at 48 Sharia Giza in Giza (tel: 348.7354) or through American Express and Thomas Cook offices. There are also cheaper first- and second-class air-conditioned trains, but no sleepers, to Alexandria, Luxor and Aswan, for which advance bookings should be made at the railway stations. The non-air-conditioned trains have only second class and third class (often without windows and very crowded) and need not be booked beforehand.

Service taxis The collective service taxis are a faster alternative than the bus, and they go just about anywhere.

The village trains give you time to enjoy the view

The fare is usually not higher than the bus, and on the main routes there are departures all day until late at night. These taxis are called 'Beejou' as they are usually Peugeot saloons seating two passengers and the driver in the front, three in the middle and two or three in the back. There is one disadvantage: the drivers often drive like sheer maniacs, as fast as they can, so that they can pick up their next load. Accidents are common and once you've taken one it will come as no surprise that they are known as 'Flying Coffins'. They are especially dangerous at night and on the Cairo–Alexandria route. There is usually a terminal for service taxis in every town and city. You can't book: just turn up and listen to the drivers shouting out their destinations. Sometimes they try to overcharge tourists; check and see what Egyptians are paying.

Car hire International car hire companies like Hertz, Budget and Avis are represented in the airport and in major hotels at most tourist centres. You can either book in advance from abroad, or arrange a car with one of the local companies. Car hire and petrol are cheap, but you have to be between 25 and 70 years old and have an International Driving Licence. Most companies now accept credit cards, but they may ask for a large deposit. Make sure the compulsory third-party insurance is included.

As the traffic is hellish in Cairo and even more hazardous outside the

An everyday Cairo traffic jam

cities, most tourists prefer to hire a car with a driver, which may also be cheaper. Misr Travel in Cairo (tel: 02/390010) and other limousine agencies provide an air-conditioned Mercedes with a driver for an hour or a few days as required, usually offering good value if there are several people. A cheaper alternative is to make an arrangement with a taxi driver who will often be pleased to change his daily routine for a small adventure, but make sure his car is up to it as well.

Driving tips Officially traffic drives on the right in Egypt, but when it comes to it, drivers will do whatever they can to get around: driving down one-way streets the wrong way, reversing back up main fly-overs if they miss the exit, and zig-zagging at speed through the traffic, often sticking out their arm to point out which direction they are going, if they notify you at all. As well as cars there are donkey carts, motorbikes, an occasional flock of sheep, people jumping off buses and many, many pedestrians. It soon becomes clear that there are no fixed rules for driving in Egypt. Anarchy reigns, so if you enjoy playing those sorts of games, Cairo is for you; if not, stick to taxis and close your eyes until you arrive.

It may seem incredible but there are relatively few road accidents in the towns. The real danger is out on the country roads and 'highways'. Most of the roads are in bad condition. Many have deep potholes and drivers will veer into the other lane without warning to avoid them. Children often play on roads, cattle wander across them and trucks suddenly stop in the middle of nowhere. Avoid driving at night as Egyptians drive without lights, and blind you with their flashlights if they see another car approaching. On country roads you may drive into a roadblock, unannounced, in the dark, or a broken-down truck or just some soldiers playing a game of cards on the tarmac. The official speed limit outside towns is 90kph.

Petrol and car breakdowns Cairo and large towns are well provided with petrol stations (*mahattat benzeen*), but they are rare in the desert and countryside. When you find a station, check how far away the next one is and fill your tank up full. Most petrol stations do oil changes and some maintenance. Egyptians love to tinker and mechanics can be found everywhere. In larger towns there may be a good range of spare parts, while in more remote places mechanics may adopt a more creative approach. Desert driving is hard on vehicles; stick to the track and carry plenty of extra water, petrol and tools.

Hitch-hiking Hitching is virtually non-existent in Egypt. You may get a ride on a truck or a van in areas where there is no public transport, but you will almost always be expected to pay something, as most locals do. Women on their own should never, ever, even consider hitching.

Student and youth travel Youth hostels in Egypt may be very cheap but can hardly be recommended. Apart from the usual night-time curfew, they close for most of the day, are out of the centre and, worst of all, they are often filthy. You will need a membership card at some hostels: for more information, check with the Egyptian Youth Hostel Association, 1 Sharia el-Ibrahimy, Cairo (tel: 02/354 0527). Museums and sights offer a 50 per cent discount and there are considerable reductions on rail and airline tickets if you can produce an official student card. An ISIC Student Card can be issued at their office in Cairo Medical University on Roda Island. Bring proof that you are a student and two photos.

There's no such thing as a free ride, but public transport is cheap

Bookshops

Here is a selection of shops which specialise in foreign language books.
Cairo:
American University Bookstore, in Hill House on the main campus, Midan el-Tahrir (tel: 357 5377)
Les Livres de France, Immobilia Building, Qasr en-Nil (tel: 393 5512)
L'Orientaliste (rare editions and prints), 15 Qasr en-Nil (tel: 575 3418)
Lehnert and Landrock, 44 Sharia Sherif, downtown (tel: 393 5324)
Zamalek Bookstore, 19 Sharia Shag-aret el-Durr, Zamalek (tel: 341 9197)
Alexandria:
Dar el-Mustaqbal, 32 Sharia Safiya Zaghlul (tel: 483 2452)
Luxor:
Aboudi Bookshop, Tourist Bazaar next to the New Winter Palace, Corniche el-Nil (tel: 373390)

Language guide

Egyptians speak Arabic, but English is taught in schools and there is usually someone happy to practise with you. Try out some Arabic and you will be surprised by the enthusiastic response, often 'Oh, you speak Arabic very well, better than me!'. Egyptians love language and they constantly play with words. The following is a phonetic transliteration from the Arabic script.

Basics

Yes	aywa or na'am
No	la
Thank you	shukran
You're welcome	'afwan
Please	min fadlak (to a man), min fadlik (to a woman)
God willing	insha'allah
Good	kwayyis
Bad	mish kwayyis

Greetings

Welcome	ahlan wa-sahlan
(response)	ahlan bik (to men), ahlan biki (to women)
Hello	(to Muslims) as-salaamu aleikum
(response)	wa aleikum as-salaam
Good-bye	ma'a salaama
Hello	(to Copts) saeeda

Good morning	sabaah el-kheer
(response)	sabaah en-nur
Good evening	masaa el-kheer
(response)	masaa en-nur

Numbers

0	sifr
1	wahid
2	itnayn
3	talaata
4	arbah
5	khamsa
6	sitta
7	sabah
8	tamanya
9	tesah
10	ashara
11	ihdaashar
12	itnarshar
13	talatarsha
14	arbahtarsha
15	khamastarsha
16	sittarsha
17	sabahtarsha
18	tamantarsha
19	tisahtarsha
20	ashreen
21	wahid wa-ashreen
30	talaateen
40	arba'een
50	khamseen
100	miyya
300	talaata miyya
1000	alf

Calendar

Sunday	youm il-ahad
Monday	youm il-itnayn
Tuesday	youm it-talaata
Wednesday	youm il-arbah
Thursday	youm il-khamees
Friday	youm il-gumah
Saturday	youm is-sabt
Today	innaharda
Tomorrow	bukra
Yesterday	imbaarih
Later	bahdeen

Directions

Where is Hotel...?	feyn funduk il- ...?
Where is the bus station?	feyn mahattat il-autobees?
Where is the restaurant?	feyn il-matam?
Where is the toilet?	feyn at-twalet?
Right, left, straight ahead	yimeen, shimaal, alatoul

Questions and remarks

Is there? There is...	fi? fi...
How much?	be-kaam?
It is too expensive	da ghaali awi
What's your name?	ismak eh? (to a man) or ismik eh? (to a woman)
My name is...	ismi...
I don't understand	ana mish faa hem (man), fahma (woman)
Go away	imshee
Impossible	mish mumkin

express mail. It helps to make the letter look as uninteresting as possible: avoid inserting photographs or other things which may appeal to someone on the way. Post offices are open from Saturday to Thursday, 8:30–3. The central post office on Midan el-Ataba in Cairo is open 24 hours.

Telephone and fax

Local calls can be made from hotels, kiosks and phone boxes. International calls can be made from Telephone and Telegraph (TT) offices, open 24 hours, most of which will also send

Media

The main foreign newspapers are available, with a few days' delay, from kiosks outside Groppi on Midan Talaat Harb, on 26th July Street in Zamalek (Cairo) and in five-star hotels. The daily *Egyptian Gazette* is published in English, as well as the weekly *Middle East Times* and *Al-Ahram Weekly*. The monthly magazine *Egypt Today* has both good listings of what is going on and interesting features.

There is daily television news in English at 8pm on Channel 2, which also broadcasts foreign movies (for schedules see the *Egyptian Gazette*).

Egyptians love to read the newspapers and there's no shortage of them in the cities

Post offices

Most airmail letters to Europe take around a week to arrive; mail to North America or Australia takes longer. Since about 15 per cent of all letters get lost, you can increase your luck by sending mail from a main post office or a five-star hotel, which should also sell stamps, or by EMS

faxes (cheaper than from most hotels). Look for the orange direct-dial phones which take phone cards (sold here) and avoid the old system whereby you have to pay a minimum of three minutes for opening the line. The main TT offices in Cairo are on Midan el-Tahrir and at 8 Sharia Adly. British Airways and Nile Hilton offer British Telecom and USA Direct services.

Crime and police

Cairo is safer than most European capitals, but tourists are considered wealthy and some Egyptians cannot resist the temptation. Always take special care of your passport, money and plane tickets. In most hotels you can deposit valuables at the reception desk for safe-keeping, but always ask for a receipt. The tourist police are more helpful to foreigners than the ordinary police.

Tourist police are usually helpful

Drugs It is illegal to bring drugs into the country. There is a serious fine for possession of drugs and mandatory sentences of life imprisonment or even hanging for anyone convicted of dealing or smuggling.

Emergency phone numbers in Cairo

Ambulance: 123
Fire Brigade: 125
Police: 122
Tourist Police: 926028 (Headquarters); 965239 (Cairo Airport); 904827 (Khan el-Khalili); 850259 (Giza Pyramids)

Embassies and consulates

A complete list of embassies and consulates can be found in the Cairo Yellow Pages. A few countries are also represented in Port Said and Alexandria. Cairo addresses include:
Australia: Cairo Plaza Tower (fifth floor), 1097 Corniche el-Nil, Bulaq (tel: 777900)
Canada: 6 Sharia Muhammad Fahmy el-Sayyid, Garden City (tel: 354 3110)
Ireland: 3 Borg Abu el-Feda (north of Zamalek Bridge), Zamalek (tel: 340 8264)
New Zealand: Represented by UK.
UK: 7 Sharia Ahmad Ragab, Garden City (tel: 354 0850)
USA: 5 Sharia Amerika Latina, Garden City (tel: 355 7371)

Egyptian embassies abroad

Australia: 1 Darwin Avenue, Yarralumla, Canberra (tel: 062/734437)
Canada: 454 Laurier Avenue East, Ottawa, Ontario K1P 5P4 (tel: 613/234-4931)
UK: 75 South Audley Street, London W1Y 8EL (tel: 0171/499 2401)
USA: 2300 Decatur Plaza NW, Washington DC 20008 (tel: 202/232-5400)

Lost property

Report any losses or thefts to the tourist police, open 24 hours in most cities. If a passport is lost, report to the tourist police first and then contact your consulate or embassy as soon as possible. For travellers' cheques or credit cards, notify the issuing company.

Health

Vaccinations No vaccination certificates are required to enter Egypt unless you are coming from an infected area. The World Health Organisation issues regular health bulletins for travellers, which you can obtain from your doctor. They may recommend polio, tetanus, yellow fever, cholera, typhoid and hepatitis A inoculations. Malaria occurs in the Delta, and may become a bigger problem, so check with your doctor in advance when you know what part of the country you will be visiting.

Precautions Although the heavily chlorinated tap water is safe to drink, it is advisable to stick to mineral water. The body risks dehydration

Pharmacies are helpful and willing to give advice on minor ailments

because of the heat, so drink at least 3 litres of fluids a day. Make sure the food you eat has been properly washed and that the place where it was prepared is clean. For the first few days, avoid eating seafood, rare meat, salads or fruits that are difficult to wash, and food from street stalls. As the sun is hot all year round it is advisable to use a high-factor suntan lotion and to wear a hat and sunglasses. Avoid iced drinks during the heat of the day and wait until after sunset to have alcoholic drinks. Take antiseptic cream for cuts as flies can spread infections, and insect repellant as mosquitoes can make life a misery and may carry malaria. Mosquito coils and plug-in machines with tablets are available in most pharmacies.

Common health complaints Almost every tourist at some stage suffers from diarrhoea, jokingly called 'the pharaoh's curse'. It is usually a matter of adjusting to the different climate and diet, and it passes in a few days if you rest, stick to plain food and drink plenty of fresh lime juice and mineral water. If you have a severe attack with cramps and/or vomiting try Imodium or Lomotil (available in Egypt), and if this doesn't work contact a doctor. Most doctors speak English or French and the hotel reception can help you find one.

Hospitals In emergencies, the following private hospitals are recommended (a cash deposit may be requested): the Anglo-American Hospital beside the Cairo Tower, Gezira (tel: 340 6162) and As-Salaam

International Hospital, Corniche el-Nil, Maadi (tel: 363 8050).

Pharmacies Pharmacists in Egypt usually speak English and are happy to recommend medicines for minor complaints. They stock a wide range of medicines, which are cheap and available over the counter (check expiry dates). Some pharmacies, like the ones on 26th-of-July Street and Sharia Brazil in Zamalek (Cairo), have more expensive imported medicines. Also in Cairo, try Ataba, 17 Midan el-Ataba (24 hours) or Isaaf, 3 26th-of-July Street, Bulaq (24 hours).

Providing water is an act of charity in a hot country

265

Camping

Egypt is not an obvious place for camping as campsites, mainly found along the coast and in the oases, often lack proper facilities and shade. The camps attached to hotels are slightly better and at least provide showers and toilets in the hotel. Before camping on a beach check with the local police and be aware that many isolated beaches are still mined (see page 221). Camping in the desert is less problematic but if you camp somewhere near water, the land is sure to belong to someone, so again ask for permission before getting into trouble.

Children

Egyptians just love children and wherever you decide to go, your children will be welcome, too. You may find a restaurant comes to a standstill as all the waiters are cooing over your blue-eyed darling, and people will stop you in the street to kiss the baby. Five-star and some four-star hotels provide high-chairs and cots, and they can usually arrange for babysitters. You may find that their attitude towards safety is different from yours, so explain clearly what you expect. You will need to take particular care of your child's hygiene, as children are even more prone to stomach bugs and other infections, and do bring a sun block (hard to find in Egypt) as the strong sun is dangerous for their skin. Disposable nappies and powdered milk can be found in most pharmacies, and baby food is sold in the bigger cities.

Children will enjoy walking in the bazaar, playing hide-and-seek in tem-

Don't worry about the children – Egyptians will keep them entertained

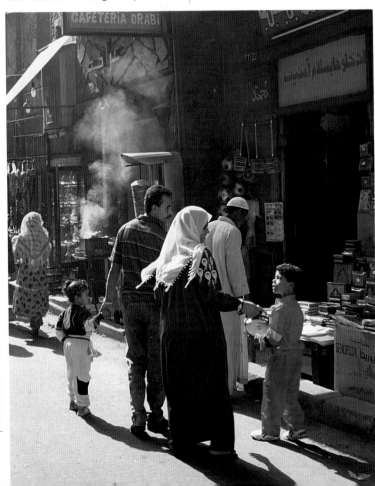

ples, riding in a horse cart or on a camel, or sailing along the Nile in a *felucca*. In Cairo there are a few special attractions for children:

Cairo Puppet Theatre, Midan el-Ataba in Ezbekiya Gardens, downtown (tel: 910954); open October–May, daily performances at 6:30pm, and also at 11am Friday and Saturday.

Cairo Zoo, Giza; open daily 6am–5pm (avoid Fridays when it is very crowded); small admission fee.

Dr Ragab's Pharaonic Village, Jacob Island, Corniche el-Nil, 2km south of Giza Bridge; open daily 9–9; admission fee for children over age 6 and adults.

Sinbad Amusement Park, near the airport; open daily 5pm–2am in summer, 2–11pm in winter, on Fridays open from 10am; admission fee for children and adults.

Clothing

Bring a few warm woollens, as well as lighter cotton clothes in autumn, spring and winter, as the temperature drops considerably once the sun has gone. In summer you will need light cotton clothes and a sweater for some cooler nights. However hot it gets, try to dress modestly and avoid shorts, sleeveless T-shirts and transparent clothes. Take good walking shoes as there is a lot of walking around the sights. A sun hat and sunglasses are essential.

Electricity

Electrical current is 220 volts AC and sockets take the standard European two-pin plug.

Opening times

In general, shops and department stores are open from 9–1 and 5–9. Shops in tourist centres may open later and stay open all day until 10pm. Some shops close on Fridays, but most close on Sundays. Museums are open daily from 9–4 and most of them close for Friday prayers from 11–1. During Ramadan the timetable changes again: most museums will close around 3pm and shops will close around 3pm but reopen from 8–10pm or later. For banks see Money matters, page 256–7.

CONVERSION CHARTS

FROM	TO	MULTIPLY BY
Inches	Centimetres	2.54
Centimetres	Inches	0.3937
Feet	Metres	0.3048
Metres	Feet	3.2810
Yards	Metres	0.9144
Metres	Yards	1.0940
Miles	Kilometres	1.6090
Kilometres	Miles	0.6214
Acres	Hectares	0.4047
Hectares	Acres	2.4710
Gallons	Litres	4.5460
Litres	Gallons	0.2200
Ounces	Grams	28.35
Grams	Ounces	0.0353
Pounds	Grams	453.6
Grams	Pounds	0.0022
Pounds	Kilograms	0.4536
Kilograms	Pounds	2.205
Tons	Tonnes	1.0160
Tonnes	Tons	0.9842

MEN'S SUITS

UK	36	38	40	42	44	46	48
Rest of Europe	46	48	50	52	54	56	58
US	36	38	40	42	44	46	48

DRESS SIZES

UK	8	10	12	14	16	18
France	36	38	40	42	44	46
Italy	38	40	42	44	46	48
Rest of Europe	34	36	38	40	42	44
US	6	8	10	12	14	16

MEN'S SHIRTS

UK	14	14.5	15	15.5	16	16.5	17
Rest of Europe	36	37	38	39/40	41	42	43
US	14	14.5	15	15.5	16	16.5	17

MEN'S SHOES

UK	7	7.5	8.5	9.5	10.5	11
Rest of Europe	41	42	43	44	45	46
US	8	8.5	9.5	10.5	11.5	12

WOMEN'S SHOES

UK	4.5	5	5.5	6	6.5	7
Rest of Europe	38	38	39	39	40	41
US	6	6.5	7	7.5	8	8.5

267

Photography

Egypt is a photographer's paradise and the light is magical. As it is usually bright outside, slow film speeds like 100 ISO or 64 ISO are recommended. Photography in most museums and sights is allowed but you will need to buy a special ticket, and even then it is forbidden to use a flash light so you will need at least 400 ISO film, which is hard to find in Egypt. Brand-name films are widely available in the tourist areas, but anything more specialised will need to be brought from abroad. Check the sell-by date as it may be old, sun-bleached stock. Film can now be processed in one or two hours in most tourist centres, but if you are a perfectionist it's better to wait until you get home, as films may get scratched or overexposed.

It is forbidden to photograph bridges, airports, railway stations, government buildings, dams or anything which Egyptians consider important to their security. Ask permission first or they may confiscate your film. Always ask people before taking their picture as some, especially villagers, religious people and women, may find it offensive.

Places of worship

Cairo and Alexandria both have several Catholic, Greek Orthodox, Protestant and Coptic churches, as well as Jewish synagogues. The following places in Cairo have services in English; times are listed in *Egypt Today* magazine.

Come prepared to take photographs...

All Saints' Cathedral (Anglican/Episcopal): 5 Sharia Michel Lutfallah (near the Marriott Hotel), Zamalek (tel: 341 8391)
St Andrew's United Church (Protestant/International): 38, 26th July Street, Bulaq (tel: 360 3527)
St Joseph's Roman Catholic Church: 2 Sharia Bank Misr, downtown (tel: 393 6677)
Jewish Synagogue: Sharia Adly, downtown (check here for information on services)

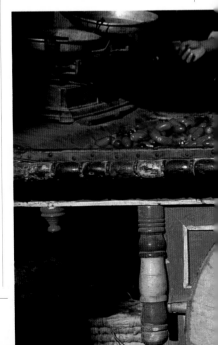

Tipping or *Baksheesh*
In Egypt you are a *khawaga* (foreigner) and *khawagas* are always rich, so they are supposed to have *baksheesh* (literally: share wealth) for everyone. It is obvious that you tip a waiter, a porter or a taxi driver, but the guard who opens a tomb or switches on the light 'specially for you', or the friendly man who wants to show you a 'special' mosque will also expect *baksheesh*. Children whose picture you took and even people who didn't do anything at all will ask for it, and alms for the poor are called *baksheesh*, too. It can be a pest as it will seem everyone wants something from you, but it is very much part of the culture. It is best to get used to paying something if someone makes your life easier – indeed, this form of bribery is often necessary to get something done – but resist giving it, apart from alms, to people who haven't done anything but are asking you because you are a *khawaga*.

Toilets
Public toilets, be it the squatting, sitting or stand-up type, are often filthy and do not provide toilet paper but a bucket of water or a squirter to splash yourself with. If you want to avoid these, look for toilets in the upmarket hotels or restaurants.

Visitors with disabilities
There are no special facilities for people with disabilities and to visit the major sights may prove a real challenge, but it will be a rewarding one. Egyptians accept disabilities as God's will and are always ready to help out. If arrangements are made beforehand it should be possible to see a lot of Egypt. Dr Sami Bishara of ETAMS Tours, 13 Sharia Qasr en-Nil, Cairo (tel: 02/575 2462) specialises in organising travel arrangements for individual travellers or groups.

Women travellers
Some Egyptian men are convinced that foreign women come to Egypt to have sex, and they can be annoying. The most important thing you can do is to dress modestly. Wear loose clothes, such as a long shirt over a long skirt or baggy trousers, covering arms, legs and curves. Be confident when you walk in the streets, don't react to verbal obscenities but shout as soon as someone touches you, and if you are dressed properly people will come to your aid. In public places, such as buses, there is often a section reserved for women. If not, sit near other women who will often protect you if there is any hassle.

...subjects are many and varied

269

Abroad

Canada: Place Bonaventure, 40 Frontenac, PO Box 304, Montreal, Québec H5A IB4 (tel: 014/861-4420)

UK & Ireland: Egyptian House, 170 Piccadilly, London W1 (tel: 0171/493 5282)

USA: 630 Fifth Avenue, Suite 1706, New York, NY 10111 (tel: 212/332-2570)

In Egypt

Don't expect to get too much help or information from tourist offices in Egypt. Some – the offices in Alexandria and Luxor for example – are really helpful. Others, as in Cairo or Aswan, can be helpful if the right person is behind the desk. Tourist offices are a good place to check for the official rates of taxis, excursions and *feluccas*. In smaller offices you will be lucky to get one of their antiquated brochures.

Local tourist offices include:

Alexandria: Midan Saad Zaghlul (tel: 03/4807611); the Marine Passenger Station at the Port (tel: 03/803494); and Misr Station (tel: 03/4925985)

Aswan: Corniche el-Nil, in the shopping arcade behind the little park at the northern end of the Corniche (tel: 097/323297)

Cairo: 5 Sharia Adly, downtown (tel: 02/391 3454); Pyramids of Giza, Giza (tel: 02/385 0259); Railway station, Sharia Ramses, Ramses (tel: 02/764214); Cairo International Airport, terminal 2 (tel: 02/245 4400)

el-Faiyum: Sharia Gumhuriya (tel: 084/322586, ext. 177)

Hurghada: Sharia Bank Misr, beyond the Sheraton (tel: 065/446513)

el-Kharga (New Valley): Sharia el-Nasser, near the Fellahin Monument (tel: 088/901205)

Luxor: Corniche el-Nil, between the temple and the Winter Palace (tel: 095/372215) and the Visitors' Centre, Corniche el-Nil, opposite Mina Palace Hotel (095/382215)

Mersa Matruh: Governorate Building (tel: 03/394 3192, ext. 7)

Minya: Governorate Building, Corniche el-Nil (tel: 086/320150)

Port Said: Sharia Filasteen (tel: 066/23868)

The Alexandrian Mosque of Abu el-Abbas el-Mursi

HOTELS AND RESTAURANTS

HOTELS AND RESTAURANTS

ACCOMMODATION

£££ = expensive
(over £50)
££ = moderate
(£20–£50)
£ = budget
(Less than £20)

CAIRO

The telephone code for
Cairo is 02.

Anglo Swiss Hotel (£) 14
Sharia Champollion,
downtown (tel: 751497).
Quite noisy and faded old-
style hotel with an airy
dining room and spacious
double rooms.
Atlas Zamalek Hotel (££)
20 Sharia Gama'a el-
Duwal el-Arabiya,
Mohandeseen (tel: 346
4175). Modern and com-
fortable hotel with busi-
ness facilities and small
swimming pool. Away
from downtown but close
to restaurants and
Western-style shopping.
Very popular discotheque
called Tamango.
Cairo Marriott (£££) Sharia
Saraya el-Gezira, Zamalek
(tel: 340 8888). The main
building is the splendid
Gezira Palace, built to
commemorate the open-
ing of the Suez Canal
(1869), and although the
rooms are in two adjacent
tower blocks, the Marriott
has retained some of the
regal atmosphere. The
Garden Promenade is a
good place to recover
from the Cairene heat
and beat.
Cosmopolitan (££) 1 Sharia
Ibn Taalab, downtown (tel:
392 3845). Grand art nou-
veau building in a quiet
backwater in the middle of
downtown. All rooms
were recently refurbished
and offer all mod-cons.
Good value and nostalgia
with a capital N.
Flamenco (££) 2 Sharia el-
Gezira el-Wusta, Zamalek
(tel: 340 0815). Modern
Spanish-run hotel with
spacious rooms, some

overlooking the river and,
on a clear day, the pyra-
mids. Located in a nice
part of Zamalek. Good
Spanish restaurant.
Garden City House (£) 23
Sharia Kamal el-Din Saleh,
Garden City (tel: 354
4969). Basic, large
and clean rooms, some
with a view on the Nile.
Half board is compulsory,
but the food is pleasant
and breakfast conversa-
tions with resident archaeologists and scholars are
interesting. The friendly
owner is always ready to
tell stories of Cairo's
heyday. Reservations are
a must.
Horus House (££) 21
Sharia Ismail Muhammad,
Zamalek (tel: 340 3977).
Very friendly and clean
hotel in the heart of
Zamalek, also rents out a
few flats for longer stays.
People usually come back
to this hotel or stay for a
while, so reservation is
necessary. Restaurant
serves cheap and good
set lunches.
Al-Husayn (£) Midan el-
Husayn, Khan el-Khalili
(tel: 918664). Definitely the
best hotel in the old part
of town. Rooms are clean
but very basic with good
views over the medieval
city. During religious festivals it is practically impossible to sleep as the party
goes on all night.
Lotus (£) 12 Sharia Talaat
Harb, downtown (tel:
750627). Friendly staff and
clean rooms, some with
bath and air-conditioning.
Mayfair (£) 9 Sharia Aziz
Osman, Zamalek (tel: 340
7315). Quiet, pastel-deco-
rated rooms with
balconies overlooking a
tree-lined street. It has a
relaxed, old-fashioned
atmosphere, and a cafete-
ria on a pleasant terrace.
Mena House Oberoi (£££)
Pyramids Road, Giza (tel:
383 3222). Deluxe rooms
with The View: the
Pyramids of Giza. Set in a
19th-century khedival

hunting lodge with a
splendid old wing; rooms
here are decorated with
taste and some antiques.
There is a less impressive
modern wing in the gar-
den. The swimming pool
also has pyramids view
and there is a divine
Indian restaurant.
Mövenpick Heliopolis
(£££) Cairo International
Airport Road, Heliopolis
(tel: 247 0077). Convenient
hotel just outside the airport. Good food and
excellent service.
Nile Hilton (£££) Corniche
el-Nil, downtown (tel:
578044). This was the first
modern international
hotel built in Egypt,
opened by Nasser in 1959.
Located in the heart of
Cairo, next door to the
Egyptian Museum and
overlooking the Nile, it
has become an institution
in the city. Wealthy
Cairenes and expatriates
meet in the Ibis Café,
Jacky's nightclub is one of
the city's best, the casino
is always crowded till the
early hours and there are
several other restaurants
as well as the Taverne du
Champ de Mars, a *fin de
siècle* café imported from
Brussels. Pleasant swim-
ming pool.
Odeon Palace (£–££) 6
Sharia Abdel Hamid Said,
downtown (tel: 776637).
Modern hotel with clean,
no-nonsense rooms and
friendly staff. Pleasant bar
on roof terrace, popular
with local intellectuals and
foreign correspondents.
Pension Oxford (£) 32
Sharia Talaat Harb, down-
town (tel: 758173). One of
the cheapest places to
stay, very popular with
long-haul travellers. Basic
accommodation with
communal bathrooms,
friendly atmosphere and
no shortage of incredible
travel stories.
Pension Roma (£) 169
Sharia Muhammad Farid,
downtown (tel: 391 1088).
Moorish façade and 1940s

atmosphere. Very clean, large rooms with high ceilings. Strongly recommended as the best budget hotel in town, advance booking preferable.

President (££) 22 Sharia Taha Husayn, Zamalek (tel: 340 0652). Friendly, modern hotel with good business facilities, located in a quiet, residential area, but close to shops and restaurants. Recommended for good value. The Cellar Bar downstairs is very popular and serves good *mezze* (appetisers).

Tulip (£) 3 Midan Talaat Harb, downtown (tel: 393 9433). Another favourite old-style hotel. Basic and clean rooms with bathroom; those in the front have a good view over the bustle of the square but tend to be noisy. Better book in advance.

Victoria Hotel (££) 66 Sharia el-Gumhuriya, Ramses (tel: 917211). Recently renovated 1930s hotel with old, polished mahogany furniture and air-conditioning. Has a pleasant terrace where couples flirt over a lemonade.

Viennoise (£) 11 Sharia Mahmoud Bassiouni, downtown (tel: 751949). Huge, quite decrepit rooms overlooking a busy downtown crossroads, but very atmospheric.

Windsor (£–££) 19 Sharia el-Alfy, downtown (tel: 915277). Faded, high-ceilinged rooms with old wooden furniture and out-of-place posters of Austria and Tyrol. It is one of the only hotels with a feel of what Cairo used to be, and a favourite for many who know Cairo. Book in advance. The lounge bar is wonderful – even more faded and totally old-fashioned!

LOWER NILE VALLEY

Asyut

Badr Hotel (££) Sharia el-Thallaga (tel: 088/329811). A middle-range hotel decorated in notorious bad taste. Rooms have fridge, video and at least one has TV. The only real restaurant in town, and the only place that might have a beer, but it's expensive for what is on offer.

Al-Haramein (£) Sharia el-Hilaly (tel: 088/320426). Very basic rooms, some with fans.

el-Faiyum

Auberge du Lac (££) Lake Qarun (tel: 084/324924 or Cairo reservation: 02/725848). Former lodge of King Farouk with pleasant rooms on the lake.

Montazah (£) Sharia Ismail el-Medani (tel: 084/324633). Simple and more or less clean in the north part of town; sometimes with hot water and fans.

Oasis Tourist Village (£) Lake Qarun (tel: 084/701565). Very basic accommodation, but on the lake.

Panorama Shakshouk (££) Lake Qarun (tel: 084/701314 or Cairo reservation: 02/725848). Newer but similar rooms to the Auberge du Lac.

Minya

Beach Hotel (el-Shati) (£) 31 Sharia el-Gumhuriya (tel: 086/322307). Clean and carpeted rooms with fans or air-conditioning.

Ibn Khasib (£) 5 Sharia Rageb (tel: 086/324535). Restored old-style rooms with fans; nice garden. In the centre of town.

Lotus (£) 1 Sharia Port Said (tel: 086/324541). Good rooms with fans. The top-floor bar and restaurant, overlooking the Nile and valley, are good for dinner or just for a beer.

PLM Azur Nefertiti (££) Sharia Corniche el-Nil (tel:

086/331515). The most comfortable hotel in town, often used by tour groups. Slightly out of the centre but with good views over the Nile. Swimming pool. Rooms may be noisy on Thursday nights as there is usually at least one wedding party going on.

Nag Hammadi

Aluminium Hotel (££) 40km from Abydos (tel: 096/581320). Comfortable, ugly Soviet-style hotel, part of an aluminium smelting plant. It's ideal as a base for visiting the temples of Abydos and Dendara.

LUXOR

The telephone code for Luxor is 095.

Akhetaton Village Club Med (££) Sharia Khaled Ibn Walid (tel: 580850). Traditional Club-Med style hotel in an Arab-esque décor, with very pleasant swimming pool overlooking the Nile and popular nightclub.

Emilio (££) Sharia Yusuf Hasan (tel: 373570). Popular with tour groups. Small rooftop swimming pool with breezy views over Luxor town and temple. Advance booking recommended.

Etap Luxor (£££) Corniche el-Nil (tel: 580944). Four-star hotel with all facilities and a heated swimming pool. Good front terrace to sip your aperitif at sunset. Rooms with views over the Nile and the Theban Hills.

Habu Hotel (£) opposite the Temple of Medinat Habu, Nag Lolah, West Bank (tel: 372477). Very simple, blue-washed rooms in traditional architecture, with a large terrace overlooking the temple and a garden. Relaxing atmosphere – strongly recommended if Luxor gets to you, or if you want to stay awhile.

Horus (£) Sharia el-Maabad, opposite Luxor Temple (tel: 372165). Modern, simple and clean rooms with air-conditioning; there are spectacular views over the temple from the front rooms. The back hangs over the *souk* (market).

Isis (££–£££) Sharia Khaled Ibn Walid (tel: 373366). Ever-expanding hotel, very popular with tour groups. It has two good swimming pools and views over the Nile; several international restaurants and a new shopping centre.

Mersam (£) Known as Sheikh Ali's Hotel, near the Noble Tombs, West Bank (tel: 372403). Basic but pleasant mud-brick rooms with fans and a quiet garden. It's run by the son of Sheikh Ali, who helped excavate the tomb of Seti I. His family, the Abdul Rassuls, were once notorious tomb robbers, but he is happy just to show people around.

Mina Palace (£) Corniche el-Nil, opposite visitors' centre (tel: 372074). Good-value rooms with air-conditioning, TV, new bathrooms and excellent views over the Nile and Luxor Temple. Pleasant roof terrace, cool beers.

Mövenpick Jolie Ville (£££) 5km out of town, Crocodile Island (tel: 374855). Probably the best resort hotel in Egypt. Deluxe bungalows set in beautiful gardens beside the Nile. Wonderful food in several restaurants, excellent swimming pool, children's activities and zoo, and – above all – immaculate service. Recommended for a longer rest after seeing tombs and temples.

New Windsor (££) Sharia Nefertiti (tel: 374306). Modern hotel between the *souk* and the Nile, with health club and swimming pool on the roof and a good international phone and fax office.

Pharaoh's (£) Between the ticket office and the Temple of Medinat Habu, Nag Lolah, West Bank (tel: 581-515-702). Slightly more upmarket than other hotels this side of the river. Clean rooms with air-conditioning or fan, some with views of the temple. Oriental restaurant and nice, kitsch beer garden.

Philippe (£) Sharia Nefertiti (tel: 372284). Very well-run hotel with roof garden. Clean rooms with bathroom and air-conditioning, views over the Nile and excellent atmosphere. Good value for money, so advance booking is recommended.

Ramoza (£) Sharia el-Mahatta (tel: 372270). Popular cheapie, close to the station and overlooking the noisy square; also popular with tour groups.

Winter Palace (££–£££) Sharia Corniche el-Nil (tel: 580422). The Old Winter Palace is a grand colonial hotel which is being refurbished as a luxurious, five-star hotel. It has long, wide corridors, a beautiful staircase, and high-ceilinged rooms with the best views of the Nile and Theban hills. Grand swimming pool in lush gardens. The new wing next door has all modern facilities but no atmosphere.

UPPER EGYPT AND NUBIA

Abu Simbel

Nefertari (££) Abu Simbel (tel: 097/316402). Located between the temple and the airport. Clean, air-conditioned rooms with swimming pool, and tennis courts for those who can brave the heat. Ideal if you want to watch the sun rise over the temple.

Nobaleh Ramses (££) Tourist City, Abu Simbel (tel: 097/311660). Less pleasant, state-run hotel, but nearer to the temple.

Aswan

The telephone code in the Aswan area is 097.

Amoun (££), Amoun Island (tel: 322555). This Club-Med resort, on its own island with a free ferry from the Corniche, overlooks Elephantine Island and the Old Cataract Hotel on one side, and the desert and more Nile on the other side. It is quite small, but a great place to relax with good-size rooms, a pleasant swimming pool and good meals. Much recommended and cheaper in summer.

Aswan Oberoi (£££) Elephantine Island (tel: 314666). The ugly tower of the hotel, which once supported a panoramic restaurant, has become one of Aswan's landmarks. Despite the architecture there are good views, efficient service, luxurious rooms and an excellent swimming pool to recommend it. A mock-pharaonic boat is used as a ferry to the Corniche.

Basma (££–£££) In front of the Nubian Museum, Sharia el-Fanadik (tel: 310901). New resort hotel, decorated by two Egyptian artists, for people who want to enjoy Aswan's pleasant climate a little longer. Beautiful pool in the patio.

Cleopatra (££) Sharia Sa'ad Zaghlul (tel: 314003). Recently refurbished rooms with air-conditioning, business facilities and a swimming pool on the roof. Good views and very central.

Horus (£) 98 Corniche el-Nil (tel: 323323). Popular, cheap hotel with basic rooms, some with a noisy air-conditioner and a view on the Nile. Quite a pleasant bar on the roof.

Kalabsha (££) (tel: 322666). Next door to the two Cataract Hotels, and part of the Pullman chain, the rooms are modest but clean and comfortable, and guests are entitled to use the Cataract swimming pool.

Mena (£) Sharia Atlas, near the station (tel: 324388). Very cheap, clean but slightly tatty rooms with air-conditioning, private bathroom and, as they advertise, a friendly laundry service.

New Abu Simbel (£) At the northern end of the Corniche el-Nil (tel: 326096). Modern, comfortable rooms with air-conditioning and carpet; some with balconies overlooking the Nile. Pleasant garden terrace that serves beer.

Old Cataract Pullman (£££) Sharia Abtal el-Tahrir, next to the Ferial Gardens (tel: 316002). One of the most romantic hotels in Egypt, recently refurbished in the old style. The spacious rooms on the Nile side have splendid views over the river and the islands. The swimming pool is set in beautiful, perfumed gardens and breakfast is served by the friendly staff on your balcony or in the impressive Moorish Hall. For a splurge, stay in the vast Agatha Christie suite or in King Farouk's.

Ramses (£) Sharia Abtal el-Tahrir (tel: 324000). New building in the centre of Aswan. Rooms have air-conditioning, private bath, telephone and views over the River Nile. Good value.

Idfu (Edfu)

Dar as-Salam (£) Sharia el-Maglis, next to the Temple of Horus (tel: 097/701727). Very basic hotel used by market traders. Cleanest hotel in town, with the luxury of hot showers, but only stay here if you must.

Kom Ombo

Cleopatra (£) Near the service-taxi stop (tel: 097/500325). Rooms, with fans, are not always clean and the bathrooms are less so. Only if you must.

WESTERN DESERT OASES

The telephone code for the New Valley Oases is 088.

Bahariya

Alpenblick (£) Behind the police station, el-Bawiti. This friendly hotel has an exotic name for its location, along with basic but clean rooms with shared bathrooms. The owner organises trips to the springs and the White Desert, and provides information on all you want to know about Bahariya.

Bir Mathar Rest House (£) In Bir Mathar, 6km from el-Bawiti. Another government rest house, with slightly more pleasant rooms than the one above, near the hot springs. Bring food and drinks as the choice may be limited.

Dakhla

Gardens (£) Beside Hamdy's restaurant (tel: 941577). Basic, clean rooms with mosquito screens and shared bathrooms.

Mebarez (£) On the main road to Farafra, Mut (tel: 941524). Modern, clean and friendly place. Rooms have fans and bathrooms, and breakfast is included. By far the best place to stay in Mut.

Poolside Rest House (£) 3km north of Mut (tel: 941530). Clean bungalows with toilet, near the hot springs. Meals are available, and there is also a camping area.

Farafra

Rest House One and Two (£) Qasr Farafra. Both rest houses offer spartan and fairly clean dormitories and, usually, cold running water.

Kharga

Hamad Alla (£) Sharia Nada, off Sharia Nasser (tel: 900638). Clean rooms with private showers and fans (some with air-conditioning) and friendly service.

Waha Hotel (£) Off Sharia Nasser (tel: 900393). Clean rooms with no fans but a few have air-conditioning. They also offer quite decent food.

Siwa

Arous al-Waha (£) At the entrance of the town. The government-run 'Bride of the Oasis', as the hotel is called, is no longer young, offering only decrepit rooms. You usually have to find meals elsewhere.

Cleopatra Hotel (£) On the main road past the market. The place to stay. New, clean rooms with bathroom and balconies overlooking Shali. Managed by the eccentric sea captain, Muhammad.

ALEXANDRIA AND THE DELTA

Alexandria

The telephone code for Alexandria is 03.

Acropole (£) 27 Rue Chambre de Commerce (tel: 805980). A top-floor neighbour to the famous Cecil Hotel. The popular Acropole has clean, simple rooms with high ceilings, old wood furniture, shared bathrooms and a lift that works most days. Still run by Greeks, so you might get a sense of Alexandria of yesteryear. Advance booking.

Agamy Palace (£–££) el-Bittash Beach (tel: 433 0230 or 433 0386). Spacious rooms with balconies overlooking the beach and a swimming pool make this a popular place to escape from noisy and crowded Alexandria.

Ailema (£) 21 Sharia Amin Fikry (tel: 482 7011). Tucked away in a side street. Basic, clean, old-style rooms, some with balconies overlooking the bay, Ramla tram station and the roof garden of the Armed Forces Club. A little quieter than most hotels in the area. The hotel restaurant does not serve alcohol.

Cecil (£££) Midan Sa'ad Zaghlul (tel: 483 7173). Alexandria's most famous hotel, with names like Lawrence Durrell, Noel Coward and Somerset Maugham in its guest book; the Pullman-run Cecil is no longer glamorous but is still the place to stay. Seaside rooms have magnificent views over the eastern harbour and the sweeping Corniche up to Qaytbay Fort. The coffee shop is a good place to hang around in the early evening; the new roof garden is perfect for sunset and sea breezes at the end of a hot day.

Holiday (£) 6 Midan Orabi (tel: 803517 or 801559). More popular with Arabs than Westerners. Rooms have wacky decoration and often several TVs, but are clean and well kept. Views over the sea and Orabi Square.

Metropole (£–££) 52 Sharia Sa'ad Zaghlul (tel: 482 1465/7). This period hotel is a little faded but retains much of its charm and is much recommended. All the rooms have high ceilings and old wooden furniture; some have sea views, and therefore also noise from the tram station. The airy breakfast room looks out over the square and the bay and, like the restaurant, has wonderful art nouveau décor. Reservations are advised.

Palestine (£££) Montazah Palace (tel: 547 3500). Not as old as the Cecil, but almost as much of an institution. Quiet, relaxing atmosphere makes it popular with Egyptian and expatriate families on weekends and holidays. All rooms have balconies overlooking the Mediterranean and/or the Montazah gardens. The Palestine's beach is cleaner than most in Alexandria.

Sea Star (formerly Admiral) (£) 24 Sharia Amin Fikry (tel: 483 1787). Clean, comfortable rooms, recently modernised. Good value for money.

Windsor (££) 17 Sharia el-Shohada (tel: 808123). Old hotel that replaced much of its old-world charm with mod cons. Some rooms have wonderful views over the Corniche and sea.

Damietta

Al-Manshy (£) 5 Sharia el-Nokrashy (tel: 057/323308). One of the only hotels in town – most visitors prefer to stay in nearby Ras el-Bahr – mostly of interest to bird-watchers.

Marine an-Nil (£) Sharia el-Mohafza, Ras el-Bahr (tel:057/528006). See el-Shatee.

Al-Shatee (£) 39, 63rd Street, Ras el-Bahr (tel: 057/528029). Both the el-Shatee and Marine an-Nil are modest hotels popular with middle-class Egyptian families wanting to avoid the summer crowds in Alexandria.

Mersa Matruh

Arous al-Bahr (£) Sharia el-Corniche (tel: 03/942419). Run-down concrete block facing the sea with basic rooms. Run by the city council, the 'Bride of the Sea' is open all year round.

Beau Site (££) 6 Sharia Osman Ahmed Osman (tel: 03/932066). Very popular Greek-run family hotel with a private beach. Friendly service and excellent food, full board is compulsory. Every night until 10 or 11pm the lounge turns into an amusing family disco. Open May–October.

Al-Gazala (£) Sharia Alma Rum (tel: 03/943519). This is a backpackers's favourite – clean and very simple rooms with communal bathrooms, often with hot showers.

Hotel des Roses (£) Sharia Galaa (tel: 03/942755). Friendly Greek-run hotel in an old villa, two blocks back from the Corniche. Half board is compulsory, as are early wake-up calls from the nearby mosque. Open June–September.

Sidi Abd al-Rahman

Alamein (££) Sidi Abd el-Rahman (tel: 03/586 3580). The best hotel west of Mersa Matrouh, this isolated, four-star resort hotel with a beautiful private beach is often booked well in advance in summer. The restaurant is not really recommended, but it is the only place to eat in the vicinity.

Tanta

Arafa (£) Midan el-Mahatta (tel: 040/336952). The only time you're likely to want to stay in Tanta's best hotel is during the *moulid* (festival). A million other people will have the same idea, so be sure to book well ahead.

CANAL ZONE AND RED SEA COAST

Hurghada

The telephone code for Hurghada is 065.

Al-Andalus (£) Sharia el-Mustashfa (tel: 447639). New hotel with quiet and clean rooms, a short walk from the beach.

La Bambola (££) Sheraton Road (tel: 442085). Clean

and pleasant three-star accommodation with small swimming pool and bus to private beach. Friendly staff.

Four Seasons (£) next door to the Luxor Palace on Sharia el-Corniche (tel: 447373). Completely new rooms with immaculate bathrooms.

Global (£) Sharia el-Sheikh el-Sebak (tel: 446623). Basic rooms with fan, shared bathrooms and a nice cafeteria on the roof.

Grand Hotel (££) Corniche Road (tel: 443751). Four-star resort hotel with several restaurants and bars, very popular with German package tourists.

Happy Land (£) Sharia el-Sheikh el-Sebak (tel: 447373). Simple, clean rooms with fans; transport to nearby private beach.

Luxor Palace Hotel (£) Opposite Three Corners on Sharia el-Corniche (tel: 447458). Basic rooms near the public beach. It's the cheapest in town, but the owner is very helpful and friendly.

Paradisio (£££) 22km north of Hurghada (tel: 447934). Beautiful and isolated, deluxe resort hotel, one of the newest and already very popular with wealthy Cairenes who have bought flats or villas in the compound.

Presidential (££) Tariq el-Sheraton (tel: 443015). Good-value rooms and nice atmosphere, but not on the beach.

Shedwan (££) Sharia el-Corniche (tel: 447007). Popular hotel for diving package holidays. Good beach and swimming pool and holiday atmosphere.

Sonesta Beach Resort (£££) Tariq el-Matar (tel: 443660). New deluxe resort hotel with all sports facilities and the usual five-star amenities and comforts.

Three Corners Village (££) 2 Sharia el-Corniche (tel: 447816). One of the first resorts in Hurghada, run by a friendly Belgian family. The rooms are clean and comfortable; swimming pool, all watersports facilities and excellent food with home-made breads and pastas. Recommended.

Isma'iliya

Hotel des Voyageurs (£) 22 Sharia Orabi (tel: 064/228304). Quickly fading, colonial-style hotel, a 'delight' for romantics who prefer nostalgia above comfort.

Isis (£) 32 Sharia Adly, Midan Orabi (tel: 064/227821). Best budget hotel in town with simple, nice interior and clean rooms with fans.

PLM Azur Etap Ismailiya (££) Fursan Island, Isma'iliya (tel: 064/768322). Fairly luxurious rooms with air-conditioning and bathroom, set on a quiet, shady island.

Port Said

Crystal (£) 12 Sharia Muhammad Mahmoud (tel: 066/222961). Basic, clean rooms, some with fans and sea views.

Hotel de la Poste (£) 42 Sharia Gumhuriya (tel: 066/229655). Another 1940s hotel and a reminder of grander days, with spacious but run-down rooms.

New Regent (££) 15 Sharia Muhammad Mahmoud, off Sharia el-Gumhuriya (tel: 066/223802). New, air-conditioned rooms with TV and bathroom, but lacking the atmosphere of the now totally decayed Regent Hotel around the corner.

Palace Hotel (££) 19 Sharia Gandhi (tel: 066/239450). One of the more pleasant hotels in town with clean rooms and cool air-conditioning, near the beach.

Sonesta Port Said Hotel (£££) Sharia Sultan Husayn (tel: 066/325511). Bland, four-star hotel with all facilities and a swimming pool.

Safaga

Menaville (££) Safaga Tourist Centre, Hurghada Road, Safaga (tel: 065/451760). New, low-rise resort hotel with rooms, chalets and cabanas; all have air-conditioning and private bathrooms. There are facilities for all watersports, tennis, fitness centre and a play area for children.

Suez

Red Sea Hotel (££) 13 Sharia Riyad, Port Tawfiq (tel: 062/223334). The only decent place to stay in Suez, with clean rooms and views over the Bay of Suez.

SINAI

el-Arish

Egoth Oberoi (££–£££) Sharia el-Fateh, el-Arish (tel: 064/351321). Luxurious rooms on the beach and a swimming pool for residents. It is the only five-star hotel in town and the only place selling alcohol – at wildly inflated prices – and often the only place where foreigners stay.

Moonlight (£) Sharia Fouad Zikry, el-Arish Beach (tel: 064/341362). Simple, cheap rooms just off the beach, some with private bathroom.

Sinai Beach (£) Sharia Fouad Zikry, el-Arish Beach (tel: 064/341713). Characterless, modern building with clean, air-conditioned rooms.

Dahab

Gulf Hotel (££) Dahab (tel: 062/640147). Basic, clean rooms near to el-Masbat. It is best known for its Black Prince Disco, the only disco worth mentioning in town and the only one selling alcohol.

HOTELS AND RESTAURANTS

Happyland (£) el-Masbat. One of the better of the many camps, run by Bedouins, with rattan huts, electricity and cold showers.

PLM Azur Holiday Village (££–£££) Dahab (tel: 062/761954). Three-star hotel in the more upmarket part of Dahab, popular with honeymooners. Good diving club and beautiful beach.

Nuweiba

Nuweiba Holiday Village (££) Nuweiba (tel: 062/770393). Air-conditioned bungalows with all the mod cons, set in a garden. On the beach it has a campsite and clean huts with fans. Excellent, fresh fish restaurant and the only bar in town serving alcohol.

Sinai Sun Camp (£) Tarabeen. Reed huts on the beach, and cold showers only.

Swelm (£) Tarabeen. Cool, Sudanese-run camp. Restaurant with cheap and good seafood.

Al-Waha Tourist Village (£–££) Nuweiba (tel: 062/500402). Simple, clean, air-conditioned bungalows located on the beach, as well as tents with the use of hot showers.

St Catherine

Monastery Hostel (£) Monastery of St Catherine (tel: 062/770945). As expected, almost monastic rooms, some with showers. Gates close at 9:30pm, but it's convenient for an early ascent. Three plain, solid meals are included in the price. Book in advance or check in early morning.

St Catherine Tourist Village (£££) Wadi el-Raha, St Catherine (reservation in Cairo, tel: 02/292 8114). Ugly, modern, deluxe complex, 1km from the monastery.

Sharm el-Sheikh

The telephone code for Sharm el-Sheikh is 062.

Clifftop Hotel (££) Sharm el-Sheikh (tel: 600251). Air-conditioned bungalows in a pleasant garden; it's no longer modern, but peaceful and quiet.

Fayrouz Hilton Village (£££) Na'ama Bay (tel: 600136). Luxurious bungalows, some with sea views. All sports facilities, including stables for horse riding. Delicious pizza and pasta buffet served in the Beach BBQ restaurant.

Kanabesh (££) Na'ama Bay (tel: 600185). White Moorish architecture with simple but comfortable rooms, lots of sitting areas and lively open-air disco.

Mövenpick Jolie Ville (£££) Na'ama Bay (tel: 600100). The smartest resort hotel: five-star, air-conditioned bungalows set in a beautiful garden. Two swimming pools, good beach and other watersports and crèche facility. Excellent restaurants, and Cactus is undoubtedly the best disco in the bay.

Pigeon Hotel (£) Na'ama Bay (tel: 600995). Cheapest place to stay with clean and nice rooms. Good place to hang out if you want to go trekking with Bedouins.

Red Sea Diving College (££) Na'ama Bay (tel: 600145). Comfortable, air-conditioned rooms, usually rented to people on a diving course. Recommended diving club.

Safety Land (£) Sharm el-Sheikh (tel: 600373). Camp with huts and tents and a private beach.

Sanafir (££) Na'ama Bay (tel: 600197). White-domed traditional architecture and laid-back atmosphere, run by an eccentric Egyptian. Good seafood restaurant and the hippest bar in town.

Motorbikes and horses for hire. Recommended as excellent value for money, so book in advance.

Shark Bay Camp (£–££) Shark Bay, 10km north of Na'ama Bay (tel: 600208). A peaceful, excellent holiday village with rooms, tents and even sleeping on the beach. There are no sharks these days, but a beautiful coral reef.

Tiran Hotel (££) Na'ama Bay (tel: 600221). New three-star holiday resort with clean, white-washed rooms in the centre of Na'ama Bay.

Taba

Taba Hilton (£££) Taba Beach, Taba (tel: 048/5783620). Typical Hilton resort, away from it all, and good for a beach-only holiday.

RESTAURANTS AND BARS

Cairenes dress up in a big way to go to an expensive restaurant and advance booking is recommended. Cheap Egyptian restaurants tend to be for men only, but they usually have a family room at the back or upstairs, where couples or single women can eat in peace.

£££ = expensive
(more than £15)
££ = moderate
(£7–£15)
£ = budget
(less than £7)

CAIRO

The telephone code for Cairo is 02.

Abu Shakra (£) 69 Sharia Qasr el-Aini, Garden City. Known as the best kebab and kofta place in town. Meat is sold by the weight here and alcohol is strictly forbidden.

Alfi Bey (£) 3 Sharia el-Alfy, downtown (tel: 771888). Wonderful, old-style restaurant with chandeliers. Over-helpful waiters serve traditional Egyptian and Levantine fare, but no alcohol.

Arabesque (£££) 6 Sharia Qasr en-Nil, downtown (tel: 574 8677). Upmarket oriental specialities served in a simple but classy décor. Popular with Egyptian film stars and French expatriates. Excellent *mulukhiya* and *Umm Ali*.

Casino des Pigeons (££) South of Abbas Bridge on the Nile, Giza (tel: 896299). Speciality of pigeon cooked in different ways, served with *mezze*.

Egyptian Pancake House (£) Between Sharia el-Azhar and Midan el-Husayn. Very good and cheap *fateers* (Egyptian pizzas, sweet or savoury). No alcohol.

Estoril (££) 12 Sharia Talaat Harb (in the passage), downtown (tel: 574 3102). Tucked away in a small passage, Estoril has a casual interior, friendly waiters and good European–Levantine menu. Often crowded with regulars, politicians and actors. Strongly recommended.

Fatayri at-Tahrir (£) Sharia el-Tahrir (two blocks to the right of Midan el-Tahrir). The man who makes the *fateers* here is a master at his job. Excellent food, but again no alcohol.

Felfella (£) 15 Sharia Hoda Shaarawi, downtown. Popular with tourists and locals for typical Egyptian food, served in an exotic décor with lots of birds and aquariums. Now Felfella has restaurants everywhere, usually good places to take kids.

Fishawi (£) In the same alley as the el-Husayn Hotel, Khan el-Khalili. This is the oldest tea house in Cairo and the family claims that they have never closed since 1773. It is a wonderful place to sit and watch the entire world go by: street vendors, schoolchildren, touts, crazy people, fortune-tellers, tourists, shoe polishers... No alcohol.

Five Bells (££–£££) 9 Sharia Adil Abu Bakr, Zamalek (tel: 340 8980). Pleasant, outdoor restaurant in summer, where a fountain splashes cooling water from a kitsch Aphrodite in the garden. Egyptian Mafia-types quickly escort their vamped-up women inside the freezing air-conditioned restaurant. Apart from the scene, they serve delicious fondues and good *mezze*.

Flying Fish (££–£££) 166 Corniche el-Nil, Dokki (tel: 349 3234). This is Omar Sharif's favourite fish restaurant. Casual décor but excellent fresh fish, shrimps and lobster.

Four Corners (£££) 4 Sharia Hasan Sabry, Zamalek (tel: 341 2961). Trendiest corner in Zamalek with four good, upmarket restaurants. La Piazza serves good Italian dishes and is even good value, but very popular. Matchpoint gathers the young crowd to watch the latest music videos with a gin and tonic; good snacks. Chin Chin serves good but expensive Chinese food. The star restaurant here is Justine, the crème de la crème of Cairene restaurants serving excellent French food in plush, padded surroundings.

Greek Club (£) 21 Sharia Bassiouni (first floor above Groppi), downtown (tel: 750759). Simple Greek food and cheap beers served to what is left of Cairo's Greek community as well as passing strangers. The restaurant overlooks the square and the roof terrace is delightful on a summer's night.

Grillon (££) 8 Sharia Qasr an-Nil, in alleyway. Pleasant outdoor terrace out back, serving Mediterranean and oriental food, but particularly popular with local intellectuals who meet here over a beer.

Groppi (£) Midan Talaat Harb, downtown (tel: 574 3244) and Groppi Garden, Sharia Adly, downtown. Both places are seriously run-down and only vaguely reminiscent of former grandeur. The pastries seem to get worse and worse, but the old waiters are friendly, and you have to go at least once. No alcohol.

Khan al-Khalili (£££) 5 Sikkat el-Badistan, Khan el-Khalili (tel: 903788). Pricey restaurant run by the Oberoi, serving Egyptian and 'European' food, in the heart of the bazaar. Tea, coffee, fresh juices and water-pipes are served on the terrace. Good for a snack and notable for the cleanest toilets in the area.

Kushary at-Tahrir (£) 169 Sharia el-Tahrir, Bab el-Luq (tel: 355 8418). The waiter claims that the one who eats *kushari* here is like the one who drinks water from the Nile: he always comes back for more. Typical, good *kushari* place. There is no alcohol.

Maroush (££) 64 Midan Lubnan, Mohandeseen (tel: 346 5350). Good Lebanese food, especially the spicy fish and shish tawook.

Nile Pharaoh (£££) 31 Corniche el-Nil, Giza (tel: 726122). Kitsch, mock-pharaonic cruise barge which sails out for lunch and dinner, offering a set menu with belly dance show and Egyptian crooner. Fun if you like this sort of thing.

HOTELS AND RESTAURANTS

Al-Omdah (£) 6 Sharia el-Gazair (next door to Atlas Zamalek), Mohandeseen. One of the best kushari places in town, serving a superior version of the national dish with the right proportions of rice, noodles, lentils and spicy sauce. No alcohol.

Paprika (££) 1129 Corniche an-Nil, Bulaq (tel: 749447). Next door to the Television Building, it is always crowded with television people. Excellent selection of *mezze*, quick service and a view of the Nile.

El Patio (££) 5 Sharia Said el Bakri, Zamalek (tel: 341 2702). The decor is dull but the Lebanese-Yugoslav chef, Nisha, never fails to surprise and delight – his Berlin Wall steak and Sardines a l'Escobar are a matter of legend. Good, inventive Mediterranean food and a bar crowded with bright young people and older habitués. Good atmosphere, sometimes with live performances or exhibitions.

Peking (££) 14 Sharia Saraya el-Ezbekiya (behind Cinema Diana) (tel: 591 2381). Tasty and fresh Chinese food in a pleasant décor. The speciality of the house is, strangely, Irish Coffee – served with accompanying bird music.

Piano Piano (£££) World Trade Centre, Corniche an-Nil, Bulaq (tel: 762810). The latest and trendiest place in town, with crowds of young, wealthy Cairenes who, after their studies abroad, hope for a bright future in Egypt. More of a piano bar, it has good music and excellent *mezze* and light meals. Book in advance.

Pub 28 (££) 28 Sharia Shagaret ad-Dor, Zamalek. Favourite watering hole of the Zamalek expatriate community, especially bachelors looking for a

listening ear. Pub atmosphere in dark décor, menu features good steaks and *mezze*.

Rigoletto (£) 3 Sharia Taha Husayn, Zamalek. Best ice-cream in town and delicious iced gateaux and cheesecake.

Seahorse (££) Corniche en-Nil (opposite the Badrawi Hospital), Maadi (tel: 363 8830). Excellent grilled fish and shrimps served with oriental rice and *mezze*. Waiters dressed as fishermen and a wonderful terrace on the Nile. Perfect for a sunny lunch in winter or a hot night in summer.

Simmonds Coffee Shop (£) 112, 26th-of-July Street, Zamalek. Good *cappuccino* and *espresso*, fresh juices and croissants, recommended for an Italian-style breakfast. Foreign journalists use it as a meeting place while real habitués use it as an unofficial office – the charming cashier girls take their phone messages! Amm Arabi behind the counter remembers exactly how his regulars take their coffee, and gives in to most of their whims. No alcohol.

Tandoori (££) 11 Sharia Shehab, Mohandeseen (tel: 348 6301). Good Indian curries in cool, marble décor. No alcohol.

LOWER NILE VALLEY
el-Faiyum
Auberge du Lac Coffee Shop (££) Lake Qarun. Pleasant restaurant looking on to the overgrown garden. Its speciality is wild Faiyumi duck.

Governorate Club (£–££) Nadi el-Muhafza, north along Bahr Sinuris. Fairly good Western-style food served in a pleasant garden with geese and ducks.

Kebabgi (£) Sharia Mustapha Kamil, Madinat el-Faiyum. The usual kebab and kofta, and a

good choice of vegetable dishes. No alcohol.

Said (£) Near the sluice on Bahr Sinuris, Madinet el-Faiyum. Best *kushari* in town. No alcohol.

Sherif's (£) Sharia Mustapha Kamil, Madinet el-Faiyum. Excellent ice-cream and sweets. Famous locally for the best *beleela* (bowl of hot milk, wheat, nuts, raisins and sugar) in Egypt.

LUXOR
Class (££) Sharia Khaled Ibn Walid, next door to Isis Hotel (tel: 095/386327). New, upmarket establishment, with very cold air-conditioning and little atmosphere. Oriental and international specialities.

1886 Restaurant and the Royal Bar (££–£££) Winter Palace Hotel, Sharia Corniche el-Nil (tel: 580422). Luxor's newest and smartest restaurant and bar, part of the old hotel's refurbishment. Neither the food nor the service live up to expectations, but the rooms are as calm and elegant as a *fin de siecle* boudoir. The bar has a pool table, if you're feeling energetic.

Kushari Sayyida Nefisa (£) Sharia Mustapha Kamel near the *souk*. Renowned for the best *kushari* in town, but a mostly male crowd. No alcohol.

Le Lotus (££–£££) Near the Novotel (tel: 095/580925). Restaurant boat run by the Novotel, offers lunch cruises to Dandara Temple and dinner cruises with oriental show.

La Mamma (££) In the Sheraton Hotel at the far end of Sharia Khaled Ibn Walid. Good, outdoor Italian restaurant, set in a garden with a pond and atmospheric Neapolitan live music. It specialises in fresh pastas and pizzas.

Marhaba (£–££) Sharia Corniche el-Nil, above the tourist office. Average, often overpriced food but the excellent roof terrace overlooking the Nile serves cool, local Stella beers.

Mövenpick Restaurants (££–£££), Crocodile Island (tel: 095/374855). The terrace restaurant beside the Nile serves excellent salads and fresh pastas for lunch, home-made ice-creams and sorbets, as well as a fantastic breakfast buffet in spring and autumn. There are two indoor restaurants, one serving a good buffet and the other pricey, but good à la carte French cuisine.

Tutankhamun (£) Near the ferry landing on the West Bank. It's worth crossing the river for some of the best food in Luxor. The friendly and chatty owner was head chef in a deluxe hotel for several years. Excellent chicken with rosemary, spinach casserole and good oriental rice. It's completely unlike the other places at the ferry landing. No alcohol.

Minya
Cafeteria Ali Baba (£) Corniche el-Nil past the Governorate Building. Good Egyptian fare – kebab and chicken are specialities. No alcohol.
Lotus (£) Top floor of the Lotus Hotel. Good meals and views, and the only place apart from the PLM that serves alcohol.

UPPER EGYPT AND NUBIA
Aswan
Aswan Moon (£) Corniche el-Nil (tel: 097/326108). Lively place with a mock-castle entrance gate and a restaurant on a floating extension. It's a favourite hang-out for *felucca* captains who come for the cheapest beer in town, the nostalgic Nubian songs and, last but not least, for the foreign girls. An amusing place for dinner, with fresh juices and 'oriental' food.

Al-Misri Tour Restaurant (£) Sharia el-Matar, off Sharia el-Suq. Tucked away, but very popular with the locals as it serves the best kebab and kofta in town. The food is served with salads and cold drinks in a décor of Islamic kitsch. Family room at the back.
Old Cataract Pullman Terrace (£) From 4pm until sunset an English tea is served, with a selection of cakes and sandwiches, and the often mentioned splendid view.
Panorama (£) Corniche el-Nil, Aswan (tel: 097/326169). Pleasant terrace along the Nile, with an huge variety of Egyptian and Europeanised dishes served by friendly waiters full of stories. Good for breakfast, lunch and dinner or just for a fresh juice or herbal tea. No alcohol.
La Trattoria (££) In the Isis Hotel on the Corniche (tel: 097/315500). Fairly boring Italian restaurant, but good enough if you're tired of kebab, kofta and other Egyptian fare.

WESTERN DESERT OASES
Bahariya
Oasis Cafeteria (£) and **Paradise Motel Restaurant** (£) On the main road. Both places serve basic menus to undemanding backpackers. A good meeting place if you want to share transport with someone.
Popular Restaurant (£) (el-Gash) opposite the police station. The owner gets angry if people ask the price of the food in advance, and he is known to overcharge if he doesn't like your face. Plain Egyptian fare.

Dakhla
Al-Dakhla Café (£) Opposite the new mosque. Good for sandwiches only.
Hamdy's (£) Off the main

road. A favourite hang-out for every tourist in town, with the best food and, for the oases, an amazingly varied menu. It plays 1970s pop music, some of which you won't have heard for a while.

Farafra
Saad's (£) On the main road. The only place to eat in town, so luckily this small restaurant is not too bad. Owners are helpful for information.

Kharga
Hotel Waha Restaurant (£) Off the main road. Chicken, rice, soup and omelette – and that's it.
New Kharga Oasis (£) Near the Fellaheen Monument. A wider variety of basic food, served with beers.

Siwa
Abduh's (£) Opposite the Yusuf Hotel. Good, cheap food, the first restaurant in town. It serves three meals a day and is also a good place for picking up information about the oasis.
East–West (£) On the main road. Serves the best food in town, mostly Egyptian fare influenced by backpackers' tastes.

ALEXANDRIA AND THE DELTA
Alexandria
The telephone code for Alexandria is 03.

Adoura (£–££) 33 Sharia Bayram el-Tonesi (tel: 800405). Popular outdoor fish restaurant where you make your choice from the day's catch. A sister restaurant has recently been opened in New York. No alcohol.
Athineos (£) 21 Midan Sa'ad Zaghlul (tel: 482 0421). Patisserie, nightclub and a vast restaurant with gilded friezes serving the usual Levantine menu. In sum-

281

mer, large windows open on to the bay.

Baudrot (£) 23 Sharia Saad Zaghlul (tel: 482 5687). This once famous patisserie serves bland pastries, but the pleasant garden filled with loving couples makes it all worthwhile.

Brazilian Coffee Store (£) Sharia Saad Zaghlul, behind the tourist office. Founded in 1929, this Greek-owned stand-up café still serves one of the better *cappuccinos* in town beneath the Brazilian flag.

Cap d'Or (£) 4 Sharia Adib, off Sharia Saad Zaghlul (tel: 483 5177). An old art nouveau bar-restaurant worth the trouble of finding for its fried fish and tasty squid casseroles. Popular with locals who pop in for beer and 1970s French music. Wild décor.

Chez Gaby au Ritrovo (££) 22 Sharia el-Hurriya. A casual restaurant, with elegant clientele, serving good pizzas and steaks; try the unusual but delicious combination of steak and shrimps. Food is also served at the popular bar. Its smarter, twin restaurant next door is less of a success.

Denis (£–££) 1 Sharia Ibn Bassam (tel: 483 0457). One of the simpler fish restaurants around the Corniche. Denis lacks the sea view, but has excellent fish and shrimps, which you choose from an iced cabinet.

Elite (£) 43 Sharia Safia Zaghlul (tel: 482 3592). Watch the world strolling by from the covered terrace or listen to the owner, Mme Christina, reminisce about old Alexandria. Very long menu of Greek and Egyptian dishes.

Hassan Bleik (£) Opposite 18 Sharia Saad Zaghlul (tel: 482 7237). Wonderful, old-fashioned and very cheap Lebanese restaurant, only open for lunch.

The plentiful choice of dishes includes delightful rice with cinnamon and chicken with grilled almonds. Leave some room for the home-made oriental sweets. No alcohol.

Mohamed Ahmed (£) 17 Sharia Shakour (tel: 483 3576). Calling itself the Great Pyramid of Alexandria, the best *fuul* and *falafel* place in town is always packed. No alcohol.

Pastroudis (£–££) 39 Sharia el-Hurriya (tel: 492 9609). The dark, red-plush restaurant is a good place to hide when history and crowds get on top of you. Another typically Alexandrian menu with dishes from all sides of the Mediterranean. Popular terrace and patisserie.

Santa Lucia (££) 40 Sharia Safia Zaghlul (tel: 482 0332 or 482 4240). One of the best and dearest restaurants in town specialising in seafood and European cuisine. The old waiters do their best to keep up the grand style. Very lively nightclub with floor show.

Spitfire Bar (£) 7 Sharia el-Bursa el-Qadima (tel: 806503). One of Egypt's most unusual bars; its walls are covered with pictures of customers and friends and memorabilia. Generally smoky and crowded, and playing loud rock 'n' roll. If the American Navy is in town you're most likely to find the ratings drinking here. Spitfire T-shirts are sold under the counter.

Tikka Grill (££) Tariq el-Gheish, el-Kashafa el-Baharia Club (tel: 805114 or 805119). Nothing tastes vaguely like a *tikka*, but the food is really good – plenty of fresh fish and meat kebabs, a free salad bar and the most peaceful view over the eastern harbour and Qaytbay Fort.

Trianon (££) Midan Saad Zaghlul (tel: 482 0986 or 482 0973). Stylish, wood-panelled restaurant serving good steaks and oriental specialities. Live piano music adds to the atmosphere. Excellent patisserie serves good-value breakfast.

Venous (£) 12 Sharia el-Hurriya and 37 Sharia Nabi Danyal (tel: 482 0956). Beautiful patisserie with mounds of pralines, biscuits and a wide variety of gâteaux.

Zephirion (££) 41 Sharia Khalid ibn Walid, Abu Kir (tel: 560 1319). A large, blue and white, family taverna overlooking the beach, well worth the excursion to an otherwise seedy suburb. Wide variety of fresh fish and Egyptian wine. Over 60 years' experience make it a very popular spot, so reservations are recommended on weekends.

Mersa Matruh

Beau Site (££) 6 Sharia Osman Ahmed Osman (tel: 03/932066). A long walk from town but worth it for Mersa Matruh's best food (set menu) and a bar overlooking the sea.

Panyotis (£) Sharia el-Tahrir. Simple Greek food – often fish – and cheap beer.

SUEZ CANAL AND RED SEA COAST

Hurghada

Arlene's (£–££) Tariq el-Mustashfa. Good American-style food, specialising in nachos and steak and lobster.

Chez Pascal (££) Next door to Three Corners Village. Excellent Belgian-run restaurant with home-made pasta, pizza and seafood specialities. Good ice-creams and pancakes. Next door, the same owners run Hurghada's hottest night spot, the Cha Cha Disco.

Felfella (£) Tariq el-Sheraton (tel: 065/442411). Part of the Cairene chain, serving good Egyptian food in a rustic décor. Good views of the sea.

Pharaohs (££) Sharia el-Bazarat. Egyptian specialities like pigeon and tagine with okra. Modern décor, good views over the ugly city of Hurghada.

Portofino (££) Tariq el-Mustashfa (tel: 065/446250). Good Italian food, nice atmosphere. The speciality is seafood fondue for two.

Scruples Steak House and Pub (£££) Sharia Nasr (tel: 065/444636). Upmarket European food with imported beef and seafood specialities.

Sun Set (£) Tariq el-Mustashfa. Fresh juices and snacks.

Young Kang (£–££) 5 Sharia el-Sheikh el-Sebak (tel: 065/446623). Chinese and Korean food with fresh seafood and Peking Duck.

Isma'iliya

George's (££) Sharia Sultan Husayn. Good, but pricey fish restaurant; the smartest restaurant in town.

Groppi (£) Opposite George's. Try this branch of the Cairo Groppi patisserie for an afternoon coffee or pastry.

King Edward (££) 171 Sharia el-Tahrir. Fairly good, varied Egyptian and 'European' menu; air-conditioned.

Port Said

Galal (£–££) Sharia Gaberti and Gumhuriya. Very good fish and seafood specialities in plain décor.

Kastan (££) Sharia el-Corniche (tel: 066/235242). A large, brightly lit restaurant with several rooms. Its friendly service and fresh fish and seafood have made it one of the city's most popular. No alcohol.

Nora's Floating Restaurant (££) On Sharia Filastin (tel: 066/326804). Pleasant daily lunch and dinner cruises on the canal. Booking in advance is recommended.

Pizza Pino (££) Intersection of Sharia Gumhuriya and 23rd of July Street. The place to be seen. Good, simple Italian cuisine and excellent ice-creams.

Cecil Reana House (££) 5, Sharia el-Gumhuriya, opposite Akri Hotel (tel: 066/225911). Korean food isn't what you would expect to find in Port Said and the staircase to the first floor isn't encouraging, but everyone from honorary consuls to passing sailors comes to Mr Pak's for a taste of the East. Spicy here means tongue-burning.

Sufer (££) Sharia Degla, behind Akri Hotel. Excellent Lebanese dishes and seafood specialities.

Suez

al-Magharbel (££) Sharia el-Gheish. Best food in town, which isn't saying much.

SINAI

el-Arish

Samar (£) On 23rd of July Street, el-Arish. Simple, good chicken, kofta and not much more. No alcohol.

Dahab

Fighting Kangaroo (£) el-Masbat, Dahab. This is a paradise for vegetarians, with inventive vegetable dishes.

Hard Rock Café (£) el-Masbat. No, not the real thing, but the music is loud and the honey and banana pancakes are delicious.

Tota (£) el-Masbat. Boat-shaped restaurant with a varied menu. Good vegetarian dishes and pizzas; famous for its delicious chocolate cake.

Sharm el-Sheikh

Beach BBQ (££–£££) Fayruz Hilton, Na'ama Bay. Italian buffet with fresh pasta prepared as you like it and a grill with fish and meat, all for a fixed price, served for dinner on the beach restaurant.

Beach BBQ (££) Mövenpick Jolie Ville, Na'ama Bay. Pleasant beach restaurant, open for lunch, with an excellent salad bar, good oriental grills and sandwiches.

Franco's Pizzeria (££) Ghazzala Hotel, Na'ama Bay. Good pizzas and pastas in a typically Italian décor.

Hilton Fish Restaurant (£££) Near the Hilton Diving Centre. Outdoor restaurant serving expensive but excellent French-inspired fish dishes in a décor where style is strangely blended with fishing nets and rods.

Na'ama Bay Grill (££) Ghazzala Hotel, Na'ama Bay. Specialities of fresh fish, lobster and meat grilled on the barbecue. Friendly staff but plain surroundings.

Sanafir Bar (£) Na'ama Bay. The bar is usually swinging after 9pm with a crowd of young trendy Cairenes, who are after some fun before they go on to the popular Cactus Disco in the Mövenpick Hotel.

Steak House (££) Kanabesh Hotel, Na'ama Bay. Sizzling steaks and salads are served in plain surroundings in this very popular restaurant.

283

Index

284

INDEX

287

288

Picture credits

The Automobile Association would like to thank the following photographers, libraries and associations for their assistance in the preparation of this book.

BRITISH MUSEUM (copyright) 30 Menthuhotpe II; 36a/37a Roman mummy case; 131 Temple of Isis, Philae. **MARY EVANS PICTURE LIBRARY** 41a Salah ad-Din; 41b Salah ad-Din; 48 Anti-British rioters; 96a British soldiers 1882; 96c Picnic on the Great Pyramid of Cheops, Giza; 184a and 184b Aswan Dam; 232a Opening of Suez Canal. **P GODEAU** 10/11 The Nile; 16b el-Muallaqa Church, Cairo; 23a Bab-el-Wagin; 24b Naguib Mahfouz; 46b British Embassy gates; 72a Mihrab of Qajmas el-Ishaqi mosque; 74/5 City of the Dead; 77b el-Qa'ah reception hall, Gayer Anderson House; 85a Sultan Barquq's tomb; 86a World Trade Centre, Cairo; 93 Imbaba camel market; 109 Marriott Hotel; 146a and 146b Siwa; 192 Dakhla Oasis; 193a Dakhla Oasis; 194a el-Kharga; 194/5 Dakhla Oasis; 195 el-Qasr; 196/7 Black Desert; 196 White Desert; 198a el-Qasr; 198b View el-Qasr; 199 Roman Fort, el-Kharga Oasis; 224 Irrigation system, Nile Delta; 227a Suez Canal; 229 Red Sea Coast; 233b Hurghada; 250b Dive site, Sinai. **T HARTWELL** 110/1 Traffic, Cairo. **J HENDERSON** 63 Step Pyramid of Zoser, Saqqara; 72c Muhammad Ali Mosque, Cairo; 152 Mortuary Temple of Hatshepsut, Luxor; 161 Valley of the Kings, Luxor. **HULTON DEUTSCH COLLECTION LTD** 13 Warren Christopher with President Mubarak; 26 Umm Kalthoum; 50/1 Sadat, Carter and Begin; 232b Suez Canal dredgers. **IMAGOS/C COE** 20b Boy and cart, Cairo; 81 Cairo grain market; 217a Qaytbay Fort, Alexandria. **B IVERSON** 167 Nefertari's tomb, Valley of the Queens. **THE MANSELL COLLECTION LTD** 36b Emperor Augustus; 45b Tourists at the Pyramids of Giza; 60a Great Pyramid of Cheops; 96b James Bruce; 125 Akhenaton; 164b Howard Carter in Tutankhamun's tomb. **JAMES H MORRIS PICTURE LIBRARY** 4a Nile scene; 5c Relief from tomb of Seti I; 6 Spices; 38 Cairo Muslims; 126 Coptic School, White Monastery; 127 White Monastery; 160 Tomb of Rameses IV, Valley of the Kings; 163 Tomb of Tuthmosis III, Valley of the Kings. **NATURE PHOTOG-RAPHERS LTD** 228 Blackspotted grunt (D A Smith); 250a Diver, Red Sea Coast (J Sutherland); 251 Clown fish (D A Smith). **REX FEATURES LTD** 51 President Mubarak; 50/1 Nasser and Tito. **A SATTIN** 31b Ramses II, Abu Simbel; 156 Ramses III, Madinet Habu. **N SCHILLER** 147 Moulid el-Husayn, Cairo; 171a and 177 Daraw camel market; 234b Red Sea Mountains. **SPECTRUM COLOUR LIBRARY** 14b Cairo el-Azhar Mosque; 28a Abydos Temple reliefs; 71 el-Azhar Mosque; 133 Roman Column, Dandara; 162 Seti I's tomb, Valley of the Kings. **ZEFA PICTURES LTD** 104 Cairo restaurant; 105 Casino, Cairo.

The remaining pictures are held in the Association's own library (AA PHOTO LIBRARY) and were taken by CHRIS COE with the exception of pages: 3, 5b, 10, 18a, 21, 27b, 30a, 33, 35, 39, 40b, 42/3a, 42/3b, 44b, 46a, 47, 52/3, 53, 54/5, 55, 56, 60b, 61b, 73, 80, 82b, 84, 86b, 88b, 92, 100, 101, 102b, 103b, 108, 113a, 113b, 114a, 114/5, 114b, 118, 119a, 119b, 121, 123, 128, 129, 130, 132, 134, 135b, 137, 138, 140a, 140b, 141, 142, 143, 148a, 148b, 151, 153, 154/5, 156, 158, 169b, 171b, 172, 173a, 173b, 174b, 175, 176a, 180/1, 182, 191, 193b, 200/1, 201, 204, 205, 206a, 207, 211, 212a, 212b, 217b, 220a, 222, 231, 234a, 235, 237a, 237b, 239a, 239b, 241a, 241b, 244, 245b, 246a, 248, 249, 252b, 255, 259, 260, 261, 265b, 266, 270, 271a.

Contributors

Series adviser: Christopher Catling   **Copy editor:** Donna Dailey
Designer: Barfoot Design   **Verifier:** Paul Murphy   **Indexer:** Marie Lorimer